Creating a transatlantic marketplace

MANCHESTER
1824

Manchester University Press

European Policy Research Unit Series

Series Editors: *Simon Bulmer, Peter Humphreys* and *Mick Moran*

The European Policy Research Unit Series aims to provide advanced text-books and thematic studies of key public policy issues in Europe. They concentrate, in particular, on comparing patterns of national policy content, but pay due attention to the European Union dimension. The thematic studies are guided by the character of the policy issue under examination.

The European Policy Research Unit (EPRU) was set up in 1989 within the University of Manchester's Department of Government to promote research on European politics and public policy. The series is part of EPRU's effort to facilitate intellectual exchange and substantive debate on the key policy issues confronting the European states and the European Union.

Titles in the series also include:

The politics of health in Europe   Richard Freeman

Immigration and European integration   Andrew Geddes

Agricultural policy in Europe   Alan Greer

The European Union and the regulation of media markets
   Alison Harcourt

Mass media and media policy in Western Europe   Peter Humphreys

The politics of fisheries in the European Union   Christian Lequesne

Sports law and policy in the European Union   Richard Parrish

The rules of integration   Gerald Schneider and Mark Aspinwall

Fifteen into one?   Wolfgang Wessels, Andreas Maurer and Jürgen Mittag
   (eds)

Extending European cooperation   Alasdair R. Young

Regulatory politics in the enlarging European Union   Alasdair Young and
   Helen Wallace

Creating a transatlantic marketplace

Government policies and business strategies

Edited by *Michelle P. Egan*

Manchester University Press
Manchester and New York

distributed exclusively in the USA by Palgrave

Published by Manchester University Press
Oxford Road, Manchester M13 9NR, UK
and Room 400, 175 Fifth Avenue, New York, NY 10010, USA
www.manchesteruniversitypress.co.uk

Distributed exclusively in the USA by
Palgrave, 175 Fifth Avenue, New York,
NY 10010, USA

Distributed exclusively in Canada by
UBC Press, University of British Columbia, 2029 West Mall
Vancouver, BC, Canada V6T 1Z2

British Library Cataloguing-in-Publication Data
A catalogue record for this book is available from the British Library

Library of Congress Cataloging-in-Publication Data applied for

ISBN   0 7190 7154 2 hardback
EAN   978 0 7190 7154 6

First published 2005

14 13 12 11 10 09 08 07 06 05   10 9 8 7 6 5 4 3 2 1

Typeset in Sabon
by Northern Phototypesetting Co Ltd, Bolton
Printed in Great Britain
by Biddles Ltd, King's Lynn

Contents

Figures and tables

Contributors

Chad Damro, University of Edinburgh
Youri Devuyst, European Commission
Michelle P. Egan, American University
Henry Farrell, George Washington University
Johan Lembke, George Washington University
Hugo Paemen, former EU Ambassador to the US
Diahanna Post, University of California-Berkeley
Martin Staniland, University of Pittsburgh
Rebecca Steffenson, Queen's University Belfast

Preface

The editor would like to thank the German Marshall Fund of the United States for the funding of a conference and report which preceded this publication. The American Institute of Contemporary German Studies hosted the conference, provided the author with research support during a Robert Bosch Foundation Fellowship, and published the conference proceedings. The Atlantic Council provided an opportunity to participate as a senior fellow in their transatlantic relations programme.

The authors of the individual chapters provide substantial insight into the current status and future prospects for the transatlantic economic relationship. They responded graciously to comments, making the job of editor fully enjoyable. Several individuals provided comments and suggestions through their conference participation and subsequent chapter readings. Thanks are due in particular to Carl Lankowski, US Foreign Service Institute; Michael Calingaert, Brookings Institution; Jacques Pelkmans, Centre for European Policy Studies; Ellen Frost, Institute for International Economics; Kalypso Nicolaidis, Oxford University; Jonathan Davidson, European Commission Delegation; and Auke Haagsma, European Commission. Valuable research assistance was provided by Charles Lor and Nino Khurditsze of American University, and Brian O'Hanlon also assisted in preparation of the manuscript for publication. Special thanks also to Bill Burros for copy-editing and formatting the manuscript, and finally to the editorial staff at Manchester University Press for the finished product.

Editor's note

Although the term 'European Community' is sometimes legally appropriate, we have generally adopted the popular usage 'European Union'.

Abbreviations

AAA	Administrative Arrangements on Attendance
AEA	Association of European Airlines
ANSI	American National Standards Institute
APEC	Asia-Pacific Economic Cooperation
APT	Asia-Pacific Telecommunity
ASA	Air Service Agreements
BSE	Bovine Spongiform Encephalopathy (mad-cow disease)
CAB	Civil Aeronautics Board
CAB	Conformity Assessment Bodies
CAP	Common Agricultural Policy
CCIA	Computer and Communications Industry Association
CDMA	Code Division Multiple Access
CE	CE Mark
CEA	Council of Economic Advisors
CERT	Canada Europe Round Table for Business
CFSP	Common Foreign and Security Policy
CITEL	Inter-American Commission on Telecommunications
DOJ	Department of Justice
DSU	Dispute Settlement Understanding
EADS	European Aerospace and Defence Company
ECJ	European Court of Justice
ECTI	EU Canada Trade Initiative
EGNOS	European Satellite Navigation Project
EI	economic internationalization
EMU	Economic and Monetary Union
EPA	Environmental Protection Agency
EPIC	Electronic Privacy Information Center
ESA	European Space Agency
ETSI	European Telecommunications Standards Institute
FAA	Federal Aviation Agency
FAQ	Frequently Asked Questions

FCC	Federal Communications Commission
FDA	Food and Drug Administration
FDI	foreign direct investment
FOMA	Freedom Of Mobile Multimedia Access
FSC	Foreign Sales Corporation
FTC	Federal Trade Commission
GATS	General Agreement on Trade in Services
GATT	General Agreement on Trade and Tariffs
GBDe	Global Business Dialogue on E-Commerce
GDP	Gross Domestic Product
GM	Genetically Modified
GMO	Genetically Modified Organism
GMP	Good Manufacturing Practice
GNSS	global navigation and satellite systems
GPS	Global Positioning System
GSM	Global System for Mobile Communications
IATA	International Air Transport Association
ICC	International Chamber of Commerce
ICN	International Competition Network
ILSA	Iran and Libya Sanctions Act
IPR	intellectual property rights
ITU	International Telecommunications Union
JCC	Joint Cooperation Committee
JHA	Justice and Home Affairs
MIA	Mergers and Acquisitions
MCR	Merger Control Regulation
MFN	Most-Favoured-Nation
MOU	Memorandum of Understanding
MRA	mutual recognition agreements
NAFO	Northwest Atlantic Fisheries Organization
NAFTA	North American Free Trade Agreement
NATO	North Atlantic Treaty Organization
NGO	Non-governmental Organization
NIC	newly industrialized countries
NIST	National Institute on Standards and Technology
NTA	New Transatlantic Agenda/Agreement
NTM	New Transatlantic Marketplace
OHG	Operators Harmonization Group
OMB	Office of Management and Budget
OPA	Online Privacy Alliance
OREGIN	Organization of European GNSS Industries
OSHA	US Occupational Safety and Health Administration
PCA	Positive Comity Agreement
PEA	Positive Economic Agenda

PRS	Public Regulated Service
QZSS	Quasi-Zenith Satellite System
SEM	Single European Market
SLG	Senior Level Group
SMP	Single Market Programme
TABD	Transatlantic Business Dialogue
TACD	Transatlantic Consumer Dialogue
TAED	Transatlantic Environmental Dialogue
TAFTA	Transatlantic Free Trade Area
TALD	Transatlantic Labour Dialogue
TBT	Technical Barriers to Trade
TCAA	Transatlantic Common Aviation Area
TDMA	Time Division Multiple Access
TEP	Transatlantic Economic Partnership
TISC	Trade and Investment Subcommittee
UMTS	Universal Mobile Telecommunications System
UNCTAD	United Nations Conference on Trade and Development
USDA	US Department of Agriculture
USTR	United States Trade Representative
UWCC	Universal Wireless Communications Consortium
W-CDMA	Wideband Code Division Multiple Access
WTO	World Trade Organization

1 *Michelle P. Egan*

Introduction

Economic cooperation between the US and EU has long been a central issue on the transatlantic agenda. Recently, however, a growing list of contentious political issues have substantially increased the usual volume of friction in the transatlantic relationship (Ludlow, 2002: 1–2; Pond, 2004; Asmus, 2003). Many expressed fears that these political rifts could also engulf transatlantic trade relations and deal a fatal blow to further liberalization of the international economy (Daft and Fitzgerald, 2004). While conflicts are inevitable between large economies with highly developed trade and investment relatioinships, the most recent generation of US–EU trade disputes have emerged at a time when the global trading system is already under severe pressure (Bergsten, 2002).

The US and EU currently have a full roster of high profile bilateral trade disputes, varying considerably in origin. While traditional trade barriers such as tariffs are generally considered inflammatory, they are no longer the primary source of transatlantic trade tensions. More attention is being given to non-tariff barriers, and particularly those trade-related domestic policies that inhibit market access. The following is only a select list of some of the major areas of contention:

- Some conflicts stem primarily from traditional demands for protection from vested interests in the form of tariffs, quotas and subsidies. In the dispute over steel tariffs initially applied by the US in March 2002, the EU won the right to impose punitive tariffs after the World Trade Organization (WTO) ruled that the US measures represented an illegal safeguard to protect its steel industry from legitimate foreign competition. The US subsequently lifted the safeguard measures in December 2003.

  In the long-running case of Foreign Sales Corporations (FSCs), tax provisions benefiting US exporters were challenged by the EU and other trade partners as illegal trade subsidies for American multinationals. The WTO determined in May 2003 that US tax policy remained non-compliant with WTO rules and granted the EU the right to apply duties of up to $4 billion. The EU has subsequently threatened to introduce a first wave of

duties in March 2004 if the US does not comply with the ruling by rewrit-
ing its tax legislation. In some aspects, the FSC saga recalls the 'banana war'
fought over the EU's banana importation scheme, with the US prevailing
repeatedly before the EU finally adapted its regime to meet WTO rules in
April 2001.

- Other conflicts stem from the imposition of economic sanctions on third
  parties to achieve foreign policy objectives. The EU has for example
  opposed efforts by the US to control the trade and investment activities of
  foreign companies through the Cuban Liberty and Democratic Solidarity
  Act (Helms Burton) and the Iran and Libya Sanctions Act (ILSA). This
  reflects differences in their respective willingness to employ commercial
  sanctions, even in the face of similar foreign-policy objectives.
- Another category of conflicts – and the most likely to proliferate in the
  future – are the result of 'behind the border' issues stemming from different regulatory systems and philosophies. Dealing with public concerns
  over new technologies and industries is at the heart of a growing number
  of trade disputes rooted in differing perspectives on the role of regulation.
  Disagreements concerning the potential health, environment and safety
  effects of biotechnology and the differences regarding privacy concerns
  with electronic commerce are the most prominent examples.
- A number of related potential conflicts stem for the new security environment following the 11 September 2001 terrorist attacks. Here the
  challenge is finding mutually acceptable means to pursue common
  counter-terrorism goals. In the case of Passenger Name Records (PNR),
  for example, the collection and exchange of airline passenger data has led
  to disagreements in methods of implementation, based largely on long-
  standing concerns over data privacy. The Container Security Initiative
  (CSI) focusing on port security and the inspection of large shipping cargo
  containers has also led to some difficulties in defining the proper balance
  between trade and transport policies and security concerns.

While traditional protectionist practices continue to generate friction in
the transatlantic economic relationship, the growth of regulatory instruments to address new challenges pertaining to trade and investment has only
served to heighten the role of regulation in international trade disputes.
Much more is involved than simply imports and exports: the growth of foreign direct investment and the development of complex supply chains and
production networks tie together the EU and US markets, which are highly
sensitive to trade disruptions (De Jonquières, 2003).

While transatlantic trade quarrels over protectionist measures have a long
history, disputes over regulatory policies and their impact on the movement
of goods and services in the transatlantic marketplace are likely to be increasingly pervasive, complex and acrimonious, 'a trend that will continue for the
foreseeable future' (Burwell, 2004: 1). Over the past several years, bilateral
relations have become increasingly strained, with a series of high profile

disputes that seem to be growing in both number and severity (Ahearn, 2002; Atlantic Council, 2003). This has significant implications for the international trading regime, as the success or failure to deal effectively with such disputes threatens to undermine progress in multilateral trade negotiations (Horlick, 2002; Bergsten, 2002). The stalled round of world trade talks has become increasingly significant for both the US and EU, since joint leadership is also more complicated and demanding in the post-Uruguay context (Pelkmans, 1999).

While the US and EU will remain the central players in any global trade round, there are growing examples of issues settled among other groupings and alliances (Pelkmans, 1999). The addition of new members has increased bargaining leverage of other groups –including developing countries – and has according to some observers made for an unwieldy trade organization (Bergsten, 2002). A determination to restart the current round of negotiations will of course bring to the fore the differences between the two sides but will be balanced by efforts to resolve them or at least propose alternative policies (De Jonquières and White, 2003; Buck, 2003). Though the US and EU share a common aim of multilateral trade liberalization, they have pursued different approaches (Zoellick, 2002). The likelihood of success depends on their willingness to negotiate politically sensitive issues rather than litigate, especially in addressing outstanding regulatory disputes.

Still, amid increasing anxiety about the survival of the transatlantic alliance, transatlantic trade has been labeled the 'stability factor' in the relationship (Lamy, 2003). Calls for greater political momentum and new strategic initiatives to revitalize the partnership should not downplay the significance of discussing matters of commercial concern. As the world's two largest economies, their bilateral relationship serves as a key anchor to global growth and prosperity (Quinlan, 2003: 7). One of the defining features is the increasing integration and cohesion of the transatlantic economy (Quinlan, 2003). As Quinlan concludes, the US and EU economies already operate to a large extent as one single transatlantic economy: globalization is not only happening faster between these two economies but their high level of integration exceeds that of any other economic relationship in the world.

Such intense economic diplomacy between the US and EU demonstrates a deep and durable partnership. Over the past four decades, the EU, as distinct from its constituent Member States, has become more important for the US as a partner in managing the global political economy. The growing importance of the non-security dimension of transatlantic relations is demonstrated by the pattern and volume of foreign direct investment and trade. The US and EU account for about two-fifths of world trade and three-fifths of world GDP. Transatlantic trade is relatively balanced, and transatlantic investment perhaps the most significant indicator of the degree to which the EU and US economies are intertwined – has accelerated at breakneck speed, far surpassing US and EU investment in other areas of the world.

Approximately one-quarter of this trade consists of transactions within firms based on their investments on either side of the Atlantic. Much of this is relatively uncontroversial with trade disputes affecting only a small percentage of overall flows (See Paemen, Chapter 2 this volume). In fact, most firms adapt to the regulatory environments in Europe and the United States without great difficulty given their familiarity with markets, institutions and investment climates (Woolcock, 1996). As US–EU economic cooperation on a wide range of issues has increased markedly in the last decade, commensurate with the importance of bilateral economic ties, those seeking to foster greater transatlantic cooperation have often focused on attempting to manage differences through regulatory cooperation (Pelkmans, 1999; Quinlan, 2003; Hamilton, 2003). Trade disputes continue, but they have been accompanied by the development of mechanisms for addressing trade tensions.

Traditional tariff and non-tariff barriers are increasingly addressed at the international level through arbitration and dispute resolution to prevent escalating trade disputes. However, an increasing number of transatlantic disputes are far less manageable at the multilateral level. The US and EU are the primary users of the international trade dispute settlement system[1] but the changing character of trade relations, and US–EU foreign economic policy in particular, has focused increased attention on bilateral dispute management. More importantly, these are not the simple trade wars of the past but rather affect such fundamental domestic issues as 'how our societies are governed or how our economies are regulated' (Hamilton, 2003: 28). Dealing with the challenges of closer economic integration means that the US and Europe face the prospect that the traditional modes of governance on both sides of the Atlantic have to change to deal with the changing dynamics of greater interdependence.

This book addresses the governance of the transatlantic market, and the efforts on both sides to tackle the increasingly important role that domestic regulations play in shaping both their bilateral and international relations. A largely unnoticed development in foreign-policy circles is the growing importance of dense networks of transnational actors, engaged in negotiations concerning specific economic and social issues that were traditionally the province of domestic institutions and agencies. This new transatlantic arena in which issues as varied as competition policy, food safety and electronic commerce have come to the forefront of discussions blurring the boundaries between foreign and domestic policy-making. Yet the nature of economic cooperation over the last decade is radically different from traditional non-security Atlantic cooperation, reflecting not only the potential of institutionalized economic cooperation in yielding policy benefits, but also structural and regulatory changes within the European Union. As Pelkmans points out, the transformation of the transatlantic relationship interacts with four global changes: the end of the Cold War, the changing distribution of power, rising globalization, and a structural shift from governments to markets (Pelkmans,

1999). While these political and economic developments have led to a re-evaluation and reconfiguration of the transatlantic partnership in the latter half of the 1990s, both sides are systematically working together to develop joint or complementary approaches toward the regulation of transatlantic markets. As a result, European and American policy-makers and business groups are engaged in new kinds of economic diplomacy. While seemingly not of the same significance as issues of international security, understanding and addressing the growing importance of regulatory issues is important for creating a climate conducive to economic growth and investment (European Council, 2003).

In light of these developments, this book analyses contemporary efforts to manage the transatlantic economy, focusing on key sectors to illustrate the growing relationship between trade and regulatory policies. This introductory chapter begins with a general overview of transatlantic relations, drawing upon select academic and policy views about the US–EU economic relationship. It provides a brief history of US–EU relations before assessing the economic elements of the relationship and the various political, economic and business interests that have led to the promotion of enhanced transatlantic economic cooperation. The chapter concludes with a summary of each of the chapters and the main themes developed in this volume.

Regulatory politics and trade

Transatlantic trade diplomacy is changing rapidly. As the transatlantic economic relationship has matured, traditional trade liberalization via tariff reductions and other measures are no longer the focus of transatlantic trade negotiations.[2] Increasingly, issues related to the role of government in regulating the economy dominate US–EU trade discussions. Progress or conflict on these issues varies by sector, as the chapters in this volume illustrate. Each chapter assesses the dynamics of transatlantic economic collaboration, coordination and competition through detailed analysis of specific sectors. It is clear from their conclusions that greater economic interdependence has brought increased political scrutiny to formerly overlooked areas of regulatory policy.

The process of extending trade policy began over thirty years ago as governments sought to identify certain regulations as non-tariff barriers that hindered market access.[3] Since then, governments have increasingly focused their attention on regulations that discriminate in favour of domestic industries. While governments agree that certain regulatory barriers do violate trade principles and obligations, it is difficult to eliminate them without infringing on the power of governments to regulate in the public interest (Lang, 1999: 1). This has important political consequences as the US and EU are grappling with a double challenge: the proliferation of regulatory obstacles that hamper cross-border trade in goods and services, and the need to find ways to protect domestic interests and promote important policy goals. Although global concerns such as cheap labour and inadequate environmental standards are generally not problematic in the transatlantic context, deep-seated differences in the nature, method and scope of regulation can lead to trade distortions and increased friction (Kahler, 1995).

For the transatlantic relationship, market access is increasingly constrained by different regulatory regimes that, intentionally or not, protect domestic producers and impact the competitive position of firms by functioning as non-tariff barriers (Egan, 2001; Vogel, 1998; Damro and Sbragia, 2003). Because market access is typically limited by different approaches to regulation in the US and EU rather than the existence of regulation per se, this means that the potential for trade disputes exists over a much wider range of issues than previously. Disputes over regulatory policy are often far less tractable than those over trade policies, reflecting deep-rooted ideological differences over the role of the government in the economy.

The US and EU have sought to manage these political consequences of different methods of regulating market operations. The two avenues of international cooperation – trade liberalization and regulatory coordination – have traditionally been associated with separate institutions and agencies, and above all with two very different negotiating cultures (Nicoläidis, 1997). As issues that encompass both external trade and domestic regulatory policy become a larger part of the transatlantic agenda, these different institutions and cultures are joined. Particularly as the transatlantic trade agenda focuses on behind-the-border issues, EU and US policy positions are often the result of competition between domestic institutions and constituencies that may have substantial impacts on the course of bilateral negotiations. The growth of regulatory trade policy creates a new dynamic bound to affect existing institutional competences, civil interests and regulatory traditions on both sides of the Atlantic.

This raises a basic question: what can be done to promote cooperation in the face of differing regulatory approaches involving entrenched domestic agencies and constituencies, who are often less willing to consider compromise in face of public pressure. Developing diplomatic strategies to promote a freer transatlantic market has involved both public and private actors which has altered the character by which trade policy is developed and implemented (Peterson, 1996). The emergence of civil society actors as well as domestic agencies in devising trade strategies has broadened the number of parties involved in shaping the policy agenda. Much of this effort has focused on creating a framework of regulatory cooperation and coordination to cope with increased economic interdependence. Though coordination has meant relinquishing some degree of regulatory sovereignty and jurisdictional control over national markets, the emergence of successful international coordination, built on mutual interests, depends on regulatory legitimacy and credible commitments (Majone, 2000).

Legal and commercial differences aside, there are different patterns of regulation that either global rules or transatlantic mechanisms need to address. Four broad categories of regulation help us analyse the relationship across different sectors and help us distinguish different patterns of regulation that impact transatlantic governance.[4] Governments can introduce pro-competitive regulation in order to promote and improve competition. They may promote strategic regulation to favour particular firms or industries through giving subsidies, awarding contracts or providing other forms of protectionism. Governments may enhance or modify existing regulation, create new regulations in order to cope with the growing complexity of markets or introduce other innovations. Finally, governments may delegate responsibility and promote self-regulation in which private actors play an increasingly important role in rule-making. All four types of regulation are in evidence in the chapters that follow, indicating that there are distinct variations in patterns of policy-making that can affect the terms of market competition. By studying differences in regulatory policies in the transatlantic context, we can learn more about the larger relationship between government and business, and the interaction between domestic politics and international pressures. And given efforts to promote a transatlantic economy, the role of regulation is an important element in understanding how policy-makers confront differences in values and objectives, institutions and processes, and legal and administrative cultures. By comparing sectors, we can determine how governments have responded to different constellations of actors and interests, as well as different types of market pressures and constraints. The chapters show that the policy dynamics vary across different issues areas: while there are grounds for optimism in areas such as competition policy (see Damro in Chapter 4) and digital policy (see Farrell in Chapter 6), there is more discord in areas such as global satellite and wireless communications (see Lemke in Chapter 5) genetically modified foods (see Post, in Chapter 7) and aviation (see Staniland in Chapter 3).

Transatlantic relations in historical perspective[5]

The Cold War consensus

From the end of the Second World War and the origins of European integration, both the US and the EU emphasized the importance of close bilateral relations. This has taken the form of both public and private interactions since the Marshall Plan, when US Government strategies and West European government responses fostered the provision of private goods in the form of investment and consumption. Support for European economic integration, despite some initial concerns about trade diversion, was framed within the security concerns of the emerging Cold War, but was also aimed at boosting demand for American products and promoting a liberal trade policy for a unified economy.

By the early 1950s, investment was flowing from the US to Europe, and all of the European countries had balance of payments deficits with the US. American companies with their technological advantages and their growing incentives to invest overseas were well placed to take advantage of a large integrated European market (Van Groeben, 1985; Pollack and Shaffer, 2001: 9).

Seeking to emulate the American experience, the European Community initially lowered traditional tariffs via the elimination of customs duties and quantitative restrictions, leading to the introduction of a common external tariff in 1968. The US relied on the mechanism of the General Agreement on Tariffs and Trade (the GATT) to foster an outward-looking orientation for the new European Community (Devuyst, 1995). In the post-war period, the dominance of the American economy meant that the US could afford to make concessions to ensure the prosperity of the Atlantic alliance.

Beginning in the 1960s, the US reconsidered some aspects of the economic relationship as it faced mounting trade and current account deficits and increased pressure to open markets and began to challenge foreign restrictive trade practices. Congressional passage of Section 301 of the US Trade Act encouraged successive US governments to assert their demands, particularly in targeting EC agricultural practices (Hudec, 1993). The US also sought to manage trade through voluntary export restraints, countervailing duties and other forms of market agreements, targeted in particular toward Japan and the newly industrialized countries (NICs) of the Asia-Pacific. Despite these concerns, the US did prevail in promoting a wide-ranging negotiating agenda in successive trade rounds that set the stage for greater liberalization by addressing new measures of protectionism in the form of non-tariff barriers (Grieco, 1990).

With slowing growth, European economies also instituted a variety of import restrictions and non-tariff barriers. Following the first oil shock and global economic recession in 1973, poor economic performance undermined both the budgetary foundations of welfare states and Keynesian demand management. The neo-corporatist class compromises and consensual incomes policies that characterized many European economies were under immense pressure. The second recession later in that decade and the spread of 'stagflation', a combination of high unemployment and high inflation, prompted largely uncoordinated national responses to the economic crisis. The trade integration model came under strain and protectionism rose across Europe. Monetary coordination was among the first casualties, as Member States also sought to maintain domestic economic activity by curbing competition, using such measures as voluntary export restraints, quotas and other technical barriers to trade (Egan, 2001; Page, 1981).

The crises of the 1970s also fostered a rethinking of national economic polices, as governments were well aware that their efforts to create national champions, protect labour markets and maintain public spending were not

stemming rising trade imbalances and deficits. While many disputes throughout the 1960s and 1970s arose from state intervention in the economy, usually
in the forms of subsidies and ownership, the shift from state to market through
the progressive liberalization and reduction of state ownership reduced some
of the earlier disagreements (*Oxford Analytica*, 1998). Greater competition via
liberalization, lower subsidies and increased pressure on welfare states accen-
tuated the greater emphasis on markets and encouraged European businesses
to become more competitive global players (Pelkmans, 1999).

Beginning in the 1980s, the European Commission led an effort to renew
economic growth and increase competitiveness by relaunching the Single
Market Programme (SMP). The US and others again raised concerns about the
terms of access for third countries. The European Community initially neglected the external implications of the 1992 SMP, with the 1985 Commission
White Paper detailing over 300 measures to remove internal trade barriers.
This did not, however, indicate a lack of interest in the relationship between
regional integration and globalization. Growing recognition of a competitiveness gap vis-à-vis the United States and Japan on the one hand, and the NICs
on the other, led to strenuous efforts to maintain overall levels of market
activity and provide conditions for viable markets (Sandholtz and Zysman,
1989). Attention focused on the strengthening of European strategies in areas
such as research and development, technical standards and regulatory coordination, as a way to improve the environment in which companies operated.
The US also began pressuring its European partners for further multilateral
trade negotiations in response to the acceleration of regionalism in Europe,
again linking European integration to international trade liberalization.

The SMP was designed to create an integrated market, encouraging European firms to increase economies of scale, and thus increase their competitive position. Despite concerns raised by the US government about 'Fortress
Europe', many US and EU businesses developed closer ties during the SMP,
as large American corporations saw this as an opportunity to increase their
market presence (Hocking and Smith, 1997). Many US multinational firms
were already viewed as European given their long-standing presence in the
Community. They were well-positioned to take advantage of the removal of
national restrictions and increased competition. American companies also
lobbied for various elements of the single market programme and gathered
information about the various restrictions they encountered across Europe in
terms of industry standards, border formalities and export licenses (Cowles,
1996). The US government generally sought to influence aspects of the SMP
through its own interagency monitoring efforts, bilateral negotiations and
studies issued by Office of Technology Assessment, International Trade Commission and Commerce Department (Devuyst, 1995; USITC, 1989; OTA,
1992).

Anxious to allay fears about protectionism, the EU sought to reassure the
US and other partners that the SMP did not represent an attempt to create

Fortress Europe (see Paemen, Chapter 2 this volume). The US persuaded the EU to alter specific aspects of its proposals, notably concerning reciprocity provisions. This had caused concern among US financial institutions whose own domestic regulatory restrictions would require change under the proposed EU legislation. The EU's malleability went only so far, however, as efforts to gain a seat in the deliberations of European standards-setting bodies were rebuffed (Egan, 2001). The EU would not allow the US to directly participate in building the single market, with EU officials arguing that the creation of the largest internal market would in itself be a catalyst for further international liberalization.

The SMP demonstrated the importance of monitoring the external implications of closer economic integration. During the past decade, the choice of regulatory policies and strategies has become a prominent focus of discussion beyond the confines of the EU. Many observers have drawn attention to the efforts by the EU to promote its policies at the global level through European leadership in the principal multilateral institutions. The primary reason for the EU's capacity to achieve such objectives is, however, its ability to promote collective action in the case of trade policy, coupled with its willingness to proceed without the US when necessary through new alliances and working relationships (see Devuyst, Chapter 9 this volume).

After the Cold War: first steps in governing the transatlantic economy
With the end of the Cold War, the US–EU political relationship required mutual adjustment on both sides of the Atlantic. The sudden disintegration of the Cold War framework raised the prospect of declining American influence in Europe and the need to keep pace with new developments, including the evolution of the EU. The nascent common European foreign and security policy and fledging defence capability now stand beside the single market and single currency. The EU has also established itself as a magnet for Central and Eastern Europe, leading to the enlargement to 25 members. The changes in Central and Eastern Europe meant that both the US and EU shifted their focus toward promoting political stabilization. Though NATO enlargement has figured prominently in this process, the recent enlargement of the EU will also alter the terms of the transatlantic dialogue.

The decline of the transatlantic relationship seemed increasingly plausible in Europe given the absence of a collective challenge from the Soviet Union. Concern over transatlantic drift led policy-makers on both sides to advocate greater institutional ties and strengthened relations. Ad hoc transatlantic consultations, usually at the margins of NATO and UN meetings, were soon deemed insufficient for Europe's growing and perceived capabilities. Transformation within Europe as the result of institutional changes and commitment to the SMP, along with the geopolitical changes after the collapse of the Berlin Wall led to a call for greater transatlantic cooperation (Baker, 1989; Gardner, 1997; see also Paemen, Chapter 2 this volume). The first Bush administration viewed the Community as playing a greater role in political and economic stabilization in the changing world order, and promoting the idea of a new policy framework to address the issue of burden sharing.

The Transatlantic Declaration adopted in 1990 laid the groundwork for a transformation of the transatlantic relationship to meet the changing demands of the post- Cold War global economy. Though the Transatlantic Declaration was later viewed as lacking in strategic focus, it went beyond simply restating existing institutional cooperative efforts, providing a political, non-security dialogue between the US and the EU, rather than its individual Member States, and creating a climate of cooperation among top officials. As Paemen notes in Chapter 2, the Declaration stressed the importance of common goals: support for democracy, human rights and social progress; peace and international security; promotion of economic stability and growth; promotion of market principles and support for multilateral trade liberalization and promotion of economic and political reform in developing countries.

By late 1994, however, the pace of political economic and economic change had overtaken the Declaration. Political leaders in Europe and the US began to ask whether a stronger transatlantic vision was necessary (Siebert, 1996; *Washington Quarterly*, 1996). Proponents such as British Foreign Minister Malcolm Rifkind and German Foreign Minister Klaus Kinkel articulated the idea of a Transatlantic Free Trade Area (TAFTA). The prospect of further negotiations received little support within the United States, and, although the European Commission had adopted a strategy paper on US–EU relations proposing a 'Transatlantic Economic Space', the proposed TAFTA would have faced a number of problems. These include conformity to WTO rules, the perception of excluding other advanced industrialized and developing countries, and the prospect that it would not cover 'substantially all trade' since it was unlikely to address liberalization in the agricultural or audiovisual sector (Devuyst, 1995: 17–18).

The New Transatlantic Agenda
Although the TAFTA was shelved, the debate had a significant outcome with the December 1995 signing of the New Transatlantic Agenda (NTA) and corresponding US–EU Joint Action Plan, establishing a framework for cooperation in areas including organized crime, terrorism, human trafficking and environmental degradation. The Action Plan consisted of 150 goals for joint action, giving the impression that every conceivable area of US–EU cooperation had been included (Hindley, 1999: p. 45). For the first time, the EU was treated not simply as a trade and economic organization, but as a political force able to partner with the US in a wide foray of diplomatic and foreign policy initiatives (Paemen, Chapter 2 this volume).

The NTA operates on the basis of (bi)annual summits of EU and US leaders,[6] which until recently coincided with the rotation of EU Presidencies, supplemented by meetings of a Senior Level Group (SLG) composed of senior government officials on both sides. The SLG and a more junior NTA Task Force make preparations for the summits, planning 'deliverables' in the area of policy cooperation and allowing each side to air matters of concern before they become major grievances (Devuyst, 2001). The SLG reports following each summit provide a sanitized but still useful overview of issues on the transatlantic agenda, including areas of agreement and disagreement in diplomatic cooperation, global challenges, economic issues and people-to-people initiatives.

The NTA also encouraged greater input from civil society through various dialogues, such as the Transatlantic Labor Dialogue, Transatlantic Environmental Dialogue and Transatlantic Legislative Dialogue (see Bignami and Charnovitz, 2001; Knauss and Trubek, 2001). While the extent of their recommendations and influence on transatlantic economic relations varies, the most influential effort has come from the Transatlantic Business Dialogue or TABD (cf Farrell, Chapter 6 this volume). As Cowles points out, business was often better equipped to think strategically about transatlantic and global market issues, so the Commerce Department and European Commission agreed that firms could contribute shaping debates on transatlantic economic issues (Cowles, 2001).

After intensive preparations, leading US and European chief executives launched the initial TABD Meeting in Seville in 1995. Modelled on the European Round Table, which had been influential in pushing the single market agenda, business was especially concerned about regulation and competitiveness. Duplicate standards and testing and certification procedures were of even greater priority than tariff reductions (see Steffenson, Chapter 8 this volume; Egan 2001). The issues promoted by the TABD have subsequently broadened to include regulatory cooperation, dispute settlement, capital markets and financial services, and electronic commerce (TABD, 2002). Both sides also invited the various transatlantic dialogues to contribute to an 'early warning' system designed to identify problems and offer proposals for possible solutions (see Paemen, Chapter 2 this volume).

The breadth of issues and joint actions covered by the NTA process led to criticisms that, though it represented an advance beyond the Transatlantic Declaration, it still lacked focus and failed to promote significant transatlantic economic cooperation. While the NTA committed the EU and US to explore the completion of a 'Transatlantic Marketplace', covering standards, certification and regulatory issues, equivalence of veterinary standards and procedures, customs cooperation, and a commitment to multilateral issues, it had no specific deadlines to encourage binding commitments (Frost, 1997).

Though more politically ambitious proposals such as TAFTA were not realized, policy-makers and business groups successfully concluded a number of agreements including those on: Mutual Recognition (1997); Competition Policy (1991, 1998); Customs Cooperation (1997); Science and Technology

Cooperation; Veterinary Procedures (1997); and Metrology and Measurement Standards (1999). However, many of these negotiations were protracted and yielded limited results, demonstrating that greater regulatory cooperation often remains difficult due to differences in domestic practices and the absence of domestic reforms needed to accomplish further economic integration (Pelkmans, 1999).

Meat on the bone? The TEP and PEA

An ambitious March 1998 proposal by the European Commission sought to give the economic elements of the NTA more coherent expression (European Commission, 1998). Spearheaded by European Trade Commissioner Leon Brittan, the proposal for a New Transatlantic Marketplace (NTM) aimed at overcoming the negative political impact of trade disputes such as the Helms-Burton and D'Amato Acts, moving beyond the modest 'step by step approach' to resolving individual problems and promoting liberalization in particular sectors. This new approach advocated a binding and comprehensive package, in essence adapting the EU's single market trading principles to the transatlantic context. This was soon made moot, however, as the proposal was effectively vetoed by France in April 1998, before formal American reaction to the proposal could be presented.

Following this setback, the European Commission, supported by the then British Presidency of the EU, proposed a less ambitious initiative in September 1998, based in part on the Transatlantic Economic Partnership or 'TEP' statement issued at the US–EU Summit in May 1998. Unlike the NTM, the TEP did not call for specific bilateral commitments to zero tariffs, a free trade area for services, an investment agreement or a bilateral dispute resolution mechanism. Instead, it contained general commitments to multilateral free-trade in the area of agriculture, industrial tariffs, investment, competition and procurement without concrete objectives or timetables (Frost, 1998). Much of the proposal reflected work already underway at the multilateral level, including improvements in enforcement and implementation in intellectual property, trademarks and customs cooperation.

Though not as far-reaching as the NTM proposal, the bilateral commitments in the TEP again focused primarily on the importance of regulatory cooperation. None of the multilateral actions represented new proposals. The TEP builds on the prior round of successful mutual-recognition agreements, since the same approach was envisioned for an increasing number of goods and service sectors. The launch of the TEP coincided with a 'mutual understanding' over the long-running dispute on US sanctions policy, encouraging political dialogue to resolve disputes over commercial foreign-policy actions, and a refrain from issuing further economic sanctions based on foreign-policy grounds.

By abandoning a broader framework, focusing instead on technical issues surrounding regulatory harmonization, the TEP does provide important

tangible goals or 'deliverables' that can be touted by both business and policymakers. These include advances in technical barriers to trade, regulatory cooperation and transparency, as well as an early warning system. Such negotiations are well suited to a climate that encompasses both regulatory and trade cultures because it requires mutual trust in each side's specific regulatory facilities and procedures, and also that testing, certification and licensing are equivalent (Steffenson, Chapter 8 this volume). But there is certainly little in the TEP that appears likely to energize transatlantic relations and generate a strong political commitment to transatlantic market integration.

Overshadowed by disputes over commercial sanctions as instruments of foreign policy, the TEP has not generated substantial results. Along with increased use of mechanisms by both sides to challenge foreign trade barriers (section 301 and special 301 in US and Article 113 and Trade Barrier Regulation in EU), demands for protection and temporary safeguards in certain sectors have also accelerated, amply documented in the respective EU and US annual reports on specific barriers that undermine restrict trade in their partners' markets (Schaffer, 2001; Paemen, Chapter 2 this volume).

To generate more momentum within the transatlantic economic relationship, the US–EU Summit in May 2002 announced a new initiative known as the Positive Economic Agenda (PEA). The PEA placed greater emphasis on new financial and regulatory developments that will likely have significant long-term consequences for the transatlantic relationship (Dam, 2003). At the core of this initiative are efforts to promote regulatory cooperation in insurance, greater coordination in financial services, public procurement and electronic tendering, and several agricultural initiatives designed to harmonize food regulations. Regulatory harmonization in the area of financial markets is especially critical given passage of the Sarbanes-Oxley legislation in the US, and the EU's effort to create a single capital market by 2005. An informal US–EU financial services dialogue has been created to address differences in financial regulation and oversight, and ensure that investment banks do not face higher compliance and operating costs or discriminate against their transatlantic counterparts in unintended ways (Dam, 2003). While efforts continue to reduce regulatory-based trade disputes, the emphasis on a unified transatlantic capital market covering accounting, audit, disclosure and corporate governance issues has broadened the impact of transatlantic economic negotiations beyond traditional trade and tariff issues.

Yet for some observers, the PEA resembles the TEP in again not being ambitious enough to add political momentum to the transatlantic economic relationship. Based on this experience, it seems more likely that future efforts to increase economic cooperation – or avoid economic conflict – will take place at the sectoral level. The disputes that currently affect the transatlantic agenda will not disappear. As the chapters in this book demonstrate, transatlantic efforts to coordinate markets reveal the depth of the underlying competition between their respective economic and social systems.

Summary of chapters

Each of the chapters in this volume reflects a focused attempt to understand an important aspect of the transatlantic economic relationship. Unlike many previous volumes on transatlantic relations (e.g. Pollack and Shaffer, 2001; Phillipart and Winand, 2001; Burwell and Daalder, 1999) this book focuses on detailed analyses of specific sectors.

Each of the chapters in this book was written for both academic and policy audiences, covering some of the most important economic issues facing the transatlantic relationship. Some cover negotiations in traditional sectors such as airlines and competition policy, which are governed by long-standing legal-institutional arrangements that shape business strategies and policies. Other issues such as data privacy, global satellite positioning and genetically modified foods are relatively new on the transatlantic trade agenda. As trade disputes increasingly garner the bulk of media attention, differences stemming from political or societal values rather than narrow economic interests will require more sophisticated economic diplomacy.

As many of the authors in this volume note, the search for markets and the promotion of liberalization has meant that the US and EU are collaborators and competitors at both bilateral and multilateral levels. Not only is market governance increasingly important for transatlantic relations, but globalization plays an increasingly important role in shaping the transatlantic economic relationship. The global aspects of that relationship, most notably in the context of the WTO, as well as the significance of specific geographic and sectoral issues such as anti-dumping, agricultural and biotechnology, determine the design of transatlantic strategic trade agendas.

Within their specific sectors, each chapter considers current trade negotiations and disputes, the record of regulatory cooperation and/or conflict, and the resulting government strategies and business responses to both policy and market developments. A renewed focus by trade specialists on regulatory issues has also increased the number of interests and constituents involved in the policy process, as business associations have found themselves confronted by consumer and environment groups seeking to influence trade negotiations.

In Chapter 2, Hugo Paemen examines the central importance of the transatlantic trade relationship in promoting liberalization in trade and investment at the bilateral and multilateral levels. While economic and political developments initiated by business and policy-makers in the post-Cold-War period have served to strengthen ties, trade tensions can and have affected its overall stability. Paemen points out that the effort to contain these disputes has resulted in mechanisms such as the bilateral early warning system and the multilateral dispute-settlement mechanism that still require further refinement and commitment.

In Chapter 3, Martin Staniland examines the impact of a long-standing international regulatory regime for the airline industry on the management of bilateral US–EU trade relations. As a result, the transatlantic aviation market has been subject to certain restrictions that reflect a long history of protectionism and nationalism. Staniland focuses on the effect of stringent regulatory protection in preventing widespread liberalization in the airline sector. Initially hampered by a fragmented market in Europe, the US has engaged in bilateral agreements with select Member States to improve market access. This has placed many recently privatized European carriers under intense competitive pressure, as well as undermining a common negotiating position throughout the EU. As Staniland notes, the response to both economic pressures and regulatory restrictions has been the creation of strategic alliances, with both sides disagreeing on the impact of such business strategies on competition. Despite common agreement on liberalization, neither the US nor the EU can agree on the terms and conditions of access for a transatlantic common aviation area.

In Chapter 4, Chad Damro describes the critical role of competition policy as corporate strategies have expanded to include a wave of mergers, acquisitions and alliances in response to the pressures of globalization. As Damro illustrates, firms are increasingly subject to multiple national jurisdictions that evaluate the competitive effects of their activities. To overcome such restrictions, the US and EU have engaged in cooperative arrangements in competition policy with regard to mergers and anti-trust measures. Damro clearly demonstrates that this effort at policy coordination has enabled regulators to avoid divergent decisions by engaging in dispute prevention. Concurrent jurisdiction has fostered extensive regulatory cooperation between the US and the EU as business behaviour has created pressures for domestic regulations to adapt to the international marketplace.

In Chapter 5, Johan Lembke argues that both the US and the EU have sought to strengthen their competitive advantage through industrial promotion efforts such as strategic regulation and financial subsidies, ensuring that their respective high-technology industries gain leverage in global markets. The security implications of such trade strategies have also generated strong transatlantic tensions as European firms seek to challenge the US monopoly over a key defence technology with significant market potential, and American firms seek to challenge EU dominance over industry standards in a key communications field. In two prominent infrastructure projects, third-generation wireless technology and global navigation and satellite systems, Lembke illustrates how the relative international competitiveness of industry leads to differential trade and regulatory efforts

In Chapter 6, Henry Farrell focuses on the development of regulatory cooperation in the area of data privacy. Controversy emerged when the EU adopted strict legal regulations that included restrictions on commercial exchanges of private information with countries lacking adequate regulatory guidelines. Since the US has advocated a self-regulatory approach, Farrell assesses the difficulties of reconciling different societal and business demands in regulating privacy, as well as the difficulties encountered in compliance with transatlantic agreements aimed at securing comparability of different regulatory regimes. Farrell demonstrates that the transatlantic dialogue has broadened to include a wide variety of interests that would traditionally have been excluded from the negotiating process. Consumer groups – most notably the Transatlantic Consumer Dialogue – have encouraged policy-makers to take account of consumer interests in their effort to manage different attitudes toward the regulation of privacy.

In Chapter 7 on food safety, Diahanna Post reviews the escalating dispute over the regulation of genetically modified foods, and the different approaches to risk assessment and risk management in the US and EU. The regulation of genetically modified foods has generated sharp disagreements over the levels and content of regulation, centred on the adoption of the precautionary principle by the EU. The EU's position is in large measure a response to consumer concerns over tightly regulating genetically modified foods, and has been roundly criticized by the US as protectionist and lacking firm scientific evidence. As Post concludes, the trade tensions between the two are further exacerbated by the European public reaction to these products, which may in the long run separate markets on both sides of the Atlantic.

In Chapter 8, Rebecca Steffenson analyses the TABD as a powerful lobbying group for businesses on both sides of the Atlantic on multilateral and bilateral trade issues, looking in particular at the case of mutual recognition agreements. For both American and European business, the issue of standards, testing and certification practices represents a key component of a more rational and accessible transatlantic market. Governments on both sides have listened to business proposals for further trade liberalization, particularly concerning issues of standards and technical barriers to trade. Steffenson convincingly argues that mutual recognition agreements promote joint coordination and mutual recognition of industry norms and standards, avoiding costly duplication and market entry barriers. However, while achieving agreement on the idea of regulatory convergence, mutual recognition agreements have largely remained a bureaucratic exercise with limited results.

While particular attention is given to US–EU relations in this volume, the relatively understudied dimension of the transatlantic relationship involving the EU and Canada provides an interesting counterpart to that of the US. As Youri Devuyst illustrates in Chapter 9, a number of trade and policy initiatives match those of the US–EU relationship, with similar efforts to institutionalize cooperation at the bilateral level over the past four decades. Devuyst provides an important survey of that relationship, with both the EU and Canada working on trade and investment issues, notably non-tariff and regulatory barriers. The efforts at policy coordination, while less visible than the summits conducted between the US and EU, have been matched by important joint actions in the spheres of both economics and security, with both the EU and Canada seeking to contribute to multilateral governance.

Conclusion: the evolving context for transatlantic trade relations

An important theme of many of these chapters is the intertwining of regulatory and trade cultures which has promoted new negotiating dynamics at the bilateral and multilateral levels. Broad changes in economics and society have occurred in post-industrial information societies, where new products and services have blurred traditional sectoral definitions that have long defined trade negotiations, increasing the number of issues on the transatlantic agenda. The range of economic disputes has expanded beyond traditional tariffs, quotas and duties into areas less amenable to resolution, with many of these issues reflecting sharp differences in public policy preferences and market and administrative practices. Though the EU and US have common trade objectives, such as market liberalization, their strategies in achieving these goals have also produced divergent proposals that must often be refined to reach consensus and agreement. Contemporary trade policy exemplifies both the potential for increased regulatory cooperation and the recurrent problems of divergent regulatory regimes in promoting a transatlantic marketplace.

A second theme is the importance of dispute-resolution mechanisms and implementation and evaluation strategies. For economic gains to be realized, the agreements reached in various sectors need to be successfully put into place. A number of chapters have highlighted the difficulties of reaching satisfactory outcomes despite what appears to be a good prospect of obtaining tangible results. This is in part due to pressure and expectations for immediate results, when in many instances discussion of technical details can, at least in the short term, yield greater uncertainty and disagreement about the long-run effects of regulatory cooperation. Many sectors have encountered obstacles and restrictions, increasing the frustration of businesses focused on deliverables. Given the largely technical nature of many regulatory processes, greater priority needs to be given to implementation and evaluation. With so much attention given to the negotiations themselves, several chapters highlight the need for improvement of existing bilateral trade rules and procedures, particularly in the competition policy and mutual recognition areas. Along with concerns about compliance with multilateral rulings,[7] there is growing pressure to improve dispute management, as well as to establish other measures to improve transparency and market confidence through enhanced regulatory cooperation and reform of existing regulatory practices.

A third and final theme is the increased role of a wide variety of socio-economic interests in shaping negotiations. While the non-governmental dialogues have varied enormously in their effectiveness and impact on the policy process, it is clear that the role of firms has become the most institutionalized and visible in shaping policy discussions. Coordination among private firms and government authorities working on trade and regulatory barriers has enabled commercial interests to provide information and establish a forum for business executives to articulate their preferences. Yet the resulting TABD represents only one facet of this relationship. Though the TABD has provided an opportunity for input by the business community into government negotiations, concern has been raised that the level of commitment and energy among executives has diminished as the range of bilateral issues under discussion has expanded in response to the changing security climate (see Lamy, 2003; Atlantic Council, 2003). The role of firms nonetheless has become a crucial factor when the particular terms of trade are debated, since their strategies ultimately reinforce efforts to seek protection from the pressures of liberalization, promote specific industrial policies, or foster strategic alliances. It is no coincidence that industry in many of the sectors in this book have made regulation and competition issues their central concern. Yet the regulatory process facilitates a variety of civil-society groups, even if they are poorly resourced or weakly engaged in the process (Young and Wallace, 2000: 2). Engaging these actors in the transatlantic economic relationship in a constructive way remains important, given the range of domestic regulatory issues that are now of direct concern in trade negotiations.

The chapters in this volume provide insights into the many dimensions of the transatlantic relationship including the often contradictory pressures between competition and collective action. Despite the often strong rhetoric, officials on both sides – as well as the business community – are well aware of the dangers of letting regulatory disputes escalate (Burwell, 2004). As the US and EU seek to mitigate the effects of transatlantic disputes created by differences in their respective domestic regulatory regimes, these chapters illustrate that transatlantic economic governance has produced an array of regulatory mechanisms with greater flexibility and innovation. The US and EU have used a variety of regulatory tools to tackle the challenges created by the international effects of domestic regulatory policy-making, with varying degrees of success. Whether those tools can keep pace with changes in the transatlantic relationship will largely be determined by both partners' political commitment to bilateral and multilateral trade liberalization, as determined by domestic societal demands and the perceived benefit of global economic development.

Notes

1 See Petersmann (2001).
2 Both the US and EU have low industrial tariffs although there are still some sensitive sectors with high levels of protection (steel, agriculture, food, textiles).
3 See for example Baldwin (1970).
4 This is based on Vogel (1996) and Egan (2001a).
5 This section draws primarily on Egan (2001b). For good historical overviews of the transatlantic relationship see also Guay (1999), Ginsberg and Featherstone (1996) and Peterson (1996; 2004).
6 The current Bush administration has decided to shift to annual summits.

7 The EU has drawn attention to the US Foreign Sales Corporation law ruled illegal by the WTO as well as the Byrd Amendment and 1916 Anti-Dumping legislation. The EU has given an ultimatum for compliance, demanding that the US amend the FSC provision to be WTO compatible or face the largest sanctions in WTO history.

References

Ahearn, R. (2002), 'US–European Union Trade Relations: Issues and Policy Challenges', Congressional Research Service, Library of Congress.

Asmus, R. (2003), 'Rebuilding the Atlantic Alliance', *Foreign Affairs*, 82:5, September/October.

Atlantic Council (June 2003), *Managing Risk Together: US and EU Regulatory Cooperation*, Washington DC.

—— (2003), *Risk and Reward: US–EU Cooperation on Food Safety and the Environment*, Washington DC.

Baker, J. (1989), 'A New Europe, A New Atlanticism: Architecture for a New Era', speech delivered in Berlin, 12 December.

Baldwin, R. (1970), *Non-Tariff Distortions of International Trade*, Washington DC: Brookings Institution.

Bergsten, C. F. (2002), 'A Renaissance for United States Trade Policy', *Foreign Affairs*, 81: 6, November/December.

Bignami, F. and S. Charnovitz (2001), in Pollack and Shaffer (eds), *Transatlantic Governance in the Global Economy*.

Buck, T. (2003), 'EU Shifts Stance on Deadlocked Trade Talks', *Financial Times*, 6 November, 2003: 12.

Burwell F. (2004), 'The Changing Transatlantic Agenda: A Lesson from the Economic Relationship', *AICGS Advisor*, American Institute for Contemporary German Studies: Washington DC, 5 February.

—— and I. Daalder (1999), *The United States and Europe in the Global Arena*, St Martin's Press.

Cowles, M. G. (1996), 'The EU Committee of AmCham: The Powerful Voice of American Firms in Brussels', *Journal of European Public Policy*, 3:3, 339–58.

—— M. G. (2001), 'The Transatlantic Business Dialogue: Transforming the New transatlantic Dialogue', in Pollack and Shaffer (eds), *Transatlantic Governance in the Global Economy*.

Daft, D. and N. Fitzgerald (2004), 'Business Can Help Bridge the Transatlantic Rift', *Financial Times*, 22 January.

Dam, K. (2003), 'A Fresh Perspective on US–EU Relations', speech to the Atlantic Council Board Dinner, Washington DC, 13 February.

Damro, C. and A. Sbragia (2003), 'The New Framework of Transatlantic Economic Governance: Strategic Trade Management and Regulatory Conflict in a Multilateral Global Economy', in M. Campanella (ed.), *EU Economic Governance and Globalization*, London: Edward Elgar.

De Jonquières, G. (2003), 'Battles among regulators could damage trade', *Financial Times*, 26 May.

—— and D. White (2003), 'US and Europe Urged to Help Revive Doha Round', *Financial Times*, 24 October.

Devuyst, Y. (1995), 'Transatlantic Trade Policy: Market Opening Strategies', European Policy Paper Series, University of Pittsburgh.

—— (2001), 'European Unity in Transatlantic Relations', in Eric Phillipart and Pascaline Winand, *Ever Closer Partnership: Policymaking in US–EU Relations*, Brussels: P.I.E. Peter Lang.

Egan, M. (1998), 'Mutual Recognition and Standard-Setting: Public and Private Strategies for Regulating Transatlantic Markets', American Institute for Contemporary German Studies Working Paper, Washington DC.

—— (2001a), *Constructing a European Market: Standards, Regulation and Governance*, Oxford: Oxford University Press.

—— (2001b), 'Creating a Transatlantic Marketplace: Government Policies and Business Strategies', AICGS Conference Report, February.

European Commission (1998), 'The New Transatlantic Marketplace', COM 125 Final, 11 March.

European Council (2003), 'Transatlantic Declaration', Annex to 12 December European Council Conclusions, Brussels.

Frost, E. (1997), *The New Transatlantic Marketplace*, Washington DC: Institute for International Economics.

—— (1998), 'The Transatlantic Economic Partnership', International Economic Policy Brief, Washington: IIE September.

Gardner, A. (1997), *A New Era in US–EU relations? The Clinton Administration and the New Transatlantic Agenda*, Aldershot: Avebury.

Ginsberg, R. and K. Featherstone (1996), *The United States and the European Union in the 1990s*, London: Palgrave Macmillan.

Gordon, P. (2003) 'Bridging the Atlantic Divide', *Foreign Policy*, January/February, 82:1, 70–83.

Grieco, J. (1990), *Cooperation Among Nations: Europe, America, and Non-Tariff Barriers to Trade*, Ithaca: Cornell University Press.

Guay, T. (1999), *The United States and the European Union: The Political Economy of a Relationship*, Sheffield: Sheffield Academic Press.

Hamilton, D. (2003), Congressional Testimony on 'Renewing the Transatlantic Partnership: A View From the US', House Committee on International Relations, House International Relations Subcommittee on Europe, 11 June.

Hindley, B. (1999), 'New Institutions for Transatlantic Trade', *International Affairs*, 75: 45–60.

Hocking, B. and M. Smith (1997), *Beyond Foreign Economic Policy: The United States and the Single European Market*, London: Pinter.

Horlick, G. (2002) 'Problems with the Compliance Structure of the WTO Dispute Resolution Process', in Daniel Kennedy and James Southwick (eds), *The Political Economy of International Trade Law*, Cambridge: Cambridge University Press.

Hudec, R. (1993), *Enforcing International Trade Law: The Evolution of the Modern GATT Legal System*, London: Butterworth.

Kahler, M. (1995), *Regional Futures and Transatlantic Relations*, New York: Council on Foreign Relations.

Knauss, J. and D. Trubek (2001), 'The Transatlantic Labor Dialogue: Minimal Action in a Weak Structure', in Pollack and Shaffer (eds), *Transatlantic Governance in the Global Economy*.

Lamy P. (2003), 'The Current State of EU–US Trade Relations', speech to Congressional Economic Leadership Council, Washington DC, 4 March.

Lang, J. (1999), 'International Trade, Domestic Regulation and Competition Policy', USIA Economic Perspectives.

Ludlow, P. (2002), 'EU–US Relations: For Better or For Worse', Euro Comment Briefing Note, 4, 4 June.

Majone, G. (2000), 'The Credibility Crisis of Community Regulation', *Journal of Common Market Studies*, 38:2.

Nicolaïdis, K. (1997), 'Mutual Recognition of Regulatory Regimes: Some Lessons and Prospects', Harvard Law School, Jean Monnet Working Paper Series, 9/97.

OTA (1992) Office of Technology Assessment Global Standards, Washington DC: US Government Printing Office.

Oxford Analytica (1998), 'European Union/US Trade Tensions', 6 August.

Page S. (1981), 'The Revival of Protectionism and Its Consequences for Europe', *Journal of Common Market Studies*, 20: 17–40.

Pelkmans, J. (1999), 'Pragmatism and Leadership: the EU's Atlantic Trade Strategy', paper presented to the American Institute for Contemporary German Studies, conference on 'Creating a Transatlantic Marketplace: Government Policies and Business Strategies', Washington DC.

Petersmann, E. (2001), 'Dispute Prevention and Dispute Settlement in the EU–US Transatlantic Economic Partnership', in Pollack and Shaffer (eds), *Transatlantic Governance in the Global Economy*.

Peterson, J. (1996), *Europe and America: The Prospects for Partnership*, London: Routledge.

—— (2004), *Europe and America: Partners and Rivals in International Relations*, Lanham: Rowman and Littlefield, forthcoming 3rd edn.

Philippart, E. and P. Winand (2001), *Ever Closer Partnership: Policy-Making in US–EU Relations*, Brussels: Presses interuniversitaires européennes/Peter Lang.

Pollack, M. and G. Shaffer (eds) (2001), *Transatlantic Governance in the Global Economy*, Lanham, MD: Rowman and Littlefield.

Pond, E. (2004), *Friendly Fire: The Near Death of the Transatlantic Alliance*, Washington DC: Brookings Institution Press.

Quinlan, J. P. (2003) *Drifting Apart or Growing Together? The Primacy of the Transatlantic Economy, Washington DC* Center for Transatlantic Relations, SAIS Johns Hopkins University.

Sandholtz, W. and J. Zysman (1989), '1992: Recasting the European Bargain', *World Politics*, 42 (October): 95–128.

Serfaty, S. (2003) *Renewing the Transatlantic Partnership*, CSIS: Washington DC, May.

Siebert, H. (1996) 'TAFTA: Fuelling Trade Discrimination or Global Liberalization' AICGS Economics Working Paper no. 19, March.

Shaffer, G. (2001), 'The Blurring of the Intergovernmental: Public-Private Partnerships behind US and EU Trade Disputes', in Pollack and Shaffer (eds), *Transatlantic Governance in the Global Economy*.

TABD (2002), Mid-Year Report.

USITC (1989), USITC Report, 'The Effects of Greater Economic Integration within the European Economic Community on the United States', USITC Report to Congress, USITC Publication 2204.

Van Groeben, H. (1985) *The EC, the Formative Years: The Struggle to Establish A Common Market and the Political Union*, Luxembourg: Commission of the European Communities.

Vogel, D. (1995), *Trading Up: Consumer & Environmental Regulation in a Global Economy*, Harvard: Harvard University Press.

—— (1998), *Barriers or Benefits? Regulation in Transatlantic Trade*, Washington DC: Brookings Institution.

Vogel, S. (1996) *Freer Markets, More Rules*, Ithaca: Cornell University Press.

Wallace, W. (2003), 'Can the Transatlantic Rift be Healed ?', *Observer Worldview Extra*, World Today Essay, 27 April.

Washington Quarterly (1996), 'Policy Forum: Transatlantic Free Trade', 19: 105–33.

Woolcock, S. (1996), 'EU–US Commercial Relations and the Debate on a Transatlantic Free Trade Area', in J. Wiener (ed.), *The Transatlantic Relationship*, London: Macmillan.

Young, A. and H. Wallace (2000), *Regulatory Politics in the Enlarging European Union*, Manchester: Manchester University Press.

Zoellick, R. (2002), 'Unleashing the Trade Winds', *The Economist*, 7–13 December.

The US–EU economic relationship

Introduction

During the second half of the twentieth Century, the US and Western Europe became the two major trading powers of the world. Together they represent about 40 per cent of world trade and about 60 per cent of world foreign direct investment (FDI). They also have become the world's two most integrated economic areas, trading about 20 per cent of their external exchanges with each other.

This ever closer transatlantic economic relationship is the result of conscious policy decisions by the governments and business communities on both sides. After the Second World War, the US strongly encouraged the liberalization of economic exchanges on the European continent, with American multinational corporations supporting this policy through massive investments. The continuing European economic integration process, as well as the regular enlargement of the number of participating countries, has no doubt exceeded the initial expectations of many, especially in the US. The two blocs were soon trading with each other as equal partners, and the increasing equality of the economic partnership became even more evident with the introduction of the single European currency in 1999.

At many times during that process, some in the US feared that European economic unification efforts would work to the detriment of American interests on the European continent. Mainly through their participation in the successive multilateral trade negotiations, the Europeans, however, have managed to roughly balance the three strides of their endeavours: deepening, widening and opening the integration process. The American agricultural community (and others in the world) maintains reservations on one aspect of this assessment, pointing to the protectionist effects of the European Agricultural Policy (CAP). Notwithstanding this criticism, which has aspects of stones and glass houses, Europe has remained a major buyer of American agricultural products during the whole period.

American concerns about the potential for introverted tendencies in Europe were at their zenith when, in the mid-1980s, the European Community under the leadership of Commission President Jacques Delors, set up a new initiative to 'complete' the single European Market. Warnings and even action programmes were launched against the dangers for the US, and the rest of the world, of a 'fortress Europe'. These concerns were proven to be misplaced. As had been the case in previous phases of the European integration, this internal initiative was soon followed by a further external opening in the form of an active participation in the Uruguay Round of multilateral trade negotiations (1986–92). As the two main economic actors, the US and the EU negotiated and cooperated intensively in order to achieve the major transformation of the GATT into a much enlarged WTO. After having been one of the main topics in transatlantic discussions for several years, the 'European fortress' theme disappeared as quickly as it had emerged.

Since the end of the Cold War this bilateral economic partnership between the US and Europe has been largely de-linked from the security context, which, until then, had exercised a kind of ameliorating effect upon possible trade conflicts between the allies. No longer inhibited by security concerns, a series of bilateral trade disputes developed their own (public) momentum (such as: the EC ban on growth hormones in meat, EC canned-fruit subsidies, EC and US subsidies in the civil aircraft sector, US measures against EC steel exports). The negative perception of these disputes (rashly proclaimed by the media as so many transatlantic 'wars') and some genuine concern about the future shape of their partnership in the new geo-political context encouraged leaders on both sides to look for some innovative ideas. Both sides also wanted the increasing role of Europe as a whole to be recognized. Some suggested the idea of a full-fledged Treaty between Europe and the US; others raised the possibility of a transatlantic free-trade zone. In December 1989 the US Secretary of State James Baker declared in a speech in Berlin that the EC and the US might 'work together to achieve, whether in treaty or some other form, a significantly strengthened set of institutional and consultative links'.

In November 1990 both sides signed a rather modest 'Transatlantic Declaration', in which they committed themselves to more regular consultations. Then, they stated that 'the increasing pace of change in the post-Cold War environment, including a number of new regional and global challenges, however, led to the more ambitious New Transatlantic Agenda (NTA) of 1995'.

The NTA was also driven by the concern of leaders on both sides that the new political situation was not without risks for the overall bilateral relationship. In the introduction to the new statement, which was signed in November 1995 at the then biennial EU–US Summit, EU and US leaders affirmed their 'conviction that the ties which bind our people are as strong today as they have been for the past half century'. They also stated that 'our economic relationship sustains our security and increases our prosperity'.

The NTA sketched out a wide scope of areas for transatlantic cooperation. In two broad sectors the existing common endeavours developed during the Cold War period would be continued and intensified:

- Promoting Peace and Stability, Democracy and Development around the world.
- Contributing to the Expansion of World Trade and Closer Economic Relations.

The two other chapters had a more innovative twist and aimed at enlarging the cooperation in order to meet the challenges and dangers of the new era for a continuing Atlantic Partnership:

- Responding to Global Challenges (e.g. international crime, terrorism, environment, biotechnology).
- Building Bridges across the Atlantic (aiming at more public support, civil society participation).

In sum, the Transatlantic Declaration and NTA recognized the new political and strategic context in which the transatlantic economic relationship is increasingly embedded.

The transatlantic economy in a new century

At the beginning of the twenty-first century, US–EU trade patterns show a great degree of balance and stability: in 2000 the US imported 11.7 per cent of its GDP, the EU 11.2 per cent. US imports from the EU represented 19.3 per cent of its total imports. EU imports from the US were 19 per cent of its total imports. The main differences concern overall trade balances. While US imports represent 23.5 per cent of world imports, US exports represent only 15.4 per cent of world totals. The same figures for the EU are more balanced, with EU imports in the same period representing 18.2 per cent of world imports, and EU exports representing 18.4 per cent of the world totals.[1] The increase of the overall US trade deficit, resulting largely from an overvalued dollar, was also reflected in bilateral US–EU trade in goods, which showed a US deficit of about $60 billion. At the same time, the US has maintained a smaller but stable surplus in trade in services. As Gary C. Hufbauer and Frederick Neumann of the Institute of International Economics note: 'mature stability rather than dynamic change is the dominant flavor of US–EU trade volumes' (Hufbauer and Neumann, 2002).

A similar and perhaps more impressive image is shown by the development of bilateral foreign direct investments. On a cumulative, historical-cost basis, EU Foreign Direct Investment (FDI) in the US grew from $228.5 billion in 1990 to $808.3 billion in 2001. The US FDI stock in the EU increased from $183.9 billion in 1990 to $640.8 billion in 2001. The EU received about 50 per cent of US FDI and supplied about 60 per cent of American incoming FDI. Like the trade figures, the investment magnitudes have been growing relative to GDP levels, but the growth figures are higher for investments than for trade, an indication of the increasing integration of the economies. Here

Hufbauer and Neumann add that: 'the investment picture is the mature closeness of an older couple' (Hufbauer and Neumann, 2002).

The driving force and the relative importance of foreign investments versus trade in integrated economies such as those of the US and the EU are further demonstrated by the fact that sales of US affiliates in Europe are considerably more important than US exports to the EU ($1.2 trillion versus $261.1 billion in 1999). The same is true for sales by European affiliates in the US compared to European exports ($1.05 trillion versus $292 billion in 1999).

The slowdown in global economic growth that started in 2000 and became more severe in 2001 and 2002, had its inevitable impact on the EU–US relations, but did not reduce their interdependency. As Martin Neil Baily observed, 'There seemed no clear reason why a cyclical decline in the United States should trigger a similar decline in Europe. And yet that seems to have happened' (Baily, 2003).

Transatlantic disputes

Much has been said and written about trade disputes between the US and the EU.[2] In their official statements, leaders on both sides never miss an opportunity to stress the relatively small part of their trading relationship that is affected by their bilateral disputes (estimated between 2 and 5 per cent). Moreover, just as increasing traffic on the highway augments the risk of accidents, the number of disputes could be expected to grow with the growing volume of trade between the two continents. It does not, however, prevent those conflicts from keeping the headlines of the media and largely determining the mood of public opinion. The reality is that they indeed involve a relatively limited amount of trade, and also that they are not limited to a special type of conflict or a specific sector of the economy. What can be said is that, with increasing integration, a new type of transatlantic issue has been added to the traditional disputes (e.g. agricultural subsidies, steel protection and taxation). They mainly result from regulatory divergences with what some would call a more ideological, societal or cultural dimension (GMOs, hormones-enhanced meat, private-data protection, environment, etc.), sometimes called 'behind-border' issues.

It is also important to underline that the most 'visible' conflicts are not always linked to most important economic issues. Those that originated in the EU have mostly related to the agricultural or the food sectors (bananas, hormones-enhanced meat, GMOs), while American measures in favour of the steel sector (safeguard measures, Byrd amendment) provoked EU action in the WTO. Legislative initiatives, which either side would qualify as 'unilateral', have also provoked conflict (Helms-Burton and Iran-Libya legislation by the US, Hushkitts, private-data protection by the EU).

An important innovation that has had a considerable impact on the way transatlantic disputes are settled is the new dispute settlement system of the

WTO. It was conceived to replace the multilateral GATT rules, which were largely inefficient in the transatlantic context. It would certainly have been unacceptable for the two main promoters of the Uruguay Round to discard the new 'Understanding on Rules and Procedures Governing Settlement of Disputes', or Dispute Settlement Understanding (DSU), with its stricter deadlines and more compelling jurisdiction when their own mutual issues were at stake. Still, it was a remarkable reversal – and a cultural shock for some of their own negotiators – that the two wily giants of international trade were ready to accept the more legalistic successor of the GATT as the ultimate referee to settle their pending as well as their future disputes.

In the first years of the DSU's existence, the American side was a more virulent complainant, putting its efficiency to the test in some highly political transatlantic cases (bananas, hormones . . .). Soon the EU took a more proactive stand and introduced its own bundle of cases (steel, anti-dumping, FSC . . .). Although some of the WTO decisions have admittedly not led to instant implementation (Anti-dumping Act of 1916, FSC for the US; bananas, hormones on the EU side), there is no doubt that the new system has introduced some degree of efficiency and predictability in transatlantic disputes. Within the total number of completed WTO-DSU cases during the period from 1995 to 2001, the US–EU disputes still represented a minority, even if some of them attracted considerable media publicity. The figures are 11 out of 54 (and a further 5 ongoing). Of these 16, 4 were cases US v. EU and the other twelve EU v. US.

As is the case with the WTO membership in general, no defendant found to be at fault has openly considered not abiding by the WTO ruling. This is a sea change from attitudes under the previous regime.

Governance of the transatlantic relationship

Trade and investment policies in the transatlantic market
The US Constitution grants Congress the power 'to regulate commerce with foreign nations and among the several states'.[3] Congress is free, after having determined the basic legislative policy, to delegate administrative authority to make regulations implementing the policy it has established. This has been done in the trade area through successive Trade Acts. Since 1979 the so-called 'fast track' procedure has been used, authorizing the president to negotiate trade agreements but making the implementation of the results dependent upon congressional approval.

In the European Union the competence and decision-making procedures for external commercial relations have been established by the EC Treaty (Treaty of Rome) in what is presently Article 133 (initially Article 113). The European Commission submits proposals and recommendations to the Council, which authorizes the Commission to open negotiations. The Commission conducts the negotiations in consultation with a special committee appointed by the Council to assist the Commission in this task and within the framework of such directives as the Council may issue to it.

In contrast with the decisive role played by Congress in the establishment and implementation of US trade policy, no Parliamentary approval is required at any stage of the Article 133 procedure on the European side. This has been a long-standing sore point between the European Parliament and the Member States, which the Parliament has repeatedly tried to change, but to no avail. It has also been invoked by critics as an element of deficient legitimacy for the action of the EU in the context of the WTO.

Because of their important share in world trade, the US and the EU are indispensable actors in any major trade initiative, especially any multilateral trade negotiation. This has again been evident, notwithstanding the increasing role of other countries, like the major developing countries, during the discussions that have led to the launching of the so-called Doha Round in 2001. Likewise, conflicts between the two majors have a tendency to reflect negatively upon the functioning of the international trading system. Dramatic examples of this reality were the suspension for many months of the Uruguay Round negotiations because of the US–EU disagreements in the agricultural sector and the failure of the Ministerial Meeting in Seattle in December 1999.

The two sides clearly do not want to rely exclusively on the WTO DSU, despite the shift in attitudes outlined in the previous section, to solve their real or potential conflicts. Highly political problems like the dispute over the Helms-Burton Act have convinced them of the limits of the system when confronted with certain types of sensitive issues. Moreover, there is the risk of the system being overburdened by the sheer number of cases if no effort is made in the direction of dispute prevention. Mainly in the wake of the New Transatlantic Agenda (NTA), new bilateral avenues were explored in order to prevent or to calm down US–EU disputes.

On the prevention side, the NTA launched the idea of a New Transatlantic Marketplace (NTM) in which 'barriers that hinder the flow of goods, services and capital between us' would be progressively reduced or eliminated. To this effect regulatory cooperation would be strengthened, in particular by encouraging regulatory agencies to give a high priority to cooperation with their respective counterparts. The NTA also promoted a series of transatlantic dialogues through which civil-society groups on both sides concerned by the issues could exchange their views and consider solutions acceptable to both sides, leading to the 'bridge-building' described above. The Transatlantic Consumer and Business Dialogues were initiated in that perspective. Of major importance in the same context were the idea and more recently the reality of a Legislative Dialogue, in which lawmakers from both sides exchange their views on the analysis and the possible solutions to common or similar problems on which they have to legislate, with the condition that dialogue take place before final decisions are made.

Mutual recognition agreements

As a result of successive multilateral trade negotiations, the transatlantic market has to a large extent become a reality between the US and the EU. Traditional trade policy barriers no longer play a decisive role between the two giants, and the trade defence instruments (Safeguard, Antidumping, Countervailing Duty measures) are only being used exceptionally.[4] This means that the somewhat hidden 'behind-borders' measures become more visible and more prominent: legislative and regulative measures, administrative practices, and other measures which do not appear as trade policy instruments, but which, intentionally or not, can have the same effect.

Not surprisingly, the US and EU have been increasingly focusing on these measures in their Annual Reports on Trade Barriers. Most can be traced to different administrative traditions or reflect the different sensitivities of the respective populations in areas like sanitary and phyto-sanitary regulations, food safety, environmental concerns, etc. The degree of centralization of governmental structures, the preferences between government-led and self-regulatory approaches, as well as between anticipatory or experience-driven regulatory traditions, especially in regard to new products and technologies (like IT and biotechnology), play an important role.

In the search for ways to reduce or eliminate the trade-inhibiting effects of these measures, the experience of the establishment of the Single European Market (SEM) has been of prime importance. After a first phase, in which the European institutions tried in vain to harmonize the divergent legislation and regulatory systems of its Member States, the principle of mutual recognition was introduced. Its basic approach is that, for the proper functioning of the market, the important element is the final result rather than the way in which the result was achieved. If the basic goals and standards of European legislation are achieved, mutual recognition allows different products, production methods, and testing and certification practices to coexist freely and competitively in a single market.

Experience has shown the advantages of the mutual-recognition approach vs. full harmonization. However, mutual recognition is easier to apply if a homogeneous regulatory and administrative environment already exists. A degree of trust in the willingness and capacity of the other parties to meet the conditions of the agreement fully is also indispensable. The enduring difficulties in certain sectors of the European market, which is largely based on the mutual-recognition approach, is an indication of the resistance of some vested (often bureaucratic) attitudes or traditions against this flexible and market-oriented approach.

In 1998 the US and the EU concluded a Mutual Recognition Agreement (MRA) covering the following sectors: telecommunication equipment, electromagnetic compatibility, medical devices, pharmaceuticals, electrical safety, and recreational craft. In 2001 a separate MRA was negotiated on marine equipment (Egan, 2001).

The conclusion of the MRAs was generally acclaimed as a substantial contribution to the further integration of the transatlantic market. In fact, it has been a limited success. From both sides there have been complaints about the implementation at the level of the regulatory and enforcing agencies, some of them being decentralized, others belonging to the private sector, especially laboratories for the testing and certification of regulated products.

In 1998, EU Trade Commissioner Leon Brittan tried to revive and formalize the idea of a 'New Transatlantic Marketplace' (NTM), which had been suggested in the context of the NTA. In substance, his proposal would have led to a free-trade zone through the elimination of all industrial tariffs and the removal of regulatory barriers to trade in goods and services. The European Council did not take up the idea, but agreed on a more modest agenda for a 'Transatlantic Economic Partnership' (TEP). The main goal was, once more, to give a new impetus to the removal of regulatory barriers as well as to the establishment of a common agenda for the next multilateral trade negotiations in the WTO.[5]

Alarmed by the continuing escalation of several ongoing trade disputes, the American and European leaders also decided at the June 1999 US–EU Summit in Bonn to develop an Early Warning System, which would be another instrument to prevent the generation of future disputes. The idea was that at an early stage potential disputes would be identified and consultations organized, particularly those concerning legislative, regulatory and policy initiatives on either side. Both the administrations and their mutual diplomatic missions were instructed to focus on those potential sources of conflict. Dialogues between the non-governmental organizations were also expected to play their part in this form of dispute prevention.

The problems addressed by the Early Warning System are likely to increase. The Foreign Trade Barriers Report of 2002, published by the Office of the US Trade Representative, states that: 'Standards-related and regulatory-based issues represent a growing element of US–EU trade relations' (USTR, 2002a: 110). Further: 'Our difficulty for US exporters is that only "notified bodies" located in Europe are empowered to grant final product approvals of regulated products' and 'subcontracting laboratories cannot issue the final product approval but must send test reports to their European affiliate for final review and approval, which delays the process and adds costs for US exporters' (USTR 2002a: 110).

The European view, as formulated in the Commission's Barriers Report, considers as a particular American problem the 'relatively low level of use, or even awareness, of standards set by international standardising bodies' (European Commission 2002b). Another problem is the continued reliance on mandatory third-party conformity-assessment procedures for many industrial products, which in many countries has been replaced by self-certification by manufacturers backed up by post-market surveillance and control. Other difficulties seem to stem from regulations at the state level, the multiplicity of standards, especially in the sectors of the environment protection, safety provisions for electrical appliances, burdensome labelling provisions, and the cost of product liability insurance.

A feeling of frustration with the slow pace of regulatory cooperation also exists in the transatlantic business community. In the briefing papers in preparation of the Transatlantic Business Dialogue meeting in Chicago in November 2002 one can read: 'Companies often face a "jungle" of different government regulations, standards, testing, certification and labelling schemes before a product can be traded and sold' (TABD, 2002: 25). The representatives of the industries on both sides reminded the US and EU governments of their long-standing request to 'apply the TABD objective of "Approved Once, Accepted Everywhere" for product requirements and conformity assessment procedures where appropriate for individual sectors' (TABD, 2002: 25).

In general, the initial ardour for further transatlantic regulatory cooperation as launched in the context of the TEP programme and through the conclusion of MRAs, has largely been lost in bureaucratic and institutional complexities, particularly at the levels of monitoring, implementation and enforcement. Next steps will require movement beyond agreement in principle to practical application. In their Briefing Papers for the 2002 TABD meeting in Chicago, industry representatives wrote: 'With the Guidelines in place, the TABD calls on governments to rebuild the momentum for EU–US regulatory cooperation and move forward in implementing the Guidelines' (2002: 25–6). They proposed specific pilot projects for that purpose, identifying the sectors of dietary supplements, cosmetics and chemicals.

No more statements needed: multilateral progress and effective implementation

In April 2002, the US and EU governments had indeed agreed on one more initiative in the sector of regulatory cooperation, the 'Guidelines on Regulatory Cooperation and Transparency'. Their goal was to promote a more systematic dialogue between the EU and the US regulators as well as greater transparency and public participation in the regulatory process. Their efforts were made less compelling, however, by the wording of the Guidelines, including paragraph 7: 'This document sets forth the Guidelines which regulators of the US Federal Government and the services of the European Commission intend to apply on a voluntary basis as broadly as possible' (USTR, 2002b).

Another effort aiming at counterbalancing the negative perception of the transatlantic economic relationship was launched by leaders at the US–EU Summit Meeting in May 2002, in the form of a 'Positive Economic Agenda consisting of an ongoing scheme of bilateral co-operation on specific sectors'. Under the previously adopted non-binding 'Guidelines for Regulatory Cooperation and Transparency', the leaders decided to 'consider the implementation of pilot projects in particular in matters relating to motor vehicle technical regulations' (European Commission, 2002a). Yet the 'Guidelines' constituted only one of seven items on the Positive Economic Agenda. The others were: financial services, sanitary and phyto-sanitary issues, insurance, organic farming and products, electronic tendering, and electronic customs. For each, indications of what was expected were rather tentative and of a general nature. The initiative thus appears as one additional effort to deal with a situation driven by forces beyond the direct control of political leaders.

It is very likely that historians will look back on the recent history of US–EU relations (since 1995) as being not particularly warm or productive. There is abundant literature, published on both sides of the Atlantic, trying to analyse the causes and successive developments of an alliance, which, mainly since the end of the Cold War, seems to have been drifting apart. The overall political context has undeniably had an important influence on what has happened in the economic sector, which is the subject of this chapter. It seems clear, however, that other, more specific factors have influenced the recent evolution of the transatlantic economic partnership.

The gradual collapse of the Soviet Union took place while the international trade negotiators were involved in the largest and most fundamental multilateral trade negotiation ever held. The United States and the European Union were the main actors in the Uruguay Round, which lasted about seven years, and which led to the creation of the WTO, a new dispute-settlement system, and new multilateral agreements on trade in services and on intellectual Property. The previous multilateral negotiations, the Tokyo Round, had taken place from 1973 to 1979. The interval between the two negotiations was a period of painful economic adjustment to the disruptions created by tenfold energy-price increases and the ensuing economic disruptions.

The US considered that another multilateral trade negotiation would be useful in that respect, while at the same time, it offered an opportunity to pursue some objectives they failed to achieve in the Tokyo Round, most particularly in the agricultural sector. The European Union was not tempted to go back to the negotiation table and resisted a new Round until 1986. Remarkably enough, after the conclusion of the Uruguay Round it was the European Union that very soon wanted to go back to Geneva, with a proposal put forward by Leon Brittan for a 'Millennium Round'. This time the US was rather reluctant before finally proposing a Ministerial Meeting in Seattle to launch a next Round in 1999. Those who participated in these developments, from the conclusion of the Tokyo Round and beyond, experienced a cycle of international trade negotiations not unlike the biblical tale of the seven lean and seven prosperous years.

The analogy would also indicate that time is overdue for another multilateral liberalization effort. It may be considered one positive development of the US–EU economic relations that during the ministerial meeting in Doha the failure of Seattle was corrected, to a large extent as a result of their common efforts. Many hope that a similar common effort in favour of a new worldwide negotiation may smooth the bilateral edges that have become sharper during the present negotiation pause.

The stakes are significant. Hufbauer and Neumann consider that in a world of expanded free trade, EU exports to the US could increase by about $44 billion and US exports to the EU by about $48 billion. Assuming a fixed ratio between FDI stock and two-way trade in merchandise and services, US owned FDI stock placed in the European Union might expand by $109 billion (some 19 per cent), whereas EU owned FDI stock placed in the US might expand by $118 billion (some 15 per cent). To make this possible, they recommend that US and EU leaders 'accelerate the resolution of market access disputes and more particularly concentrate on the industrial policy disputes, rather than on the "ideological" conflicts (often based on environmental or bio-safety concerns in the EU and unilateralist tendencies in American policy-making)' (Hufbauer and Neumann, 2002: 12–13).

More progress at the multilateral level will be necessary, with positive bilateral spillover. It appears, however, that the largest obstacle to a smoothly functioning transatlantic market is not the basic motivation of the governments or of economic operators. We have learned that initial political impulses for trade liberalization increasingly meet resistance at the level of implementing and enforcing agencies on both sides. These bodies and the officials staffing them often consider that, independently of their personal inclination, they cannot 'negotiate away' their authority, which results from the existing statutory legislation. In order to overcome this hurdle the governments need to do more than publish solemn statements at summit meetings. The legislative authorities on both sides need to be actively associated (through the legislative dialogues) and convinced of the need to participate in a common effort. Where necessary, they must also resist the special interests opposed to change.

Conclusion

Near the middle of 2003 neither the overall geopolitical situation nor the respective economic growth patterns seemed to favour a new impetus for the transatlantic economic cooperation. The US has had a sharper decline in economic growth than Europe but seems also to have the better chances for an earlier recovery, although the timing is far from certain. The relative weakness of the dollar compared with the euro will probably reinforce this scenario, but the uncertainties about the war against Iraq, the likelihood of increased oil prices and deeper deficits make rational forecasts even more hazardous.

The multilateral trade negotiations in the WTO have been given a 'Doha Development Agenda'. This puts the interests of the developing countries squarely in the middle of the negotiations and will require the industrialized countries to adjust their strategies accordingly. Since the WTO Cancun Ministerial Meeting collapsed in September 2003, negotiations will have to be extended beyond the original time frame for completion. This means that the multilateral negotiating process will continue during an electoral year with presidential elections in the US and the appointment of a new European Commission, and the enlargement of the European Union with the accession of ten new member states. Notwithstanding a much larger field of active participants in the negotiations, US–EU cooperation remains a decisive factor for the success of the negotiations.

For the moment the US government, like many others, seems rather focused on the extension of its network of bilateral and regional agreements (with Chile, Singapore, Morocco, Latin America). The business communities on both sides of the Atlantic do not show great interest in the multilateral Round. For most companies, especially the larger ones, the transatlantic market has already become a reality they feel comfortable with, so that they are rather looking for improvements on the side of regulations in other areas such as taxation.

For all these reasons a pause seems to have been entered into as far as further transatlantic regulatory cooperation is concerned. But those who think that the increasing integration of the two markets is as inevitable as desirable have already appealed for another initiative to 'close the Atlantic divide' (Eizenstat and Paemen, 2002).

Notes

1 Unless indicated otherwise, US–EU economic statistics are derived from the US Department of Commerce, www.doc.gov and the European Commission http://europa.eu.int.
2 For a comprehensive review, see: Pollack and Shaffer, 2001.
3 See the US Constitution, Art. I § 8.
4 In 2001 the US had again recourse to safeguard measures in the steel sector against a large number of countries, included the EU.
5 See the 2129th Council Meeting (General Affairs), 12560/98, Press 369.

References

Baily, M. (2003), 'The Year in Review: A Turning Point?', Washington DC: Institute for International Economics Working Paper.

Egan, M. (2001), 'Mutual Recognition and Standard Setting: Public and Private Strategies for Governing Markets', in Pollack and Shaffer, *Transatlantic Governance in the Global Economy*.

European Commission (2002a), 'EU and US Agree to Launch Positive Economic Agenda at EU–US Summit', Press Memo 2002/85, Brussels, 3 May. Available at www.europa.eu.int/comm/external_relations/us/sum04_02/me02_85.htm.

—— (2002b), 'Report on United States Barriers to Trade and Investment 2002', Brussels, November 2002. Available at http://europa.eu.int/comm/trade/bilateral/usa/usa.htm.

Eizenstat, S. and H. Paemen (2002), 'Closing the Atlantic Divide', *Financial Times*, 24 July.

Hufbauer, G. C. and F. Neumann (2002), 'US–EU Trade and Investment: An American Perspective', Washington DC: Institute for International Economics Conference Paper. Available at www.iie.com/papers/hufbauer0502.htm.

Pollack, M. and G. Shaffer (eds) (2001) *Transatlantic Governance in the Global Economy*, Lanham, MD: Rowman and Littlefield.

TABD (2002), CEO Issue Briefing Papers for the Annual TABD Conference, Chicago, October.

United States and European Union (1995), 'New Transatlantic Agenda and Joint Action Plan', US–EU Summit, December.

USTR (2002a), '*National Trade Estimate Report on Foreign Trade*', also available at www.ustr.gov/reports/index.shtml.

—— (2002b), 'United States and European Commission Agree on Guidelines for Increased Regulatory Cooperation and Transparency', Press release 02/42, April 12. Also available from http://ustr.gov/releases/2002/04/02-42.htm.

Long-haul liberalization: will transatlantic air transport ever be deregulated?

Introduction

In November 2002, the European Court of Justice (ECJ) delivered a ruling on the regulation of international aviation that was widely described as 'historic' and likely to revolutionize in particular the organization of air transport across the North Atlantic. For example, Richard Branson, the chairman of Virgin Atlantic Airways, wrote: 'The world of international aviation changed on [5 November], and it changed permanently and for the better. There is now no going back. We are on the verge of a breakthrough that will transform this industry, and not a moment too soon' (Branson, 2002). The editor-in-chief of *Air Transport World* commented similarly that the ECJ's ruling was 'a historic decision likely to reshape international aviation and aeropolitics in ways that cannot be foreseen'(Flint, 2002).[1]

The aim of this chapter is to examine the character of transatlantic air transport as a trading sector and to explore the major issues arising and emerging in regulating this sector. In particular, it will examine the impact of recent deregulation in the EU and the US on airlines operating transatlantic services and the rationale for the recent wave of strategic alliances between EU and US (and other) airlines. Lastly, it will compare strategies for further liberalization now being pursued or proposed and will assess their feasibility, given the airline industry's long history of nationalism and protectionism and the recent ECJ judgment.

Transatlantic air services

The transatlantic aviation market exemplifies both the phenomenal growth and the recurrent problems of the airline industry. Transatlantic routes developed later than those between Europe and Asia and Africa (which developed before the Second World War as a matter of imperial strategy) and those within the western hemisphere developed by Pan American and other US carriers. True commercial service to the United States only began after the Second World War: even as late as 1949, fewer than 300,000 passengers a year were crossing the North Atlantic by air and it was only in 1957 that the number crossing the Atlantic by air exceeded those travelling by sea.[2]

The introduction of jet airliners in the late 1950s (and of large wide-body aircraft such as the Boeing 747 in the 1970s) increased reliability and productivity, leading in turn to lower fares and yet more passengers. In 1980, more than 16 million passengers flew across the North Atlantic: by 1990, this figure had jumped again to 30,340,000, with a forecast of 51,800,000 by 2001 – a fifty-fold increase in passenger traffic since 1957 (Ott, 1993: 65). Passengers carried on transatlantic flights now represent approximately 14 per cent of all passengers carried worldwide by air, partly because transatlantic flights connect the world's two largest domestic air transport markets – the European and the US markets with 28.4 per cent and 41.35 per cent, respectively, of the world's air traffic (*Air Transport World*, 1999: 54).

Economically, the transatlantic market is an important generator of revenue for both European and North American airlines. In 1998, services between the EU and the US produced a total revenue of $20 billion for participating airlines (with $10 billion of the total coming just from routes between the UK and the US). North Atlantic routes are especially important for EU airlines which have historically relied more on long-haul international routes than their American counterparts. In 1992/3, six of the European flag carriers flew more than 30 per cent of their international mileage on North Atlantic routes (Lehmann Brothers, 1993).[3] Profit figures for particular markets and routes are hard to obtain, but it has been reported that Lufthansa in the early 1990s was deriving some 30 per cent of its profits from transatlantic services (*Financial Times*, 1992; *Financial Times*, 1993).[4] For some smaller carriers, dependence on transatlantic traffic was even greater: in the late 1990s, some 60 per cent of Aer Lingus's revenue and half of its profits came from its transatlantic routes (Brown, 2001).

Despite the prodigious growth in traffic across the North Atlantic, this market has been chronically afflicted by what has been described as 'profitless growth syndrome'.[5] In the 1950s and 1960s, overcapacity and low profits stemmed from the adoption of 'tourist' and then 'economy' fares, from the multiplication of airlines flying across the Atlantic, and (in the early 1960s) from the addition of aircraft and services by airlines that had been hurt by decolonization in Africa and Asia. In the 1970s, excess capacity arose from the simultaneous introduction of wide-bodied aircraft and the recessionary effects of the first OPEC oil shock. In the 1980s and 1990s, fares continued to fall, partly due to the advent of budget carriers such as Laker Airways, People Express and Virgin Atlantic.

Overcapacity has led to periodic fare-wars and has caused a continuing drop in the 'yield' that airlines get from seats sold.[6] During the 1990s, airlines on transatlantic routes saw their yields fluctuate between 6.6 and 8.0 US¢ per passenger kilometre, falling to 6.3 in US¢ per passenger kilometre in 2000 (AEA, 2001: I-8). With the advent of alliances, airlines have become more skilled at managing supply, putting on fewer flights and using smaller aircraft on certain routes. But in the transatlantic market profitability remains elusive, despite the persistence of stringent regulatory protection.

The Chicago Convention and international regulation

Regulation of air travel between Europe and the US still rests on the foundation provided by the 1944 Chicago Convention on International Civil Aviation and the array of bilateral Air Service Agreements (ASAs) concluded between individual states within the framework of this Convention. The bilateral agreements have traditionally stipulated what routes may be flown between airports on the territories of the signatories and with what frequency; they may also contain limits on capacity (seats offered) and provisions for authorizing fares. Finally, they empower states to designate one or more carriers to exercise the traffic rights obtained through ASAs: states have typically vested these rights in their national 'flag carriers' such as British Airways (BA) and Lufthansa. Until the 1980s (and still in many areas of the world), fares were coordinated by the designated airlines through traffic conferences held by the International Air Transport Association (IATA). The resulting combination of restricted traffic rights and coordination in setting fares led to comfortable airline duopolies, both within Europe and on intercontinental routes, with some airlines even engaging in pooling of revenues. Meanwhile, until 1978 the US domestic market was subject to control of routes and fares by the Civil Aeronautics Board (CAB).

An important corollary of the management of trade by bilateral agreements was the application of standards of nationality to airlines. ASAs invariably contained a stipulation that airlines benefiting from the designation of traffic rights must be 'substantially owned and effectively controlled' by nationals of the countries concerned. To protect such rights, many countries imposed (and still impose) restrictions on the proportion and type of shares that may be held by foreign citizens. For example, under US law, at least 75 per cent of the voting stock of a US airline must be owned by US citizens. Moreover, the president and at least two-thirds of the board of directors and 'key management officials' of US airlines must be US citizens.

What effect has deregulation in the US and liberalization in the EU had on the Chicago regulatory framework? On the American side, deregulation had two consequences, one deliberate, the other inadvertent. Quite deliberately, the Carter administration (which sponsored the Airline Deregulation Act of 1978) set out to apply the same principles to international markets that had been applied by Alfred E. Kahn and his colleagues to the US domestic market. Under Carter and succeeding presidents, the outcome was a series of so-called 'open-skies' agreements which permit, without restriction, airlines registered in the countries concerned to fly between any points in their own countries and in the other countries. As well as providing open entry to routes, 'open-skies' agreements usually remove restrictions on the setting of fares as well as on frequency and capacity.

While these agreements have undoubtedly led to an expansion of routes, an increase in traffic and in some cases lower fares, they are only liberalized ASAs. They remove restrictions on routes flown, on the number of carriers allowed to fly on such routes, on fares charged and on numbers of seats offered. But they do not relax nationality requirements: under the Netherlands-US open-skies agreement of 1992, for example, only airlines of demonstrable Dutch and US nationality may fly between airports in the Netherlands and airports in the US. The European Commission has therefore opposed the conclusion of 'open-skies' agreements between Member States and the US, arguing that, despite the liberalizing effect of such agreements, the exclusivity of their nationality provisions make them incompatible with the single market.

Such provisions are, in the Commission's view, an affront to the right of establishment of firms throughout the single market and thus obstruct the full realization of the single market programme. Because of the EU's liberalization 'packages' in the late 1980s and early 1990s, a French airline (say) may now fly at will between any airport in France and any airport in Germany, as well as between two or more airports in Germany. But because of the persistence of bilateral agreements with countries outside the EU, the French carrier may not offer scheduled services between a German airport and an airport in a 'third country' (such as the US). Since the authors of the liberalization packages regarded the right of EU airlines to offer services from any point within Member States to any point outside as integral to the single-market programme, the persistence of nationality provisions in ASAs with third countries represents a barrier to completion of the market, no matter how much such agreements offer an opportunity to expand services and to make air travel more accessible and affordable.

The European Commission's objections to the American strategy of signing 'open skies' agreements with Member States were deepened, at least in the early 1990s, by an unexpected consequence of American deregulation, namely, the consolidation of the American airline industry and the expansion of the resulting 'megacarriers' on routes outside the US. Before 1978, the only American airlines flying significant scheduled services across the Atlantic were Pan American and TWA, both of which were suffering a progressive loss in market share, partly because of expansion in the number and capacity of European and other carriers on transatlantic services and partly because of the weakness (or, in Pan Am's case, the complete absence) of a domestic 'feeder' network to sustain international flights.[7] By 1991, when Pan Am finally entered bankruptcy and TWA was selling off routes to prevent following suit, competing airlines with powerful domestic hub-and-spoke systems (mainly American, Delta and United) were expanding their transatlantic services substantially, to the alarm of major European carriers such as Air France and Lufthansa.[8]

By offering low fares and frequent service, US airlines were in fact able to capture a substantial share of the transatlantic market. By 1993, the European airlines' share of the market had shrunk from 68 per cent (in 1962) to 48 per cent. The impact of the 'American invasion' was particularly dramatic in Germany and France: by 1992, 61 per cent of traffic between the US and Germany and 71 per cent of traffic between the US and France (respectively, the second- and third-largest transatlantic markets) was being carried by US airlines. The British market was largely immune to this 'invasion' because of the highly restrictive provisions of the so-called 'Bermuda II' UK-US bilateral of 1977 that permitted only two US and two British airlines to fly between Heathrow and American destinations.[9]

Faced with this American 'invasion', European airlines clamored for protection, arguing that the American carriers were unreasonably exploiting clauses in post-War ASAs that allowed them 'unrestricted capacity increase and the ability to open new routes almost at will' (Sparaco, 1993).[10] Further, they complained bitterly about the provisions of US Chapter 11 bankruptcy law that allowed carriers such as Continental to continue operating while technically in bankruptcy. Both France and Germany demanded renegotiation of their ASAs with the US (and France actually renounced its ASA in 1992, transatlantic services continuing on the basis of annual agreements). Both countries felt obliged to resist pressure for liberalization until Air France and Lufthansa had undergone drastic restructuring preparatory to privatization and were better able to compete with the more powerful American carriers, especially given the simultaneous pressures created by liberalization of air services within the European single market.

While the American campaign for 'open skies' – not surprisingly – attracted few sympathizers in the larger EU Member States, it was very tempting to smaller states, such as the Netherlands, which had for many years been frustrated in their efforts to gain extra traffic rights to American cities. In the intense diplomacy surrounding the negotiation of ASAs, such countries (and especially those with ambitious carriers such as KLM) were prevented from obtaining the new transatlantic traffic rights they wanted by application of a 'balance-of-benefits' principle which allocated rights in rough proportion to the size of market in each country. States with larger domestic markets, such as France, Germany and the UK, thus obtained greater access to the American market than did the Belgians, Dutch and Scandinavians. Even when smaller states did get new routes, they usually did so only after much pressure including some pressure completely unrelated to aviation and in the face of intense opposition from airline and labour lobbies in the US.

The prospect of unrestricted access to the US market under an 'open-skies' agreement was therefore extremely tempting to the governments and airlines of smaller EU Member States, and in 1992 the Dutch became the first to sign an open-skies agreement with the US. This agreement was received with predictable hostility by most American airlines, who claimed that it traded away the American market in return for access to the very small Dutch market. But it served a larger (and quite explicit) American strategy of divide-and-rule that was designed to put pressure on the larger and more protectionist Member States: islands of liberalization would be created within the single market and the lower fares and greater capacity resulting from liberalization would attract passengers from neighbouring countries.

While the Netherlands open skies agreement actually did little to increase direct competition on routes to the US, it did demonstrate the potential of liberalization for lowering fares and attracting new customers. Between 1992 and 2000, the number of passengers carried between Amsterdam and the US grew from 1.7 million to over 4.5 million (Mendes de Leon, 2002: 303). By 1995, Schiphol airport in Amsterdam had overtaken Charles de Gaulle in Paris as the fourth-largest European 'gateway', the number of transatlantic passengers flying through Amsterdam having grown by 74 per cent between 1989 and 1994.[11] The propensity for open-skies arrangements to lower fares was shown on routes between Germany and the US following signature of an open skies ASA between the two countries in 1996. Here, fares which had risen by 50 per cent between 1993 and 1996 dropped by 10 per cent in the two years following the agreement (Marchick, 1999).

Beneficial as such liberalization was for both airlines and passengers, it did nothing to loosen nationality restrictions. Similarly within the EU, while the liberalization 'packages' for air transport removed nationality requirements for the operation of services within the single market, they widened the perimeter of nationality rather than abolishing it. The new legislation created a broader 'nationality' category, in the form of 'Community carriers': to have this status (and to exercise the rights of free establishment and operation throughout the single market), an airline must be 'owned and continue to be owned directly or through a majority ownership by Member States and/or national of Member States. It shall at all times be effectively controlled by such states or such nationals'.[12] Ironically, the privatization of state-owned airlines has in fact been accompanied by new regulation of ownership in the form of 'golden shares' and other devices for preventing foreign takeovers.[13]

By creating the category of 'Community carriers', the three EU liberalization 'packages' for air transport did make it possible in principle for European airlines to establish themselves in other countries and to take over other carriers. But the only substantial purchase of shares made by one European flag carrier in another was Swissair's purchase of 49.5 per cent of Sabena – a transaction precisely intended to give a non-Community carrier access to the single market.

The problem for would-be mergers has been that while the EU abolished all Chicago-type ASAs between Member States, such bilaterals and their accompanying nationality rules continue to govern flights between EU Member States and 'third countries' (including the US). Thus if, for example, Iberia were to buy controlling equity in TAP-Air Portugal, the transaction would not affect the latter's traffic rights within the single market, unless the Commission raised questions to do with competition. But third countries might object that TAP was no longer a 'Portuguese' airline and they might therefore threaten to withdraw its rights on long-haul routes as, reportedly, the US government threatened to do to KLM in 2000 when the Dutch carrier was in merger talks with British Airways (Baker, 2000). Such threats are serious for airlines such as the EU flag carriers that rely so heavily on long-haul routes and discourage mergers within the EU, however legal they would be.

The same inhibitions affect foreign investment in American airlines. Though SAS, KLM and BA have, at different times, invested in American airlines, all eventually wrote off their investments. Substantial though they were, such investments could not lead to control of management because of the statutory prohibition on a foreign carrier owning more than 25 per cent of the voting stock of an American airline. The alternative strategy, of establishing a foreign subsidiary, is impractical because the principle of 'cabotage' (applied almost universally) prohibits a foreign airline from offering service on domestic routes: thus Air France may not pick up passengers in Washington and fly them to Atlanta, just as Delta may not pick up passengers in Paris and fly them to Nice.[14]

The alliance system

Faced with all these restrictions, the response of both American and EU airlines has been to create alliances. Prevented from merging and from directly entering each other's markets, the airlines have adopted a second-best solution that enables them to tap traffic in foreign markets through coordinated marketing and scheduling.

The earliest transatlantic alliances were established in the late 1980s by arrangements between SAS and Continental and between KLM and Northwest.[15] Since then, virtually all the major EU and US carriers have led or joined alliances.[16] Though these relationships have often been unstable, sometimes contentious and usually confusing to the observer, they now seem to have settled into a more enduring pattern, just as they have become more comprehensive in membership.[17]

As Tables 3.1 and 3.2 indicate, the alliances have also acquired a significant degree of control over the transatlantic and global markets. In 2000, nearly 77 per cent of seats on North Atlantic flights were offered by airlines participating in the five transatlantic alliances, with the Oneworld alliance, led by American and BA, alone controlling nearly 27 per cent of these seats. In 1999, the same five alliances controlled over 49 per cent of the world's scheduled passenger traffic, with the Star Alliance (including Lufthansa and United) flying over 289 million passengers that year.

Table 3.1 Transatlantic market shares of major airline alliances and non-allied carriers, 2000

Alliance	% of seats on Europe-US services	of which (%):	
Oneworld	26.7	BA	13.5
		American	9.0
Star Alliance	17.6	United	8.5
		Lufthansa	6.9
Sky Team	17.2	Delta	11.1
		Air France	6.1
KLM/Northwest	8.5	Northwest	5.5
		KLM	3.0
Qualiflyer Group	6.9	Swissair	3.0[a]
Unaligned	23.1	Continental	6.3
		Virgin Atlantic	6.1
		US Airways	3.1

Source: AEA (2001: 1–8).

Note: [a] The Qualiflyer group ceased to exist except as a merger of frequent-flyer programmes in 2002.

Table 3.2 Global traffic and market shares of major airline alliances, 1999

Alliance	Total passengers, 1999 (million)	% of world traffic, 1999	Members' traffic: millions and (world rank)[a]		
Star	289.3	18.5	United Airlines	87.0	(2)
			Lufthansa	41.9	(8)
			SAS	22.0	(14)
			BMI British Midland	6.5	(40)
Oneworld	183.9	11.8	American Airlines	81.5	(3)
			British Airways	36.6	(10)
			Iberia	21.9	(15)
			Finnair	6.1	(45)
			Aer Lingus	6.3	(42)
Sky Team[b]	173.5	11.1	Air France	37.0	(9)
			Delta	105.5	(1)
			CSA Czech	1.9	(95)
Qualiflyer[c]	54.2	3.5	Swissair	13.3	(27)
			Sabena	10.0	(33)
			Air Portugal	4.8	(56)
Wings	72.9	4.7	KLM	15.5	(22)
			Northwest	57.5	(4)
(All alliances)	(773.8)	(49.6)			
WORLD	1,560	100			

Source: AEA (200: I-14).

Notes: [a] Major US and European members only. [b] Subsequently joined by Alitalia. [c] The Qualiflyer group ceased to exist except as a merger of frequent-flyer programmes in 2002.

What benefits do airlines get from membership of alliances? Creation of larger organizations does not, as such, produce benefits: economies of scale in the airline business peak at a fleet of roughly twenty aircraft.[18] Indeed, one of the costs of alliances has turned out to be the need for new coordinating committees and the resulting extra travel and use of managers' time.[19] But the alliances do offer substantial economies of scope through the creation of networks that generate huge numbers of new connections at very little cost. Such connections are made by the device of 'code-sharing' in which airlines apply their own designator codes and numbers to flights operated by other carriers. (For example, a flight operated by BA as 'BA348' might also be marketed by Aer Lingus as 'EI868' and by Iberia as 'IB234' – but in reality the flight would be entirely by a BA aircraft with a BA crew.) As an official of Airports Council International has put it succinctly, code-shares 'expand an airline's hub and spoke network, and therefore their market. They give smaller carriers access to major routes and major carriers access to thinner routes. They also allow carriers to depict services to cities which they do not actually serve, giving the impression of a much bigger route structure than in fact is the case' (Howe, 1998: 31). Alliances thus increase dramatically the number of 'city-pairs' available to alliance members and their customers, and this increase in 'network connectivity' enables airlines to increase the 'feed' to their own – and their partners'– hubs.[20]

Expanded networks have therefore led to increased traffic and higher revenue. KLM, for example, claimed that in 1994 alone its alliance with Northwest expanded its passenger traffic by some 100,000 and brought in an additional $100 million in revenue, while Northwest attracted roughly 200,000 new passengers and generated between $125 million and $175 million in extra revenue. Similarly, Lufthansa reported that in 1997 the new Star Alliance was adding between DM250 million and DM270 million to its revenues.[21]

On the cost side, alliances have also enabled airlines to achieve 'synergy' savings by sharing assets and services. Alliance members can save by joint marketing and by sharing check-in and other ground facilities (such as aircraft maintenance): by joint scheduling, they may also use fewer aircraft and achieve higher payloads (Doganis, 2001: 76–7).[22] Finally, they may save by joint purchasing of supplies and even aircraft.

How far alliance partners actually make such savings depends, however, on the degree of integration they have achieved: apart from the five global alliances, many agreements are limited marketing alliances, typically involving code-sharing on selected routes. Even regarding the global 'strategic alliances', some observers question whether integration has yet reached the level at which sizeable savings can be made.[23]

While alliances have clearly benefited the airline industry, the benefits for passengers are more debatable. The alliances claim that they help passengers by offering them a larger range of connecting flights (with shorter delays) and at lower fares than they would find by using non-allied carriers.[24]

Research supports the claim regarding fares: Brueckner and Whalen have shown that passengers travelling on allied airlines commonly pay as much as 25 per cent less than those flying on the same or a comparable route using non-allied airlines.[25] Further savings are achieved when a passenger flies on a route covered by an open-skies agreement.[26]

While open skies agreements offer the possibility of greater competition (and therefore lower fares), the transatlantic alliances do have an obvious potential to reduce competition. This is paradoxical since the US has invariably required an open-skies agreement as a condition for giving anti-trust immunity that allows airlines to integrate their marketing and operations and thus potentially reduce competition!

With nearly 80 per cent of transatlantic flights being operated by the five major alliances, the issue of competition has attracted the attention of both regulatory authorities and the few remaining non-allied carriers. Critics claim that many of the advantages derived by airlines from alliances depend on actions reducing competition (such as coordinated scheduling and reduced capacity) and they argue that alliances are as intentionally anti-competitive as earlier arrangements for fixing prices and pooling revenue.[27]

While it may be that 'managing competition' was one goal of airline executives in entering alliances, the main issue is how far choice has actually been reduced by the marketing and operational practices of the alliances. As the respected aviation economist Rigas Doganis points out, the alliances have been quite successful in squeezing rivals out of their hubs. On the US side, American Airlines progressively withdrew from several European services as it was challenged by the Star and Qualiflyer alliances (Doganis, 2001: 75). On the European side, the advent of alliances has been accompanied by even greater dominance of hubs such as Amsterdam and Frankfurt by the home-based carriers.[28]

But, as Doganis also notes, the rivalry between alliances (and their skill in reducing transfer times) means that passengers often have a significant choice in routing. Thus a passenger traveling from, say, Kansas City to Florence might choose between connections on Oneworld, SkyTeam, Star or Wings, with the kind of itineraries and times indicated in Table 3.3.[29]

Table 3.3 Sample alliance itineraries for journey from Kansas City, Missouri, to Florence, Italy, 1 March 2003[a]

Alliance	Via	Carriers	Shortest elapsed time
Oneworld	St Louis, Gatwick	American/American/BA	17h 25m[b]
SkyTeam	Cincinnati, Paris	Delta/Delta/CityJet	13h 40m
Star Alliance	Chicago, Munich	United/Lufthansa/Lufthansa	13h 55m
Wings	Detroit, Amsterdam	Northwest/KLM/Meridiana	16h 0m

Sources: Alliance and airline websites.

Notes: [a] Excludes Qualiflyer alliance. [b] To Pisa.

The real reduction in choice is for passengers dependent on alliance hubs where competition on non-stop services has diminished.[30]

Critics also argue that code-sharing – the basic marketing tool of alliances – is fundamentally deceptive of consumers to the extent that it disguises the actual source of the 'product' bought by a passenger. In both the EU and the US, airlines are required to indicate clearly in schedules and other relevant documents when a service is operated by a carrier other than that whose designator is attached to the flight number.

Code-sharing may lead a passenger to fly on an airline that has inferior service or, worse still, lower safety standards than the passenger's preferred carrier. The issue of safety standards was first raised in practice in 1998 by the fatal crash of a Boeing 727 operating a service between Colombia and Ecuador advertised by Air France with its own 'AF' flight designator as part of a through service from Paris. The service was in fact operated not by Air France aircraft and crew but by TAME, the commercial wing of the Ecuadorian Air Force. Early in 1999, Air France and Delta ended their code-sharing arrangements with Korean Air Lines because of concerns about the latter's safety record.[31] Critics further claim that the benefits of merging frequent-flyer programmes (a common feature of alliances) may be exaggerated and that such programmes are unfair marketing devices.

Regulating the transatlantic market

Such issues of commercial practice, as well as the more fundamental regulatory issue of traffic rights, have led to continual and sometimes heated discussion about the scope of and terms for future liberalization of transatlantic air transport. While the US has, until recently, been fairly permissive toward alliances (though insisting on open skies as a condition for their approval), the EU has actively investigated both the practices and the impact of alliances, while also claiming authority to negotiate on behalf of Member States over traffic rights on routes between the EU and 'third countries' (such as the US).

The regulatory issue facing alliances is generally framed as one of impact on competition (though specific questions of consumer protection and even safety may be raised). The US government requires specific approval for code-sharing (which until recently has been very limited on US domestic services): the EU does not require such approval but does examine the impact of code-sharing on competition within the EU and on services between the EU and third countries (Oum and Park, 1997: 135). Since 1987, the European Commission has investigated both mergers and strategic alliances and has regularly imposed restrictions and conditions on such arrangements in the interest of protecting or promoting competition. To this end, it has required the airlines concerned to give up specified routes, to surrender runway slots and/or to sell shares in other airlines. Initially, it applied such scrutiny only to mergers and acquisitions within the single market, but since

1998 it has systematically examined the transatlantic alliances that EU airlines have joined.

While the Commission has imposed specific and sometimes stringent conditions, notably for approval of the Lufthansa-SAS-United alliance and the American Airlines (AA)-BA alliance, the net effects have been small.[32] In the former case, Lufthansa decided to appeal against the Commission's recommendation that the partners reduce frequencies on hub-to-hub flights and give up 93 slots at Frankfurt and 15 at Copenhagen for use by competitors.

In the AA-BA case, the partners decided to abandon their strategic alliance after the Commission ruled that they should give up 267 slots (including 50 on hub-to-hub routes) so as to encourage competition on services between Heathrow and the US.[33] Though the two airlines continued to seek a marketing alliance, they were opposed strenuously by several major American carriers, and the US Department of Transportation ruled in January 2002 that they should surrender 224 slots at Heathrow as a condition for receiving anti-trust immunity. At this point, American abandoned the alliance with BA, having apparently concluded that the price required was too high.

Thus neither ruling has made much, if any, difference to the market shares controlled by the carriers concerned. As Table 3.4 indicates, in November 2002 Oneworld controlled 52.4 per cent of traffic on US flights to the UK, while the Star Alliance controlled 67.5 per cent of traffic on flights from the US to Germany. (SkyTeam controlled 66.8 per cent of passengers on flights to France, and Wings controlled 74.4 per cent of traffic from the US to the Netherlands.)

The American approach in the AA-BA case and others has (as noted above) been to link approval of alliances to liberalization of traffic rights. Thus the US made conclusion of an open-skies agreement with the UK a condition for providing anti-trust immunity for the AA-BA alliance. This requirement presented the alliance partners with a delicate calculation of costs and benefits. On the one hand, they were anxious to reap the large prospective benefits for each airline's network offered by the alliance, as well as all the other advantages enjoyed by the existing alliances. On the other hand, an open-skies agreement would have led to increased competition (mainly from other American carriers) at Heathrow (where services to the US are limited to two US airlines – American and United – and two British carriers – BA and Virgin Atlantic).[34] Such an agreement would have reduced the rents enjoyed by the existing oligopoly.[35]

The peculiarly intractable case of the UK–US relationship aside, both the .EU and the US agree on the desirability of further liberalization of transatlantic air services. But they differ on the route to such liberalization and on the conditions to accompany it. The EU (with the support of the Association of European Airlines) favours the creation of a transatlantic common aviation area (TCAA), to be negotiated directly between the Commission and the US government (with the possible addition of Canada).[36] Under the TCAA,

Table 3.4 Alliance and airline shares of transatlantic routes, November 2002

Routes	Total passengers (from US only) and US airlines' share %	Alliance shares %		Individual airlines' shares %	
US–UK	908,563 (37.8)	Oneworld (AA, BA, etc.)	52.4	BA	38.1
				Virgin Atlantic	15.7
				American	14.3
		Star (United, Lufthansa, etc.)	10.9	United	10.9
				Continental	5.1
		SkyTeam (Delta, Air France, etc.)	4.2	Delta	4.2
				US Airways	3.3
		Wings (Northwest, KLM, Continental)	5.1		
US–Germany	354,743 (43.5)	Star	67.5	Lufthansa	51.3
		SkyTeam	11.5	United	16.2
		Oneworld	3.6	Delta	11.5
		Wings	*	USAirways	8.0
				American	3.6
US–France	279,818 (48.9)	SkyTeam	66.8	Air France	50.3
		Oneworld	11.1	Delta	16.5
		Star	8.7	American	11.1
		Wings	6.7	United	8.7
				Continental	6.7
US–Netherlands	229,089 (57.3)	Wings	74.4	Northwest	36.3
		Star	6.8	KLM	32.5
		SkyTeam	5.9	United	6.8
		Oneworld	*	Delta	5.9
				Continental	5.6

Source: Adapted from Landler (2002), based on data from ECLAT Consulting (given the date of publication, the data used in this source must refer to seats sold for November 2002, rather than passengers actually carried).

* Data not available because the alliances concerned do not have non-stop flights between the countries concerned.

the existing ASAs between Member States and the US would be superseded by a single free-trade area: EU and US airlines would be free to fly between any points in the single market and the US. Current nationality rules would be relaxed to allow for transatlantic mergers and acquisitions, with the corollary that existing restrictions on cabotage would be lifted: thus, say, Alitalia (or perhaps a US branch or affiliate of Alitalia) would be able to fly on domestic routes within the US, while United (or its Italian branch) would be able to fly on routes within the EU.[37]

While advocating a TCAA, the European Commission has also pursued legal action in the European Court of Justice (ECJ) against eight Member States who have signed bilateral ASAs with the US, on the grounds that such agreements rest on exclusive nationality clauses that are inconsistent with Community legislation. Seven of the Member States (Austria, Belgium, Denmark, Finland, Germany, Luxembourg and Sweden) have signed open-skies agreements with the US. The Commission included the UK in its action since in 1994 the British government had insisted on holding talks with the US government on revision of its ASA, against the expressed wish of the Commission that it not do so. The Commission did not initially include the Netherlands (which had signed the first open-skies agreement with the US) and France (which concluded a phased-in open-skies agreement with the US in 1998) in the list of states taken to the ECJ.

In pursuing these cases, the Commission has also sought the support of the ECJ for its claim to take over negotiating authority for ASAs with third countries from the Member States. On 5 November 2002, the ECJ ruled that the open-skies agreements violated EU law by discriminating against other Member States (and their airlines) (Dombey and Done, 2002; *Financial Times*, 2002).While this ruling was greeted by the Commissioner for Transport and Energy as 'historic', it did not in fact give the Commission the exclusive negotiating competence it wanted for negotiating traffic rights with third countries.[38]

The November 2002 ruling thus provided (as the *Financial Times* noted) only partial satisfaction for any of the parties and it 'created many new uncertainties about the way ahead' (*Financial Times*, 2002). While it seemed to invalidate the open-skies agreements, some observers concluded that it did not actually annul them (though the Commissioner herself declared that they were now 'null and void') (*Financial Times*, 2002; Dombey, 2002). Moreover, the lack of exclusive negotiating authority for the Commission implied that such a mandate would have to be extracted from the Council of Ministers and exercised in conjunction with relevant Member States.

Finally, the European Commission's own goals sometimes seem to be contradictory. While claiming to promote competition as part of its mandate under the single-market legislation, it has also spoken (especially under the leadership of the current commissioner, Loyola de Palacio) of the desirability of greater consolidation of the European airline industry. Indeed, the Commission's own press release on the ECJ decision noted that bilateral agreements concluded by Member States had 'effectively prevented the European industry from consolidating into economically stronger, international businesses' (European Commission, 2002).[39] Critics of the Commission's willingness to approve restructuring aid for national airlines during the 1990s might well argue that it has itself contributed quite effectively to preventing such consolidation.

Meanwhile, the US position remains one of preferring to achieve further liberalization through bilateral ASAs. The US has also indicated that it will continue to regard the open-skies agreements as valid. It has now concluded 21 open-skies agreements with European states, with Greece, Ireland, Spain and the UK outstanding.[40] While the US has formally welcomed the idea of a transatlantic common aviation area, it has expressed reservations about proposals for allowing domestic services by foreign airlines and for abolishing limits on foreign ownership.[41] Moreover, labour interests are sure to resist any liberalization that is seen as threatening job security: the main airline pilots' union in the US has already claimed that the alliances have reduced the opportunities for transatlantic flying available to its members.[42]

The US Department of Defense, for its part, is concerned about the implications of foreign ownership for national security. Under the Civil Reserve Air Fleet (CRAF) programme, US airlines commit themselves (voluntarily) to making available earmarked aircraft from their fleets (along with crew members) for use by the Department of Defense in time of national emergency. The Department of Defense has expressed the fear that a foreign owner or majority shareholder might, for political reasons, deny it the use of such aircraft. Airliners are crucial for transporting troops, since the US Air Force has concentrated on building a fleet of cargo and tanker aircraft and has relatively few purely passenger aircraft.

Conclusions

Despite progress in liberalizing bilateral ASAs and the recent proposals for a TCAA, the prospects for complete free trade in transatlantic air services are murky. While privatization has reduced the direct stake that European governments have in their flag carriers, a residual nationalism and the survival of nationality requirements in ASAs stand in the way of free cross-border investment, even within the European single market. Until nationality requirements are abolished or radically changed, airlines will be reluctant or unable to move from alliances to full mergers with foreign carriers and they will be prevented from starting new long-haul services at will.

A major step toward resolving this problem would be to abolish the requirement for 'substantial ownership' in bilateral ASAs while leaving that for 'effective control' by nationals.[43] The effect of such a change would be to give airlines a right of establishment abroad and to encourage cross-border investment. BA, for example, could then set up an American affiliate (with American board members) which would be eligible for designation by Washington as a US carrier on international routes: similarly, US Airways, for instance, could establish itself as an EU 'Community carrier'. Given the abolition of the 'substantial-ownership' provision, both affiliates could presumably operate on both domestic and international routes.

As regards the liberalization of traffic rights, in principle several strategies are possible. One is a form of regional free-trade area (such as the TCAA). Another is a multilateral or plurilateral liberalization agreement, in which countries – regardless of region – guarantee open-skies on any routes between them.[44] Such an agreement was signed in August 2000 by Brunei,

Chile, New Zealand, Singapore and the US and provides for open-skies conditions in both routing and pricing. The problem with both the multilateral and plurilateral formulas, however, is that the countries taking part will still need bilateral ASAs with third countries – those outside the constituted free-trade area – and, for purposes of these ASAs, they will presumably have to maintain the present nationality provisions, which in turn may continue to obstruct consolidation of airlines *within* the liberalized zone.

Ultimately and logically, the only way to cut through the knot of nationality requirements and ASAs will be through some form of global agreement to liberalize international air transport. The obvious forum for such an agreement is the General Agreement on Trade in Services (GATS), leading to inclusion of air transport in the domain of the WTO. But the history of air transport (more particularly, of the 'hard' traffic rights) in the Uruguay Round suggests that the GATS is both an obvious and a hopeless arena for liberalization of this sector. Air-traffic rights were in fact the only potential item for the agenda of the Uruguay Round to be unanimously rejected by all participants. The GATS does provide for general liberalization of aviation-related activities such as marketing and aircraft maintenance, but traffic rights are firmly excluded (though their exclusion is subject to periodic review).

While a full transatlantic common aviation area may still be some way in the future, the ECJ judgment does create the likelihood of further challenges to the existing bilateral system. Indeed, as *Aviation Week* noted, the Commission has already encouraged Member States 'to begin the process of formally abrogating their bilateral agreements with the US over a period of twelve months'(Barrie, 2002). It is certainly unlikely that any Member State will now try to renegotiate a bilateral with a third country until the issues raised by the ECJ decision are clarified, if not resolved. On the airlines' side, the next logical step would be for an EU airline to explore the new dispensation by announcing the start of transatlantic services from a hub in another Member State: thus Air France, for example, might announce its intention to start transatlantic service from London. Given the ECJ judgment, the British government would probably hesitate to deny it authority, for fear of provoking the Commission.[45]

Two serious problems stand in the way of such an initiative. One is the attitude of the US government, which has (as noted above) made it clear that it sees no reason to abandon the bilaterals it has negotiated over the last ten years. Thus, whatever the attitude of the British government, Washington would not accept Air France's proposed services from London because France is not a party to the UK–US bilateral. The second problem is more commercial and less discussed, namely, that such an initiative would not fit with the hub-and-spoke system developed by (in this case) Air France and with the present strategy of the SkyTeam alliance. Except as a way of irritating BA and the Oneworld alliance, it is hard to see why Air France would want to start services from either Gatwick or Heathrow, even if Washington allowed it to do so. It might take some British and US passengers away from BA and other incumbents, but it would have no 'feed' traffic except from passengers who, for reasons best known to themselves, might choose to fly via London when they could fly nonstop from Paris or another SkyTeam hub (such as Rome or Milan). As Cathy Buyck notes (and the Commission recognizes) national carriers tend 'to sit on their hubs' (Buyck, 2003: 37).

A more dangerous situation for incumbents would arise if a domestic rival, linked to another alliance (such as, in the London case, BMI British Midland – a Star Alliance member) were to begin transatlantic services, drawing on 'feed' from an alliance network. But the current alliances have so far shown little inclination to invade each others' hubs and, ironically, the kind of consolidation favoured by the Commission would probably reduce this kind of potential competitive threat even more. The American carriers already have (apart from Heathrow) ample access to most of the European airports under the open-skies agreements and have shown little enthusiasm for a transatlantic common aviation area, which might lead to challenges to their domestic dominance.

In truth, a more fundamental question than that of transatlantic regulation now faces the airline industry on both sides of the Atlantic, namely, the viability of all 'full-service' airlines in the face of the challenge from low-cost carriers such as EasyJet, Ryanair and Southwest Airlines. Recent analysis suggests that by 2013 Southwest will become the largest airline in the US and that by 2020 the *combined* domestic market share of seven of the largest carriers in the US will have shrunk to about 45 per cent.[46] Within the EU, Ryanair expects to be carrying between 40 and 60 million passengers annually by 2010, and executives of both Ryanair and EasyJet expect their airlines to dominate the European market by that date (Sparaco, 2002: 60).

This situation, apart from ending the lives of some national airlines, may lead to a segmented industry, with the remaining national airlines and some US carriers surviving by concentrating on long-haul routes through three or four alliance systems.[47] A more intriguing prospect would arise if the current low-cost carriers or some new international counterparts were to decide to extend their commercial strategy to long-haul routes (following the earlier examples of Laker Airways and People Express) and even to start operations abroad. Then a true 'free-trade' revolution would occur in an industry that has long been a fortress of nationalism and protectionism.

Notes

1 For other comments on the significance of the judgment, see *Flight International* (2002) and Goeteyn (2002).
2 Contrary to popular myth, air travel's initial success in beating the ocean liners was due not to the advent of jets, but to the introduction of low fares on services flown by advanced piston-engine and turboprop aircraft (Heppenheimer, 1995: 192–5).

3 In 1992, KLM obtained 33.9 per cent of all its revenue from transatlantic services, followed by British Airways with 30.7 per cent and Swissair with 24.9 per cent.

4 Overall, in the early 1990s, services across the North Atlantic represented 11.6 per cent of all international traffic carried by airlines belonging to the Association of European Airlines (AEA) but they generated roughly 20 per cent of the group's revenues; by 2000, the percentage of the AEA members' total traffic contributed by transatlantic services had dropped slightly, to 8.78 per cent; AEA, 2001: I-8, IV-5.

5 'Note' (by H. E. Marking and William T. Seawell) in Friedman (1976), no page number. This work described the transatlantic market as in a 'sick condition' with losses 'chronic and widespread'.

6 Passenger yield is defined as 'passenger revenue per revenue-passenger-kilome-tre'– that is, for one passenger transported one kilometre (AEA (2001: IV-14)).

7 In 1946, Pan Am and TWA carried approximately 92 per cent of all passengers on air services between North America and Europe. By 1956, fifteen airlines were operating across the North Atlantic and the share of the two US carriers had fallen to 53 per cent: by 1962, nineteen airlines were carrying passengers across the Atlantic, and the US share had fallen to 32 per cent (Davies, 1964: 461, 471; Sampson, (1984: 110).

8 Such expansion was possible because the French and German ASAs, among others, had liberal provisions for the expansion of capacity. Certain airlines (such as Continental and Northwest) expanded as a way of generating revenue to stave off or survive bankruptcy.

9 The American carriers' share of US-UK traffic only rose from 54.2 per cent in 1989 to 55.0 per cent in 1992 – a frustrating outcome for them, considering that passengers on services between the UK and the US represented 34.9 per cent of all passengers carried across the North Atlantic.

10 A further issue for European airlines has been that earlier ASAs give so-called 'fifth-freedom' rights to US carriers. 'Fifths' allow (in this case) a US airline flying across the Atlantic to pick up or disembark passengers at a European airport and to fly them to or from a third country, within or outside Europe. Such an operation is only possible, however, with the agreement of the third country concerned.

11 The potential for market expansion was shown dramatically in the case of a new service between Amsterdam and Minneapolis, launched in April 1994 jointly by KLM and Northwest Airlines. Starting with a capacity of 1,942 seats each week, capacity on this route was increased to 9,758 seats weekly by mid-summer to cope with demand: in August, a second daily flight was scheduled for the remainder of the season.

12 Regulation 2407/92, Article 4. It will be no consolation (though perhaps a sur-prise) to would-be purchasers of EU airlines to discover that EU legislation on licensing does not apply to hot-air balloons (or to ultra-light aircraft). For the text of the Regulation and a discussion of licensing provisions, see Adkins 1994: Appendix 9 and Chapter 10, and Havel 1997: 388–92, 391.

13 On changes in ownership and more generally on the role of governments in the ownership and management of European airlines, see Staniland 2003b.

14 But ASAs sometimes allow flights carrying international traffic between domestic points: BA, for example, flies between Baltimore and Charlotte as a continuation

of its service between London and Baltimore. But it is not allowed to pick up Charlotte-bound passengers in Baltimore or vice versa.

15 Various marketing and technical agreements existed earlier, but none had the scope and formality of the alliances between the major European and US airlines formed from 1986 onward.

16 By 1999, the total number of airline alliances in the world had risen to roughly 500.

17 In 1999, the Boston Consulting Group reported that two-thirds of current alliances had lasted more than three years, whereas between 1992 and 1995 some two-thirds had collapsed (*The Economist*, 1999). But in 1999 J. A. Donoghue noted that 'alliance churn' was continuing, with airline employees having trouble remembering what current arrangements were in force (Donoghue: 1999).

18 Doganis points out that the unit-costs of larger airlines are in fact often higher than those of smaller airlines (Doganis, 2001: 71).

19 The Star Alliance, for example, set up 24 committees to monitor different aspects of co-ordination and the chief executive of a participating airline reportedly complained that 'time [was] wasted in endless committee meetings' (*The Economist*, 1998: 68; *The Economist*, 2002: 54). According to Joan M. Feldman, 'British Airways once estimated that alliance staff spent two-thirds of their time attending or travelling to meetings', while Jürgen Weber, the CEO of Lufthansa, said that alliances took 'a third of his time' at one point in the late 1990s (Feldman, 1998: 30). For similar complaints by the former CEO of Swissair, Philippe Bruggisser, see Feldman (1997: 32).

20 For instance, between 1993 and 1998 the number of passengers transferring at either end (or both ends) of Star Alliance flights between Chicago and Frankfurt tripled – an increase that the alliance attributed to easier (or, as the airlines prefer to say, 'seamless') online connections. In the case of the KLM-Northwest alliance, the number of connecting passengers on flights between Amsterdam and the US tripled between 1988 and 2000 (Mendes de Leon, 2002: 303–4 and Chart 3). In 2000, the US Department of Transportation reported subsantial increases in international traffic between smaller US cities (such as Birmingham, Alabama, and Portland, Oregon) and Europe (cited in Zuckerman, 2002).

21 In 1995, a US GAO study (GAO, 1995) found that between 1991and 1994 KLM and Northwest had increased their traffic annually by 350,000 passengers, while their combined market share on North Atlantic routes had gone up from 7 per cent to 11.5 per cent: some of this increase was due (as noted above) to the open-skies agreement between the US and the Netherlands. An earlier report (Gelman Research Associates, 1994) found significant (though unbalanced) increases in revenue from the alliance between BA and the then USAir. Park and Zhang (1998a: 17) found from an examination of four alliances operating between 1992 and 1994 that many carriers had 'greater traffic increases on their alliance routes than those on their non-alliance routes': during its alliance with USAir, BA increased its traffic by 8.3 per cent more on routes shared with its partner than on routes it operated alone, while Lufthansa and United 'increased traffic by 10 per cent more and 8 per cent more, respectively, on their alliance routes than on their non-alliance routes.' For other studies of the impact of alliances on the finances and traffic of airlines, see for example Brueckner (2001), Morrish and Hamilton (2002), Oum and Park (1997), and Park and Zhang (1998b). Between

1996 and early 1998, Continental Airlines' revenue from passengers connecting in Paris 'more than doubled' following a marketing agreement between it and Air France in October 1996 (Sparaco, 1998).

22 One unexplained change concerns the overall market share between US and EU carriers. From the mid-1990s onward, the share of capacity on North Atlantic routes controlled by European carriers (both EU and non-EU airlines) went up sharply – from slightly over 48 per cent of all capacity on bilateral (so-called 'third-freedom' and 'fourth-freedom') services in 1993 to 54 per cent in 1995 and to just under 57 per cent in 1997: the European market share then dropped slightly, to 55.75 by 2000 (AEA, 2001: I-8).

23 For example, a recent trade report (*Airline Financial News*, 2002) noted that many analysts had concluded that 'none of the alliances has yet attained the depth of cooperation [needed] to make major cost savings to the business'.

24 For research demonstrating reduced delay of between 12 per cent and 25 per cent on transatlantic flights using alliance services, see Park and Zhang (1997).

25 See Brueckner and Whalen (2000) and Doganis (2001: 94). Brueckner and Whalen also found that fares on transatlantic journeys involving several legs were between 18 per cent and 28 per cent cheaper using allied rather than non-allied airlines. In a more recent study (Brueckner, 2000a and 2000b), Brueckner claimed that fares were 27 per cent lower on services provided by the Star Alliance than on comparable journeys involving non-allied carriers and argued that in this case anti-trust immunity and code-sharing together yielded an annual benefit of $100 million for consumers. The reason for the difference is that allied airlines engage in 'cooperative pricing' in charging for the section of the journey each flies. Thus, for example, for a flight between Stockholm and Kansas City, say, via Frankfurt and Chicago, on the Star Alliance, SAS would charge a lower 'pro-rated' fare for the Stockholm to Frankfurt sector and United for the Chicago to Kansas City sector than they would if the passenger were traveling by non-allied carriers. The allied airlines have a shared incentive to attract business, whereas with non-allied carriers each airline 'inevitably tries to milk its one leg of the ticket journey for as much money as it can' (*The Economist*, 1999).

26 In 1997, David Marchik of the US Department of Transportation reported that during the previous year, fares had dropped by 17 per cent on services between the US and European countries that had signed 'open-skies' agreements with the US (Marchik, 1999).

27 A former airline executive, Randy Malin, reportedly said: 'Alliances have two purposes: Stop competing and jointly beat up on the other guy. The rest is fluff' (quoted in Feldman (2000: 48) The main mechanism for coordinating prices was the traffic conferences of the International Air Transport Association (IATA): before liberalization, many European airlines practised 'pooling' of revenues as well as coordinated scheduling.

28 By 1998, KLM and its partners and affiliates controlled nearly 71 per cent of slots at Amsterdam, while BA and its affiliates and franchisees controlled 66 per cent of slots at Gatwick (BA also controlled nearly 40 per cent of slots at Heathrow); SAS and its partners controlled 74 per cent of slots at Copenhagen (Doganis, 2001: 81–2).

29 For a detailed comparison of transatlantic alliance services, see Doganis (2001: 92–3, Tables 4.6 and 4.7).

30 Doganis (2001: 99) argues that the most serious threats to competition 'are not in the creation of long-haul alliance networks as such but appear to be linked more with growing hub dominance and the creation of alliances monopolies on short or medium-haul routes'. Brueckner (2000 a and b) has noted the possibility that fares would be *higher* for passengers travelling only between alliance hubs, since in such cases the alliance partners would have the opportunity to earn a rent from operating side by side. But his earlier data suggested that no anti-competitive effect had yet been detected on 'gateway-gateway' services.

31 For a useful short discussion of the issue of safety standards, see Havel and Eastmond (2001: 13, 115–16).

32 Doganis (2001: 97–8). In July 2002, the Commission announced that it had decided not to oppose continuation of the transatlantic alliances created by Air France, KLM and Lufthansa (*The Economist*, 2002: 51).

33 In this case, the particular issue was the fact that the partners controlled 98 of 153 (64 per cent) weekly flights between Heathrow and JFK, New York: they also had a substantial collective presence on routes to Dallas-Fort Worth, Chicago and Miami. The Commission further required them not to pool their frequent-flyer programmes (or instead to allow other airlines to participate in them) and it placed restrictions on their use of computer reservation systems.

34 Table 3.4 shows that in November 2002 the 'Heathrow Four' controlled 79 per cent of traffic from the US to the UK: while BA and Virgin Atlantic operate transatlantic flights from both Gatwick and Heathrow, United and American only fly to Heathrow.

35 In 1998, British Midland (now BMI-British Midland) published research showing that business-class fares between Heathrow and American cities were as much as 92 per cent higher than those between continental cities and the US. (For example, such fares between Heathrow and the US were charged at a rate of 0.94 £ per mile, compared to 0.49 £ per mile for comparable fares between Amsterdam and the US.) The same business-class fares were being charged between Heathrow and Los Angeles as between Heathrow and Auckland, New Zealand, though the latter journey was twice as long (as cited in Churchill, 1999). *The Economist* (2002: 51) has noted that even now business-class fares between Heathrow and the US are still nearly 60 per cent higher than those between Frankfurt and equivalent US cities.

36 On the AEA's position, see AEA (1999).

37 The AEA document (1999: 8) argues that 'within the TCAA, the principle that airlines should be free to provide services should go hand in hand with the right of establishment, so as to permit cross-border mergers, acquisitions and new entry'.

38 The ruling states that Community law 'does not, in itself, establish an external community [EU] competence in the field of air transport which allows [the Commission] to conclude international agreements' (quoted in Dombey, 2002).

39 On the day that the ECJ decision was announced, the Commissioner herself was reported to have come 'storming down the stairs to the press room' and to have declared: 'This is a historic decision that is going to have some enormously positive consequences for the consolidation of the European aviation industry' (quoted in Dombey, 2002). For a discussion of the strain between the Commission's simultaneous pursuit of 'competition' and 'competitiveness', see Staniland (2004).

40 In response to the November 2002 ruling, a US State Department spokesman said that the existing agreements '[remained] in force as the legal basis for air services between the US and individual EU Member States' (quoted in Dombey and Done, 2002).

41 Though the report of a commission on the US airline industry in 1993 had recommended raising the permitted level of foreign ownership to 49 per cent of voting stock, Congress has not acted on the recommendation.

42 The Air Line Pilots' Association (ALPA) in the US has claimed that under code-sharing arrangements an increasing proportion of transatlantic services has been allocated to the European partners (and their crews) (Duane E. Woerth, President of ALPA, cited by Havel and Eastmond (2001: 13,115 and notes 91 and 92). As Table 3.4 indicates, the percentage of all traffic carried from the US to the four main European destinations by US airlines in November 2002 was below 50 per cent in all cases, except that of the Netherlands: interestingly, the lowest American market share (37.8 per cent) was on routes to the UK, many of which are affected by restrictions on access to Heathrow. As regards the Netherlands, the KLM–Northwest alliance reportedly reached an arrangement with pilots that guaranteed an even split of transatlantic flying (Feldman, 2001b: 122), though in November 2002 Northwest seems to have carried more than KLM. Overall, it is not clear why the alliances would allot more flights to European carriers, which typically have higher labour costs than their American counterparts.

43 Parallel changes would have to occur in national regulations. In the so-called 'APEC' multilateral, signed by Brunei, Chile, New Zealand, Singapore and the US in 2000, the requirement for 'substantial ownership' has been removed while that for 'effective control' by nationals remains. Thus a US airline could not simply establish itself in Chile as a Chilean airline but it could invest substantially in an existing Chilean carrier (see Feldman, 2001a: 43).

44 A 'plurilateral' agreement differs from a 'multilateral' agreement only in the sense that the former is composed of a network of separate bilateral ASAs, while the latter comprises a general and shared zone of liberalization: the form is different, but the effect is the same. Havel and Eastmond (2001: 13, 116) suggest that both forms of agreement would need one or more competition tribunals.

45 Interestingly, in late November 2002, both BA and Virgin Atlantic came out in favour of the Commission's assuming negotiating authority – as Douglas Barrie notes, a change of position by BA, which had previously backed negotiation of a new bilateral with the US (Barrie, 2002). Rod Eddington, the chief executive of BA, also declared support for the creation of a TCAA.

46 See Velocci (2002: 52), quoting Edmund S. Greenslet of ESG Aviation Services. The seven carriers concerned are Alaska Airlines, American, Continental, Delta, Northwest, United and USAirways. The same study suggests that by 2020 the New York-based carrier JetBlue will have displaced Delta as the third-largest US carrier.

47 Sparaco (2002: 60), quoting EasyJet and Ryanair officials.

References

Adkins, B. (1994), *Air transport and E.C. Competition law*, London: Sweet & Maxwell.

Air Transport World (1999), 'A Soft Landing', July, 54.

Airline Financial News (2002), 'Global Alliances Vulnerable to Shakeups in Four Areas', 10 June.

Association of European Airlines (1999), *Towards a Transatlantic Common Aviation Area: AEA Policy Statement*, Brussels.

—— (2001), *Yearbook 2001*, Brussels.

Baker, C. (2000), 'British Airways Calls off KLM Merger', *Airline Business*, October, 9.

Barrie, D. (2002), 'Europe Delivers Blow to Bilateral Deals', *Aviation Week and Space Technology*, 25 November, 42.

Branson, R. (2002), 'Fair Competition: A True Revolution in Flight', *Aviation Week and Space Technology*, 2 December, 78.

Brown, J. M. (2001), 'Aer Lingus Gears Up in Flight for Survival', *Financial Times*, 29 October, 20.

Brueckner, J. K. (2000a), 'International Airfares in the Age of Alliances: The Effects of Codesharing and Antitrust Immunity', Working Paper, University of Illinois at Urbana-Champaign.

—— (2000b), 'The Benefits of Codesharing and Antitrust Immunity for International Passengers, with an Application to the Star Alliance', study prepared for the Star Alliance.

—— (2001a), 'The Economics of International Codesharing: An Analysis of Airline Alliances', *International Journal of Industrial Organization*, 19, 1475–98.

—— (2001b), 'Airline Alliances Benefit Consumers', *Policy Forum*, 14:3, 1–4.

Brueckner, J. K. and W. T. Whalen (1998), 'The Pros and Cons of Airline Alliances', *Policy Forum*, 12:1, 1–3.

—— (2000), 'The Price Effects of International Airline Alliances', *Journal of Law and Economics*, 43:2, 503–45.

Buyck, C. (2003), 'The EU's "Historic Judgment"', *Air Transport World*, January, 36–7.

Churchill, D. (1999), 'Taking a Tough Line', *Director*, October.

Davies, R. E. G. (1964), *A History of the World's Airlines*, Oxford: Oxford University Press.

Doganis, R. (2001), *The Airline Business in the Twenty-First Century*, London: Routledge.

Dombey, D. (2002), 'Long Haul ahead in "Open skies" Struggle', *Financial Times*, 6 November.

Dombey, D. and K. Done (2002), '"Open Skies" Deals Illegal European Union Court Rules', *Financial Times*, 6 November, 1.

Donoghue, J. A. 1999, 'Alliance Churn', *Air Transport World*, November, 5.

The Economist (1998), 'Mergers in Mind', 26 September, 68.

—— (1999), 'Flying in Circles', 17 July, 57.

—— (2002), 'Signs of Life', 3 August, 51–4.

European Commission (2002), 'Open Sky Agreements: Commission Welcomes European Court of Justice Ruling', Press and Communications DG, 5 November, IP/02/1609.

Feldman, J. M. (1997), 'Swissair: Time to Deliver', *Air Transport World*, June, 31–8.

—— (1998), 'Making Alliances Work', *Air Transport World*, June, 27–35.

—— (2000), 'Alliance Costs Start Building', *Air Transport World*, June, 41–8.

—— (2001a), 'Drip, Drip, Drip', *Air Transport World*, March, 42–6.

—— (2001b), 'Alliance Imbalance', *Air Transport World*, June, 121–3.

Financial Times (1992), France and US Fail to Resolve Air Route Row', 6 April, 3.

—— (1993), 'Lufthansa in Link Talks with American', 6 April, 4.

—— (2002), 'New EU Flight Plan', 6 November, 14.

Flight International (2002), 'Opening the Skies', 12–18 November, 3.

Flint, P. (2002), 'The Devil is in the Details', *Air Transport World*, December, 5.

Friedman, J. J. (1976), *A New Air Transport Policy for the North Atlantic: Saving an Endangered System*, New York: Atheneum.

GAO (1995), 'Airline Alliances Produce Benefits, but Effect on Competition is Uncertain', US General Accounting Office, GAO/RCED-95-99, April.

Gellman Research Associates (1994), 'A Study of International Airline Codesharing', Report submitted to the Office of Aviation and International Economics, Office of the Secretary of Transportation, US Department of Transportation, Washington DC, December.

Goeteyn, G. (2002), 'Is the End of the Chicago Convention Era in Sight?', *Airline Business*, December, 78.

Havel, B. F. (1997), *In Search of Open Skies: Law and Policy for a New Era in International Aviation*, The Hague: Kluwer Law International.

Havel, B. F. and A. C. Eastmond (2001), 'The Path to Open Skies: Transcending Global Alliances', *Issues in Aviation Law and Policy*, CCH Incorporated.

Heppenheimer, T. A. (1995), *Turbulent Skies: The History of Commercial Aviation*, New York: John Wiley.

Howe, J. (1998), 'Code-sharing: Fraud or Favour?', *Interavia Business and Technology*, June, 30–2.

Landler, M. (2002), 'Europe's Highest Court Voids Air Treaties with the US', *New York Times*, 6 November, C1.

Lehmann Brothers (1993), 'European Airlines: A Turbulent Decade', 14 September.

Marchik, D. (1999), 'Clearing the Air', *Financial Times*, 14 July, 10.

Mendes de Leon, P. (2002), 'Before and After the Tenth Anniversary of the Open Skies Agreement Netherlands–US of 1992', *Air and Space Law*, 28:4 and 5, 280–313.

Mims, A. B. (1999), Acting Assistant Secretary for Aviation and International Affairs, Department of Transportation, testimony before the Aviation Subcommittee of the Transportation and Infrastructure Committee, US House of Representatives.

Morrish, S. C., and Hamilton, R. T. (2002), 'Airline Alliances – Who Benefits?', *Journal of Air Transport Management*, 8:6, 401–7.

Ott, J. (1993), 'Competition to Force New Airline Structures', *Aviation Week and Space Technology*, 15 March, 63–7.

Oum, T. H. and J.-H. Park (1997), 'Airline Alliances: Current Status, Policy Issues, and Future Directions', *Journal of Air Transport Management*, 3:3, 133–44.

Oum, T. H., J.-H. Park and A. Zhang (2000), *Globalization and Strategic Alliances*, New York and Oxford: Elsevier Science, Pergamon.

Park, J.-H. and A. Zhang (1997), 'The effects of Intercontinental Alliances: Cases in the North Atlantic Market', University of British Columbia and City University of Hong Kong, Working Paper.

—— (1998a), 'On the Effects of Strategic Alliances on Partners' Outputs', mimeo, April (also published in 'Transportation Research – Part E', *Logistics and Transportation Review*, 34:4 (December 1998), 245–55).

—— (1998b), 'An Empirical Analysis of Global Airline Alliances: Cases in North Atlantic Markets', mimeo, August (also published in *Review of Industrial Organization*, 16:4 (June 2002), 367–84).

Sampson, A. (1984), *Empires of the Sky: The Politics, Contests and Cartels of World Airlines*, New York: Random House.

Sparaco, P. (1993), 'Eurocarriers Must Fight for American Market Share', *Aviation Week and Space Technology*, 31 May, 35.

—— (1998), 'Air France will Retain Double US partnership', *Aviation Week and Space Technology*, 23 March, 37.

—— (2002), 'Low-cost Carriers Steal the European Show', *Aviation Week and Space Technology*, 18 November, 59–61.

Staniland, M. (2003), *Government Birds: The State and Air Transport in Western Europe*, Boulder, CO, Rowman and Littlefield.

—— (2004), 'Competition Versus Competitiveness in the European Single Aviation Market', in Miriam L. Campanella and Sylvester C. W. Eijffinger (eds), *EU Economic Governance and Globalization*, London: Edward Elgar.

Velocci, A. L., Jr. (2002), 'Can Majors Shift Focus Fast Enough to Survive?', *Aviation Week and Space Technology*, 18 November, 52–4.

Zuckerman, L. (2002), 'Travel Advisory: Correspondent's Report: Antitrust Laws an Issue in Airline Alliances', *New York Times*, 28 April, Section 5, 3.

Sole of discretion: competition relations in the transatlantic marketplace

Introduction

Competition relations are a fundamental component of bilateral and multilateral economic policy-making in the transatlantic marketplace and the international political economy. Since the 1890 United States' Sherman Antitrust Act, the gradual proliferation of European and other national competition policies reflects the emergence of free market economies throughout the world.[1] These competition policies – broadly including merger control, cartel and monopoly policies and state aids – operate as regulatory tools to prevent anticompetitive business activity from undermining the benefits of competition in a domestic free market economy.[2] However, as markets internationalize, the implementation of competition policy is no longer simply a behind-the-border matter of regulating domestic economic activity. Competition relations now increasingly intersect with trade policies and create new challenges for the implementation of domestic and international public policy.

Nowhere are the new pressures on domestic competition policies more evident than in the transatlantic marketplace, where officials in Washington and Brussels frequently regulate anticompetitive business activity that concurrently impacts the domestic markets of the United States (US) and the European Union (EU).[3] Transatlantic efforts to prevent such cross-border anticompetitive business activity have historically relied on the unilateral and extraterritorial enforcement of domestic laws. This extraterritoriality, most frequently exercised by the US, led to the creation of national 'blocking' and other retaliatory measures in Europe.[4] As a result, transatlantic disagreements in individual competition cases typically escalated into a politicized tit-for-tat of extraterritoriality versus retaliatory countermeasures.

Despite this historical adversity and tendency toward unilateralism, EU–US competition relations since 1991 are now more appropriately characterized as cooperative bilateralism. This improved relationship can be disaggregated into three distinct processes of policy coordination: rule-making, implementation and exploratory institutional cooperation. Beginning with rule-making cooperation, EU and US competition regulators created a formal framework

– via three separate agreements – to increase implementation and exploratory institutional cooperation in transatlantic competition relations. The framework emphasizes dispute prevention as a corrective to the uncertainty and political tensions arising from dispute resolution through extraterritoriality and retaliatory countermeasures.

This chapter argues that the discretionary authority enjoyed by EU and US competition regulators allows them to play a decisive role in creating, implementing and expanding this cooperative framework. Reflecting the preferences of the regulators, the framework has also allowed for degrees of substantive and procedural convergence. These developments also largely reflect the preferences of European and American business interests. Despite the occasional politicization of high-profile competition cases, the transition to dispute prevention has led to considerable increases in policy coordination and significantly reduced the likelihood of transatlantic competition disputes. Some outcomes of the process of cooperative bilateralism remain subject to disagreements. However, the overall record of cooperation in transatlantic competition relations has prompted the EU's Competition Commissioner Mario Monti to claim that they might serve as a model for transatlantic cooperation more generally (2001a: 2).

The first section of this chapter provides a discussion of how fundamental changes in the international economy have altered business strategies and government approaches to international cooperation in competition policy. Second, the chapter describes the three bilateral agreements that form the basis for the formal framework of transatlantic cooperation in competition relations since 1990. The third section assesses the empirical record of EU–US competition relations in practice across three distinct processes of transatlantic cooperation – rule-making, implementation and exploratory institutional – and comments on the potential for substantive and procedural convergence given institutional differences in the EU and US competition policies. The chapter concludes with a summary of findings and suggests avenues for further research in transatlantic competition relations and international regulatory relations.

Economic internationalization and transatlantic cooperation in competition relations

Economic internationalization and business strategies

Throughout most of the 1980s, changes in the international economy prompted changes in business activity. This economic internationalization (EI) reflects an expansion of markets from the domestic level to the international level, caused by economic liberalization, deregulation and technological development.[5] As firms and markets internationalize, they become active in multiple national jurisdictions and, therefore, subject to multiple and mutually-exclusive domestic competition laws. EI, at least tacitly, also

includes the expansion of domestic corporate strategies, activities and orga-
nizational structures to the international level.[6]

EI has dramatically increased rivalry among firms, both within and across
national borders, which can significantly change business strategies. A common business response to the new pressure of EI, especially in the developed
economies, is to increase foreign direct investment (FDI) by pursuing mergers with firms in other jurisdictions (UNCTAD, 2000: 13).[7] Such mergers are
often intended as a means to attain internationally competitive economies of
scale and enhance overseas market access with new distribution networks
and locally-familiar reputations. More specifically, firms pursue internationally oriented mergers in order to access strategic proprietary assets, gain market power and market dominance, achieve synergy gains, become larger,
diversify and spread risks, exploit financial opportunities, and reap personal
benefits (UNCTAD, 2000: 154).

These changing business strategies and the resulting increases in FDI
(specifically via mergers) raise questions about the private sector's role in
transatlantic competition relations. In general, business interests in Europe
and the United States support closer cooperation between competition
authorities. This support was witnessed during negotiations over the three
agreements formalizing the present EU–US framework for cooperation (see
below).[8] Such support is, however, conditional. Possibly the most important
condition relates to the exchange and protection of sensitive business information while competition regulators are cooperating in individual cases.[9]
Sensitive business information may include a firm's trade secrets, proprietary
information, and information relating to business strategies, investment
plans and marketing goals and methods. Without formal guarantees of protection for such information, business interests are unlikely to support
transatlantic cooperation in competition policy.

Even when formal bilateral agreements include such guarantees, the business position on the treatment of sensitive information varies significantly
between merger and non-merger cases.[10] In concurrent jurisdiction merger
cases, merging firms must officially notify EU and US competition authorities of their intent to merge by submitting a Form CO and Hart-Scott-Rodino
filing, respectively.[11] These pre-merger notification forms often contain business information that is sensitive vis-à-vis competitors who could use it to
their advantage against the merging firms. Due to its sensitivity, domestic EU
and US laws provide firms rights of confidentiality over this business information.[12] If firms officially waive these rights, EU and US competition regulators can freely exchange such information at their discretion, but not
necessarily make it public or otherwise available to the merging firms' competitors. Absent such waivers, the competition authorities cannot exchange
this information with each other, which may limit their ability to cooperate.

It is now common for firms to waive their rights to confidentiality in
merger cases. The reason is simple: firms prefer regulatory approval of a

merger as soon as possible. When competition regulators in multiple jurisdictions can freely exchange information at their own discretion, they are
able to compare their analyses and coordinate their respective legally pro-
scribed timetables for reviewing the merger.[13] Thus, by allowing multiple
regulators to exchange this information, the firms may ultimately expedite
the review process. Waivers of confidentiality may also increase the likelihood that regulators in all relevant jurisdictions will reach similar decisions
on the transaction. Similar, or convergent, regulatory decisions are important
for merging firms because a merger can be delayed when different regulators
reach divergent decisions on whether to approve completely, conditionally
approve or prohibit the transaction. This is particularly important in merger
cases where firms are required to file pre-merger notifications in a large number of jurisdictions. For example, as Waller argues,

> most major transnational mergers or acquisitions end up filing for antitrust
> review in multiple jurisdictions, including many countries in which they have
> little or no actual operations or sales. The current record appears to be the
> Exxon-Mobil merger, which may ultimately involve the filing of up to 40 pre-
> merger notifications in different jurisdictions'. (2000: 574–5)

While waivers of confidentiality in merger cases are common today, this
was not always the case. Since 1991, firms had to learn the modalities of
this new procedure and become confident that the competition regulators
would not leak, whether intentionally or unintentionally, the sensitive information to their competitors. Because waivers of confidentiality are now
common practice in merger cases, when merging firms decide not to waive
their rights, competition regulators may actually perceive this behaviour
as evidence that the firms have something to hide.[14] Such a perception can
slow the merger-review process as the regulators scrutinize the transaction
through their own resources and without the benefit of input from regulators in other jurisdictions.

In non-merger cases (i.e., broadly, cartel and monopoly investigations),[15]
the domestic EU and US laws governing confidentiality also protect sensitive
information that firms provide to competition authorities. However, in such
cases, firms are less likely to waive their rights to confidentiality. Unlike
merging firms, firms under investigation in non-merger cases do not notify
competition authorities of their intent to engage in a specific behaviour.
Rather, non-merger cases are those in which the competition authorities
open an investigation on their own initiative (or based on third-party complaint) into an allegedly anticompetitive behaviour. The firms that are targeted for investigation are then immediately placed on the defensive as they
build a case to convince the regulators in multiple jurisdictions that their
behaviour is not anticompetitive.

This distinction is responsible for a crucial difference in the degree to
which some firms support transatlantic cooperation in the implementation of
competition policy in individual cases.[16] While merging firms typically desire

the sharing of information between EU and US regulators, firms facing non-merger competition investigations are less likely to desire such exchanges. Firms facing non-merger investigations do not necessarily want a competition investigation to be expedited. Rather, these firms may seek to use the information asymmetry to prevent the coordination of investigations in multiple jurisdictions and, in turn, play one regulator off against the other as an obstructing and delaying tactic. Such behaviour is primarily, though not exclusively, expected if the firms are guilty of the alleged anticompetitive behaviour. If a firm is engaging in anticompetitive behaviour that adversely affects multiple jurisdictions, by restricting certain information exchanges between the respective regulators, it may be able to hide incriminating evidence. This is particularly important for firms, whether European or American, facing non-merger competition investigations in the US because domestic law in that jurisdiction provides for criminal sanctions against guilty parties (e.g., prison sentences for corporate managers and executives). In contrast, the EU's domestic law only provides for – albeit, sometimes very large – administrative fines for such anticompetitive behaviour.

In the transatlantic marketplace, business interests have been careful to protect their rights to confidentiality when EU and US competition regulators exchange information in multijurisdictional cases. In merger cases, firms are concerned primarily that competitors could acquire sensitive business information provided to regulators. In non-merger competition investigations, firms are concerned primarily that sensitive business information could incriminate them. Reflecting these shared concerns regarding the treatment of sensitive business information in the transatlantic marketplace, each of the three formal EU–US agreements discussed in the next section explicitly respects domestic provisions that protect the confidentiality of such information.

Economic internationalization and government policies

EI also challenged government competition policies. As EI changed opportunities and incentives for firms, governments had to change their behaviour if they hoped to manage business activity that increasingly occurred across or outside their national borders but still affected their domestic market. Before the onset of EI, EU and US competition policies primarily focused on managing competition in their respective domestic markets. However, as EI impacted markets and, thus, changed business strategies, governments were faced with the prospect of applying their domestic competition policies to an increasing number of potentially anticompetitive activities of foreign firms. In addition, domestic competition policies would have to address the potentially anticompetitive activity of domestic firms that affected the international economy and, thus, the interests of other states.

The application of domestic competition policies to increasingly international business activity raises the prospect that different domestic competition policies may overlap and come into conflict. For example, competition regulators in different national jurisdictions may reach divergent regulatory decisions on how to treat a given multijurisdictional merger. These divergent decisions may directly conflict when one regulator approves a merger and the other prohibits the transaction. More commonly, divergent decisions are simply disagreements over the precise remedies (e.g., divestment of assets, implementation of licensing agreements) that firms must meet in order to gain approval of a merger.

As discussed above, these divergent decisions are not in the interest of most, primarily merging, firms. In addition, divergent decisions are generally not in the interest of competition regulators because they can prompt politicians to intervene with the intent of resolving the dispute. Competition regulators prefer limiting political interventions because, in the words of the EU Competition Commissioner Mario Monti, such decisions are 'a matter of law and economics, not politics' (European Commission, 2001). From the regulators' perspective, dispute resolution via political intervention – including threats and the actual imposition on foreign firms of various punitive measures based in domestic law – raises the prospect that competition decisions may be linked to trade disputes and other non-competition issues.[17] As a result, the final outcome of the investigation is uncertain and may not reflect the initial analysis and decision of the competition regulators.

In the transatlantic marketplace, politicians historically intervened with threats and the actual exercise of extraterritorial action in order to resolve divergent competition decisions. These political attempts at dispute resolution frequently prompted retaliatory countermeasures from the target jurisdiction, which increased the uncertainty of the final competition investigation.[18] This behaviour also increased the likelihood of multisectoral trade wars that threatened to destabilize bilateral relations and, more generally, the international economy (ICPAC, 2000: 41).

As EI increased the cross-border nature of business activity throughout the 1980s, EU and US regulators were faced with the prospect of reaching divergent decisions in an increasing number of cases. US and EU competition regulators also viewed overseas domestic developments as contributing to an unacceptable imbalance in transatlantic competition relations that was likely to trigger an increase in political interventions.[19] For the EU and US competition regulators, the twin prospects of EI and domestic institutional developments would likely prompt an increasingly untenable reliance on dispute resolution via political interventions.

The formal framework of transatlantic competition relations

To avoid the looming problems presented by EI and domestic institutional developments on both sides of the Atlantic, EU and US competition regulators opted to create a formal framework for dispute prevention.[20] Notably, this cooperative framework was not established through treaty-making processes that require political ratification procedures. The regulators instead pursued bilateral agreements that could be negotiated and signed under their discretionary authority. By binding each other into a formal framework, regulators on both sides of the Atlantic could be more certain of the behaviour of their overseas counterparts. The resulting 'rule-making' policy cooperation was designed to avoid divergent decisions and limit the need for dispute resolution via destabilizing political interventions. As a result transatlantic relations experienced a seminal transition from adversarial unilateralism to cooperative bilateralism. The agreements underpinning the formal framework are reviewed in detail in this section and also provide the basis for other processes of cooperation discussed below.

The 1991 bilateral agreement
The 1991 EU–US Bilateral Competition Agreement established the basic cooperative framework between EU and US competition regulators.[21] This original effort at rule-making cooperation formalized a process of discretionary competition policy coordination that emphasizes information exchanges and introduces the principle of 'comity' into transatlantic competition relations.

In order to avoid jurisdictional conflict, EU and US competition regulators agreed that divergent decisions had to be prevented from occurring in the first place. Thus, their objective was to design a framework for dispute prevention, not dispute resolution. Reflecting this objective, the central components of the resulting EU–US Bilateral Competition Agreement include:

1 notification when competition enforcement activities may affect the 'important interests' (Art. 2, Para. 1) of the other party;
2 exchange of non-confidential information;
3 coordination of action;
4 conduct of enforcement activities, 'insofar as possible' (Art. 4, Para. 3), that are consistent with objectives of the other party; and
5 consultation.[22]

The Bilateral Agreement also reduces the potential for EU–US jurisdictional conflict by formalizing the exchange of non-confidential information at multiple stages of competition investigations. In individual competition cases, the agreement emphasizes that one competition authority will officially notify the other that it is reviewing a case that may affect the important interests of the other party. Acting as an alert system, such notifications are made 'far enough in advance . . . to enable the other Party's views to be taken into account' (Article 2). After the initial notification, further cooperation can take numerous forms in the investigative and remedial phases of a competition case. Generally, 'the two sides try to synchronize their fact-finding actions and coordinate their respective approaches on the definition of relevant markets, on points of foreign law relevant to the interpretation of the case, and on possible remedies to ensure they do not conflict' (Devuyst, 2001: 324).

Possibly the most unique component of the Bilateral Agreement is the introduction of the international legal principle of comity. Comity can be distinguished as two distinct types: traditional and positive. Traditional comity (Article VI) requires a party conducting a competition investigation to *consider* the important interests of the other party to the agreement.[23] This principle has inspired intensive daily cooperation as EU and US competition regulators strive to coordinate their respective positions and remedies in order to avoid creating a harmful effect in the other's market.

While the term 'positive comity' cannot be found in the Bilateral Agreement, the legal principle is clearly articulated in Article V. Positive comity differs from traditional comity in that it allows one party to *request* that the other party open an investigation into a competition case that is located outside the requesting party's jurisdiction but affects the requesting party's important interests.[24] In such cases, the requested party would inform the requesting party whether they plan to initiate an investigation, which may eliminate the need for the requesting party to open its own investigation.[25] By allowing one party to request an investigation of activity that occurs outside its jurisdiction, the positive comity provision of the Bilateral Agreement is intended to reduce the need for the requesting party to enforce its domestic competition laws extraterritorially. In addition, by refraining from conducting a simultaneous investigation, the requesting party reduces the likelihood that a divergent decision will be reached.[26]

Conscious of the limits of their discretionary authority, the competition regulators agreed that 'Nothing in this Agreement shall be interpreted in a manner inconsistent with the existing laws, or as requiring any change in the laws, of the United States of America or the European Communities or of their respective States or Member States' (Article IX). The Bilateral Agreement is also flexible enough to allow for the use of extraterritoriality in cases of concurrent jurisdiction. As such, the Agreement stipulates that 'Nothing in this Article . . . precludes the notifying Party from undertaking enforcement activities with respect to extraterritorial anticompetitive activities' (Article V), regardless of action or inaction by the notified party. In other words, EU and US politicians maintain the right to intervene in cases in which they perceive divergent decisions as threatening national and/or constituent interests. The regulators included this phraseology, in part, in the hope of assuaging any political concerns that might arise regarding their discretionary authority to engage in such rule-making cooperation.

Despite the regulators' efforts to draft an agreement that was within their discretionary authority, the French Government (supported by the Netherlands and Spain) challenged the legality of the agreement on the basis that the Commission had overstepped its authority to sign the Bilateral Agreement.[27] The ECJ delivered its final judgment in the case in 1994, finding in favour of the French position.[28] The ECJ's decision legally annulled the Bilateral. However, following internal negotiations and exchanges of interpretive letters with the US competition officials, the Council and the Commission promptly issued a joint decision on 10 April 1995.[29] The Joint Decision officially approved and implemented the Bilateral, noting 'The Agreement shall apply with effect from 23 September 1991' (Article 2), the date the Commission originally signed the agreement.

The 1998 Positive Comity Agreement

The primary intent of the 1998 Positive Comity Agreement (PCA) was to clarify how positive comity should work in practice. The PCA asserts that 'The competition authorities of a Requesting Party may request the competition authorities of a Requested Party to investigate and, if warranted, to remedy anticompetitive activities in accordance with the Requested Party's competition laws' (Article III). These requests will typically be made when one competition authority is better placed to acquire the necessary information to conduct an investigation. In such a case, the PCA creates the presumption that the competition authorities of a requesting party 'will normally defer or suspend their own enforcement activities in favor of enforcement activities by the competition authorities of the Requested Party' (Article IV).

Because domestic EU and US laws require competition regulators to initiate investigations into mergers that meet certain thresholds, the PCA does not apply to merger cases.[30] However, in non-merger cases, the PCA provides specific conditions under which a positive comity referral will be made. For example, referrals will normally be made when the anticompetitive activities in question do not have a 'direct, substantial and reasonably foreseeable impact on consumers' in the requested party's territory (Article IV). If a requested party feels the anticompetitive behaviour is seriously detrimental to its domestic consumers, that party has the right to conduct a simultaneous investigation of its own. This decision to conduct a simultaneous investigation is discretionary and is in no way abrogated if the party has made a positive comity request.

The PCA procedures increase implementation cooperation by requiring the requested party – 'on request or at reasonable intervals' – to update the requesting party of the status of the investigation. Should the requested party be unable to deal 'actively and expeditiously' with or update the other party on a positive comity request, the requesting party is free to initiate its own investigation. Under the PCA, all positive comity investigations and updates must conform to the domestic statutory requirements of the respective parties for protecting confidential information (Article V). As such, the PCA does not threaten the interests of firms regarding the exchange of sensitive business information.

The 1999 administrative arrangements on attendance

Unlike the Bilateral Agreement and the PCA, the Administrative Arrangements on Attendance (AAA) are not binding on the signatories. Rather, the

AAA offers an example of rule-making cooperation in which the regulators perceived the need to formalize and clarify procedures that were already taking place on an informal, ad hoc basis under the framework of the Bilateral Agreement and PCA.

When conducting their respective competition investigations, EU and US regulators frequently meet with the targeted firms and third parties as a way to increase their information on the market impact of the activity in question. These meetings are known as 'oral hearings' in the EU and 'pitch meetings' in the US. As provided for in the EU's domestic-competition provisions, oral hearings are held by the Competition Directorate General and conducted by an independent Hearing Officer.[31] In the US, the Department of Justice's (DOJ) Antitrust Division and the Federal Trade Commission (FTC) hold their own respective pitch meetings.

In 1997, the US DOJ and FTC issued separate requests to attend the EU's oral hearings in three merger cases: Boeing/McDonnell Douglas, Guinness/ Grand Metropolitan and WorldCom/MCI. After reviewing these requests, the Competition Directorate General (specifically, the Hearing Officer) invited officials from the US competition regulators to take part as observers in the oral hearings. Because the US officials attended the hearings as observers, they were not authorized to participate or otherwise intervene in the proceedings.

The Commission's decision to accept the US's requests for attendance 'took into account that the US authorities were examining the same transactions and that attendance in the hearings could improve cooperation and coordination of enforcement activities' (Devuyst, 2001: 136). Based on these initial experiences, the EU believed that further attendance at foreign hearings could prove beneficial to the analysis of concurrent-jurisdiction competition cases (i.e., reduce the likelihood of divergent decisions). As a result, the Commission approached the US competition authorities to establish a clear framework for attendance requests based on reciprocity. The explicit requirement of reciprocity again reflects the desire of the EU competition agents for balance in their relations with the US competition regulators.

The resulting AAA formalized a discretionary procedure for allowing representatives of foreign competition authorities to attend internal meetings in cases of mutual interest (i.e., concurrent-jurisdiction competition cases). Based on the AAA, reciprocal exchanges of attendees are now a common feature of the review process for concurrent-jurisdiction competition cases. As Commissioner Monti argues 'it has now become standard practice for representatives of the antitrust agencies to attend oral hearings in cases involving close EU–US cooperation – a virtually unprecedented step forward in EU–US regulatory cooperation' (2001b: 3).[32]

When requests for attendance are granted, the prevailing laws protecting confidential information in the host jurisdiction apply to the guest regulators. As such, the host competition authorities will typically consult with the targeted firms before an arrangement for attendance is confirmed. Unless the firms have agreed to waive their right to confidentiality, guest competition regulators are asked to exit the meeting when confidential information is being discussed. As such, the AAA does not threaten domestic laws on confidential information and conforms to general business interests on both sides of the Atlantic.

By simplifying the procedure for attendance into a standard practice, the AAA reduces information asymmetries and, again, reduces the likelihood that competition regulators will reach divergent decisions.[33] By reducing the likelihood of divergent decisions, the AAA (like the Bilateral and PCA) also reduces the likelihood of political intervention.

The record of transatlantic competition relations

In practice, cooperation in transatlantic competition relations can be understood as three distinct processes of policy coordination: rule-making, implementation and exploratory institutional cooperation. To varying degrees, EU and US competition regulators emphasize the importance of substantive and procedural convergence across each of these three processes as means to increase the likelihood of future transatlantic cooperation. Evidence of substantive convergence is found most readily in the overwhelming number of convergent decisions reached in individual concurrent-jurisdiction competition investigations (see below). At the same time, convergence of the domestic procedures through which EU and US competition regulators conduct their respective investigations remains more elusive.[34]

The Bilateral Agreement, the PCA and the AAA provide examples of rule-making cooperation that formalize binding and non-binding cooperation in the transatlantic marketplace. When negotiating and signing these agreements, the EU and US competition authorities were mindful of remaining within their discretionary authority. This rule-making cooperation represents a conscious attempt by the competition regulators to increase their discretionary information exchanges and, notably, introduce the principle of comity into bilateral competition relations. In general, the formal framework of transatlantic competition relations is designed to increase substantive convergence (i.e., convergent decisions in individual competition cases) as a means to enhance dispute prevention.

Following from the formal framework, EU and US competition regulators engage in implementation cooperation on individual competition cases. Reflecting the notion of traditional comity, the competition authorities coordinate those investigations that may affect the other's important interests. This coordination is intensive, occurring on a daily basis via phone, faxes and email exchanges. As former FTC Commissioner Robert Pitofsky argues:

It is hard to imagine how day-to-day cooperation and coordination between enforcement officials in Europe and the United States could be much improved. Within the bounds of confidentiality rules, we share, on a regular and continuing basis, views and information about particular transactions, coordinate the timing of our review process to the extent feasible, and almost always achieve consistent remedies. (2000)[35]

The success of implementation cooperation also can be seen in the number of notifications exchanged between the EU and US competition regulators. As provided for in the Bilateral Agreement, notifications occur when one competition authority informs the other that it is initiating an investigation that may affect the important interests of their foreign counterpart. Table 4.1 illustrates the number of total EU–US competition notifications since formal cooperation began in 1991.

Table 4.1   EU and US competition and merger notifications, 1991–2000

Year	EU competition notifications	US competition notifications			Merger notifications[b]	
		FTC	DOJ	Total	EU	US
1992[a]	26	20	20	40	11	31
1993	44	22	18	40	20	20
1994	29	16	19	35	18	20
1995	42	14	21	35	31	18
1996	48	20	18	38	35	27
1997	42	12	24	36	30	20
1998	52	22	24	46	43	39
1999	70	26	23	49	59	39
2000	104	26	32	58	85	49

Source: European Commission (2001), Report to the Council and European Parliament, 8.

Notes: [a] Notifications since 23 September 1991. [b] The numbers reported for EU and US 'competition notifications' include both merger and non-merger notifications. The table separates out merger notifications in the last two columns to demonstrate that they account for the bulk of all transatlantic competition notifications.

Once a notification has been made, the competition authorities proceed to cooperate on a number of substantive and procedural matters that are central to domestic enforcement activities, including factual investigations and the coordination of remedies. As such, the increasing levels of notifications in Table 4.1 reflect the commitment of the EU and US competition regulators to coordinate their competition investigations in order to increase the likelihood of convergent decisions. Table 4.1 also demonstrates that EU and US competition regulators exchanged more than 800 notifications during the 1990s of competition cases that involved the other's important interests. Considering this volume of concurrent-jurisdiction competition cases, it is noteworthy that only two instances of divergent decisions escalated into significant transatlantic political disputes: the 1997 Boeing/McDonnell Douglas and 2001 GE/Honeywell merger cases.[36] This finding suggests that exchanges of information and coordination of substantive analyses by regulators may increase the likelihood of convergent decisions and reduce the likelihood of political intervention in individual competition cases.

The final process of transatlantic cooperation can be labeled 'exploratory institutional'. This process is the most recent and experimental in EU–US cooperation in competition relations and illustrated at the bilateral level in the establishment of the EU–US Mergers Working Group (MWG) in 1999.[37] The MWG is an ad hoc forum mandated to study different approaches in the EU and the US to the formulation of remedies and the scope for convergence of merger analysis and methodology. The creation of the MWG was undertaken entirely at the regulators' discretion as a means to address important new areas for cooperation. Reflecting its ad hoc nature and discretionary focus, the MWG's membership is flexible, it does not produce documentation available to the public and its future agenda will vary depending on regulatory needs.

The MWG faces significant obstacles created by institutional differences in domestic in EU and US competition policies.[38] For example, EU and US competition regulators may prioritize different substantive objectives in their respective competition investigations, which can increase the likelihood of divergent decisions in concurrent-jurisdiction competition cases. These differences reflect distinctive historical and legal institutional developments on either side of the Atlantic.[39] In practice, they can lead to substantive divergences in the definition of relevant product and/or geographic markets, which can result in dramatically divergent market-analysis calculations and, ultimately, divergent competition decisions. Similarly, procedural differences embedded in domestic EU and US competition policies – such as different timetables for competition investigations, different evidence-gathering tools and different roles for the judiciary – can impede the transatlantic coordination of competition investigations.

Despite these domestic institutional differences in EU and US competition policies, some signs of convergence are emerging. Substantively, the overwhelming majority of transatlantic regulatory decisions in individual concurrent-jurisdiction competition cases are convergent (see above at Table 4.1). Procedurally, limited convergence is also occurring. For example, the MWG's work in the area of merger remedies has already produced practical results. Through the MWG, the Commission received useful comments from US competition authorities on a preliminary draft of its recent notice on remedies.[40] Commissioner Monti was candid in commenting on lessons learned from the US and the role of the MWG in the EU's preparation of this notice:

> I have no hesitation in acknowledging that the Commission's approach to remedies as set out in the Notice was influenced by the FTC's previous study on the divestiture process, which demonstrated that some remedies secured by the FTC had proved less effective than intended. Furthermore, the EU and US

antitrust authorities discussed their respective approaches to remedies within the framework of a working group on merger control [i.e., the MWG]. The exchange of expertise in this group proved invaluable to the drafting of our Notice on remedies. (2002: 2)

While the MWG's initial agenda focused on convergence in merger review, it is conceptualized as a very informal and ongoing forum that can evolve to address future areas of concern and potential convergence in transatlantic competition relations. Though procedural convergence is possible, these future efforts will likely concentrate on measures to enhance substantive convergence. In any case, further convergence of EU and US competition policies, whether substantive or procedural, will most likely be seen in areas under the discretionary authority of the competition regulators.

Conclusions

Despite aberrant, high-profile competition cases, such as the Boeing/McDonnell Douglas and GE/Honeywell merger cases, the norm of transatlantic competition relations since 1991 is best characterized as cooperative bilateralism. The emergence of cooperative bilateralism is particularly surprising considering the traditional, adversarial unilateralism of transatlantic competition relations.

Because EI changed business strategies – as witnessed, for example, in increasing FDI and internationally-oriented mergers – EU and US competition regulators were prompted to adjust their behaviour. Always conscious of the limits of their discretionary authority, the regulators decided to pursue a formal framework for bilateral cooperation. The resulting framework emphasizes dispute prevention by regulators as a means to obviate the need for dispute resolution by politicians. The regulators implement this dispute prevention by increasing information exchanges (and incorporating comity considerations) with the intent of reducing the likelihood of divergent decisions in concurrent-jurisdiction competition cases.

The transition to cooperative bilateralism in the transatlantic marketplace occurred despite different domestic institutions of competition policy in the EU and US. Regardless of these persistent obstacles, substantive convergence (i.e., consistent decisions in simultaneous investigations) remains a high priority for EU and US competition authorities. In addition, regulators continue to pursue avenues for procedural convergence (e.g., investigation coordination).

Further research on the modalities of international competition relations is strongly encouraged, especially considering the inclusion for the first time of competition policy in the WTO's Doha Round of trade negotiations. Such research may begin with questions about the possibility of substantive and procedural convergence in the transatlantic marketplace and the international political economy. In addition, comparisons with efforts in other policy areas would be useful to assess Commissioner Monti's claim that transatlantic cooperation in competition relations can serve as a model for transatlantic cooperation more generally. Such studies would benefit from a systematic analysis of the role of different (both merging and non-merging) firms in and across these various policy areas.

The chapter also reveals the pressing need for a cross-disciplinary research agenda on the causes and consequences of international competition relations, particularly in studying the role of public and private actors in promoting inter-state cooperation and conflict.

Notes

1 Usage of the general moniker 'competition policy' is more common in Europe while 'antitrust' is more frequently used in the United States to cover many of the same policies. For simplicity, the current chapter generally uses the term 'competition policy' regardless of the specific policy or jurisdiction in question.

2 In general, the goal of competition policy is to increase economic efficiency (i.e., allocative, productive and dynamic/technological) in a free market economy. As Nicolaides argues, 'Economic theory suggests that efficiency is usually, but not always, improved by rivalry among firms. To encourage rivalry, competition policy prohibits practices and policies that seek to exclude or discriminate against rival firms or that intend to reduce competition among incumbent firms' (1994: 9).

3 The term 'European Community' is still legally correct when referring to activities that fall under the rubric of the Single Market (Pillar I), including competition policy. For simplicity, this chapter refers to only the 'European Union', regardless of whether the activity in question is legally subsumed under the competency of the European Community.

4 For examples, see Griffin (1998).

5 Much of this EI follows from the liberalization of international commerce through successive rounds of trade negotiations in the GATT.

6 For a study that challenges some of the typical assumptions of the impact of EI on business strategies, see Doremus et al. (1998).

7 This trend is witnessed in the fact that overall FDI inflows have increased dramatically since the 1980s, especially in the developed economies. Cross-border mergers and acquisitions (M&As) represent a substantial source of these overall FDI flows. For example, as UNCTAD reports, 'The ratio of the value of cross-border M&As to world FDI flows reached over 80 per cent in 1999. M&As are particularly significant as a mode of entry for FDI in developed countries' (2000: 13). Similarly, Held et al. argue that, since 1990, mergers and acquisitions 'have accounted typically for a third to over a half of all FDI flows' (1999: 243).

8 For an example of this support for the 1998 EU–US Positive Comity Agreement, see International Chamber of Commerce (1997). Of course, the ICC membership is not representative of all business interests. Comprehensive and systematic international business attitudes toward transatlantic cooperation in competition relations are diverse, but likely vary depending on the size of the business, their exposure to import competition, their dependency on export markets, the sector in question and cyclical conditions in a geographic and/or sectoral or product market.

9 For example, see ICC (1999) and Parisi (1999).

10 It should be added that strategies in individual competition cases also vary between the firms targeted in a given investigation (whether merging or non-merging firms) and their competitors.

11 These notification requirements, which also apply to mergers that are exclusively domestic in their effect, are based in the EU's Merger Control Regulation (MCR) and the US's Hart-Scott-Rodino Act (HSR). The MCR and HSR contain specific thresholds at which firms must officially notify competition authorities of their intent to merge.

12 Ham (1993: 588) provides a very useful list of the domestic legal constraints in both the EU and the US which protect confidential information. These include the EU's Regulation 17, parts of the US Code and the Federal Trade Commission Act. See also Parisi (1999).

13 Of course, if there are fundamental problems with a merger, waivers of confidentiality are unlikely to improve the likelihood that the merger will be approved.

14 From the perspective of merging firms facing a regulatory prohibition of their transaction, they may choose not to waive their right to confidentiality in order to prevent the EU and US competition authorities from coordinating their timetables for investigations and final decisions. The idea behind this strategy is that approval of one authority will pressure the other to approve the merger despite any potential reservations to the contrary by the latter. However, in practice, such a strategy can create even greater problems for the firms by extending the investigation and creating the perception that they have something to hide.

15 For the purposes of the current discussion, 'non-merger cases' do not include state aid investigations. State aids include Member-State governments of the EU, which creates a different dynamic for the sharing of information and transatlantic cooperation.

16 Of course, this distinction does not hold for the more general support which business has provided for the creation of the formal framework of EU–US cooperation in competition policy.

17 For a discussion of the linkage between trade and competition policy, see Damro (2004).

18 A frequently cited example of the problems that can arise over multijurisdictional competition cases is Laker Airways (British Airways Bd. v. Laker Airways Ltd, 1985 A.C. 58 [1984]). For more extensive discussions of this historically adversarial transatlantic relationship, see Damro (2003) and Devuyst (2001).

19 For example, US competition regulators feared the possibility of increased political disputes because the EU was believed to be a 'maturing' international economic actor with competition regulators who could now exercise their merger review extraterritorially and impose remedies on US firms even if the US competition authorities disagreed. This perception of maturation was based on three domestic developments in the Union: the 1988 Wood Pulp doctrine of extraterritoriality and the pending completion of the Single European Market and the Merger Control Regulation. The EU's concerns arose from the willingness of the US to use Section 301 and the Exon-Florio Amendment to Section 501 of the Omnibus Trade and Competitiveness Act of 1988.

20 In the EU, the primary competition regulator is the European Commission, or more specifically, the Competition Directorate and the Merger Task Force. In the

US, the primary competition regulators are the Department of Justice's Antitrust Division and the Federal Trade Commission.

21 Limited voluntary EU–US cooperation had occurred previously under a series of OECD Recommendations on Restrictive Business Practices Affecting International Trade. On these non-binding recommendations, see OECD (1999: 7–9). In contrast to these OECD Recommendations, the Bilateral Agreement has a much more operational and binding character (Devuyst 2000: 324).

22 For a thorough analysis of the content of the Bilateral Agreement, see Ham (1993).

23 Traditional comity is also sometimes referred to as 'negative' comity. A basis for traditional comity in international competition relations can be found in the non-binding OECD Recommendations. However, moving beyond the OECD's non-binding regime, the 1991 Bilateral Agreement embodied both variants of comity for the first time in a binding agreement relating to competition matters (Ham 1993: 594).

24 A legal distinction may also be made between a request that a foreign jurisdiction open or expand an investigation and a request for assistance in a foreign jurisdiction's investigation (OECD 1999: 3). See also OECD (1999: 5–6) for a treatment of further definitional issues of positive comity.

25 If an investigation is initiated on the basis of positive comity, the Bilateral Agreement requires the requested party to update the requesting party on the investigation and inform them of any relevant decisions taken in the investigation.

26 It should be noted that much scepticism surrounds the actual employment of positive comity. For discussions of these limitations, see Waller (2000), Janow (2000: 41) and Ham (1993: 595).

27 The US competition regulators had clear discretionary authority to enter into such an 'executive agreement' as provided for under the 1972 Case-Zablocki Act. As a result, the Bilateral Agreement was not challenged in the US.

28 See Case C-327/91 France v. Commission [1994] ECR I-3641. For a discussion of the ECJ's judgment, see Riley (1995).

29 See OJ 1995 L131/38. Or OJ L 95 of 27.4.95, pp. 45–6.

30 On these pre-merger notification thresholds, see the EU's Merger Control Regulation and the US's Hart-Scott-Rodino Act.

31 In merger cases, oral hearings are held by the Merger Task Force, but still conducted by an independent Hearing Officer.

32 It is possible that a request for attendance could be denied. The AAA mentions that attendance will be granted for 'appropriate' cases. Thus, a competition authority can 'decline to invite attendance by the requesting competition authority, if it believes that the other's attendance would adversely affect the proceedings or would otherwise be inconsistent with important interests' (Devuyst 2001: 137).

33 However, reciprocal attendance does not guarantee convergent decisions. For example, see the 1999 BOC/Air Liquide merger.

34 According to Kagan, limitations on procedural convergence should not be surprising: 'Particularly resistant to transnational harmonization, it appears, are procedural and institutional aspects of national legal systems: their methods of adjudication and public administration, their modes of drafting statutes, penalizing illegal behavior, and managing relations between regulatory agencies and regulated firms' (2000: 3). For a useful discussion of substantive and procedural convergence

in competition relations, and the limits thereof, in EU and US competition policy, see Venit and Kolasky (2000).

35 For similar arguments, see Devuyst (2001), Monti (2001a), Parisi (1999) and Van Miert (1998).

36 For a discussion of the Boeing/McDonnell Douglas merger, see Damro (2001). On the GE/Honeywell merger, see Burnside (2002) and Evans (2002).

37 At the multilateral level, the EU and the US have also cooperated over the last two years to facilitate the establishment of the International Competition Network (ICN). Instead of a formal international organization, the ICN is an informal venue for discussions on the multilateralization of cooperation in competition policy. For more on the ICN, see Damro (2004). In addition, at the multilateral level, the EU and the US continue to engage each other in the OECD and, more importantly, recently agreed to add competition policy to the current Doha Round of trade negotiations in the WTO.

38 For useful discussions of the institutional differences between EU and US competition policy, see Majone (2000: 279), Campbell and Trebilcock (1997), Doern and Wilks (1996: 328–34), and Doern (1995).

39 While the US promulgated the 1890 Sherman Act to protect individual entrepreneurs from large trusts, the EU developed competition policy as a way to encourage economic integration and to create the SEM. In practice, this difference and significant changes in the priorities of US competition policy have led to perceptions that the US may look more closely at the impact of a merger deal on consumers (i.e., increased choices, decreased prices) while the EU may look more closely at the impact of a deal on competitors. The resulting differences in objectives (consumer protection versus market integration) can lead to different substantive final decisions in competition cases.

40 Commission Notice on remedies acceptable under Council Regulation (EEC) No 4064/89 and under Commission Regulation (EC) No 447/98, OJ C 68, 2.3.2001. pp. 3–11.

References

Burnside, A. (2002), 'GE, Honey, I Sunk the Merger', *European Competition Law Review*, 2, 107–10.

Campbell, A. N. and M. J. Trebilcock (1997), 'Interjurisdictional Conflict in Merger Review', in L. Waverman, W. S. Comanor and A. Goto (eds), *Competition Policy in the Global Economy: Modalities for Cooperation*, London: Routledge.

Damro, C. (2001), 'Building an International Identity: The EU and Extraterritorial Competition Policy', *Journal of European Public Policy*, 8:2, 208–26.

—— (2003), *Economic Internationalization and Competition Policy: International and Domestic Sources of Transatlantic Cooperation*, PhD Dissertation, Pittsburgh, University of Pittsburgh.

—— (2004), 'International Competition Policy: Bilateral and Multilateral Efforts at Dispute Prevention', in B. Hocking and S. McGuire (eds), *Trade Politics*, 2nd edn, London: Routledge.

Devuyst, Y. (2000), 'Toward a Multilateral Competition Policy Regime?', *Global Governance*, 6:3, 319–38.

—— (2001), 'Transatlantic Competition Relations', in M. A. Pollack and G. C. Shaffer (eds), *Transatlantic Governance in the Global Economy*, Lanham, MD: Rowman and Littlefield.

Doern, G. B. (1995), 'A Political-Institutional Framework for the Analysis of Competition Policy Institutions', *Governance*, 8, 195–217.

—— and S. Wilks (1996), 'Conclusions: International Convergence and National Contrasts', in G. B. Doern and S. Wilks (eds), *Comparative Competition Policy: National Institutions in a Global Market*, Oxford: Clarendon.

Doremus, P., W. Keller, L. Pauly and S. Reich (1998), *The Myth of the Global Corporation*, Princeton, NJ: Princeton University Press.

European Commission (2001), 'Monti Dismisses Criticism of GE/Honeywell Merger Review, Deplores Politicization of the Case', Press Release No. 47/01, 18 June.

Evans, D. S. (2002), 'The New Trustbusters: Brussels and Washington May Part Ways', *Foreign Affairs*, 81:1, 14–20.

Griffin, J. P. (1998), 'Foreign Governmental Reactions to US Assertions of Extraterritorial Jurisdiction', *European Competition Law Review*, 19, 64–73.

Ham, A. D. (1993), 'International Cooperation in the Anti-Trust Field and in Particular the Agreement between the United States of America and the Commission of the European Communities', *Common Market Law Review*, 30, 39–62.

Held, D., A. McGrew, D. Goldblatt and J. Perraton (1999), *Global Transformations: Politics, Economics and Culture*, Stanford, CA: Stanford University Press.

International Chamber of Commerce (1997), 'ICC Comments on EU–US Positive Comity Agreement', Policy Statement of the Commission on Law and Practices Relating to Competition, 12 March.

—— (1999), 'ICC Recommendations to the International Competition Policy Advisory Committee (ICPAC) on Exchange of Confidential Information Between Competition Authorities in the Merger Context', Policy Statement of the Commission on Law and Practices Relating to Competition, Doc 225/525, 21 May.

ICPAC (2000), *Final Report*, Washington, DC, US Government Printing Office.

Janow, M. E. (2000), 'Transatlantic Cooperation on Competition Policy', in S. J. Evenett, A. Lehmann, and B. Steil (eds), *Antitrust Goes Global: What Future for Transatlantic Cooperation?* Washington, DC: Brookings Institution Press.

Kagan, R. A. (2000), 'How Much Do National Styles of Law Matter?', in R. A. Kagan and L. Axelrad (eds), *Regulatory Encounters: Multinational Corporations and American Adversarial Legalism*, Berkeley, CA: University of California Press.

Majone, G. (2000), 'The Credibility Crisis of Community Regulation', *Journal of Common Market Studies*, 38:2, 273–302.

Monti, M. (2001a), 'The EU Views on Global Competition Forum', speech at the American Bar Association Meetings, Washington DC, 29 March.

—— (2001b), 'Prospects for Transatlantic Competition Policy', speech at the Institute for International Economics, Washington 30 March.

—— (2002), 'The Commission Notice on Merger Remedies – One Year After', speech at the Centre d'économie Industrielle, Ecole Nationale Supérieure de Mines, Paris, 18 January.

Nicolaides, P. (1994), 'The Role of Competition Policy in Economic Integration', in P. Nicolaides and A. van der Klugt (eds), *The Competition Policy of the European Community*, Maastricht: European Institute of Public Administration.

OECD (1999), 'CLP Report on Positive Comity', DAFFE/CLP(99)19, Paris.

Parisi, J. J. (1999), 'Enforcement Co-operation Among Antitrust Authorities', *European Competition Law Review* 20:3, 133–42.

Pitofsky, R. (2000), 'EU and US Approaches to International Mergers – Views from the US Federal Trade Commission', speech at EC Merger Control 10th Anniversary Conference, EU Competition Directorate and International Bar Association, Brussels, 14–15 September.

UNCTAD (2000), *World Investment Report 2000: Cross-border Mergers and Acquisitions and Development*, Geneva.

Van Miert, K. (1998), 'The Transatlantic and Global Implications of European Competition Policy', speech at North Atlantic Assembly Meeting, Palais Egmont, Brussels, 16 February.

Venit, J. S. and W. J. Kolasky (2000), 'Substantive Convergence and Procedural Dissonance in Merger Review', in S. J. Evenett, A. Lehmann and B. Steil (eds), *Antitrust Goes Global: What Future for Transatlantic Cooperation?*, Washington DC: Brookings Institution Press, 79–97.

Waller, S. W. (2000), 'The Twilight of Comity', *Columbia Journal of Transnational Law*, 38, 563–79.

Government-business strategies and transatlantic economic relations: between hegemony and high technology[1]

Introduction

American and European public- and private-sector organizations are involved in two of the highest-profile and highest-stake technology infrastructure projects ever undertaken: the advancement of (1) the third generation of wireless communications and the launch of wireless Internet (3G), and (2) the next generation of global navigation and satellite systems (GNSS). This chapter provides a comparative analysis of government-business strategies and transatlantic economic relations in examining these high-technology developments. Europe and the United States have very different starting positions: Europe benefits from a position as regional hegemon (unchallenged dominance) at home and a commanding international position in wireless cellular communications through the so-called Global System for Mobile Communications (GSM), whereas the United States has enjoyed an extraordinary position as a global hegemon in satellite navigation through the Global Positioning System (GPS), a sector where Europe had virtually no presence in the 1990s. However, developments in the last decade could result in a new international division of labour, with the United States gaining a stronger position in the wireless sector and Europe gaining in the field of satellite navigation through its planned Galileo system.

A traditional assumption is that the European Union – for historical, structural and cultural reasons – is more prone to explicit, intentional and corporatist industrial policy than the United States, especially in leading-edge technologies. The United States is commonly associated with a more fragmented industrial policy and system of political economy (Bingham, 1998; Nester, 1997). The conventional wisdom would suggest that EU industrial policy considerations trump security considerations in the fields of satellite navigation and wireless Internet. The EU objectives to promote security-oriented considerations and the need for autonomous military capabilities represent no more than a mask for industrial policy interests. Moreover, it would suggest that American security considerations trump explicit industrial policy considerations in the field of satellite navigation, while its approach toward wireless Internet is the result of a free-market policy tradition. It would also suggest that the US policy for satellite navigation is based on the fact that the United States assumes the major burden of security throughout the world, whereas the European Union and Japan can spend more resources on coordinated industrial policies.

This chapter contends that collective support for high-technology development depends largely on variation in relative economic and industrial competitiveness and that it better explains behaviour and strategies for satellite navigation and wireless Internet in the European Union and the United States (Gourevitch, 1986: 56; Milner, 1988; Grossman and Helpman, 1994: 835). The relative international positions of EU and US (and Japanese) economies and high-technology capabilities are different today compared to those of the 1980s and 1990s and have been strengthened in several areas, followed by EU and US industrial support that in many instances has become more global in orientation. The US approach to wireless Internet, influenced by a relatively weaker competitive position in industrial terms, has been aimed at creating a level playing field and objecting to EU industrial policy. It eventually supported a free-market orientation, but only after aggressive lobbying on the part of a number of industrial coalitions against the interests that promoted American CDMA (code division multiple access) technology. Its approach to satellite navigation has been aimed at both supporting national security priorities and, through explicit industrial policy considerations, GPS as the dominant global standard.

While traditional industrial policy traditions still bear a role on behaviour and strategies, the promotion of large-scale technology infrastructures in Europe and the United States cannot be primarily understood along the traditional distinctions of free trade versus protection, or of an Anglo-Saxon versus a European model of political economy (Milner and Yoffie, 1989). The relative international competitiveness of economies, industries and firms, which shapes behaviour and strategies for high technology, play a more important role than traditional industrial policy traditions. In order to stimulate productivity, job creation, tax revenues and an information society, the EU and US industrial strategies for satellite navigation and wireless Internet have been aimed at promoting worldwide technology infrastructures and at gaining advantage through alliances with other centres for support for their industrial policy ambitions.

The two developments examined in this chapter provide interesting illustrations of government-business strategies within the transatlantic relationship. Technological progress implies that societies become increasingly dependent on large-scale infrastructures for their functioning (such as transport, telecommunications, information technology and energy). The need for efficient technology infrastructures to support commerce, communication, mobility, and navigation – and the need to protect such public goods from unintentional and intentional interference – is clear to decision-makers in the economic, political and military sectors. As markets and technologies evolve, the character of state support demanded by industry also changes, which in turn triggers a need to explore a more nuanced form of industry support that corresponds to the realities of global competition (Lembke, 2002c).

Industrial and corporate strategies to control the dominant architectural standards in new cutting-edge technologies – within a context of a gradual move toward decentralized industrial structures, cross-national networks and alliances, and flexible regulatory policies – illustrate a new mode of competition and governance in relatively more global and liberalized industries, sometimes referred to as Wintelism (Borrus and Zysman, 1997; Hart and Kim 2002a, 2002b). Changes in industrial strategies and government approaches may result in various formal and informal public–private constellations at the same time as further integration of the transatlantic economy may reduce the feasibility of certain policy options open to governments (Egan, 2001; Smith, 2001; Hocking and McGuire, 2002). The relationships between equipment manufacturers, operators, software and content providers, and other industrial players, are also changing to new value chains and business structures in both the terrestrial wireless and the satellite navigation sectors.

Governments clearly have a potentially important role to play in the development of high-technology infrastructures. From the perspective guiding this analysis, what may be called strategic liberalism, public actors try to use a variety of tools to tweak the rules of the world economy and structure global competition in ways that enhance job creation and overall competitiveness in cutting-edge high-technology sectors. According to this perspective, the public sector should – in a prescriptive sense – influence the business environment by creating rules and procedures to foster healthy market competition, innovation capacity, the availability of competitively priced products and services, and productivity (competitiveness). In order to maximize general welfare (generate wealth, increase user choice and meet security priorities), political institutions may seek to elicit the support of those actors and sectors on whom they rely for political support, for example by giving a positive boost to leading industrial actors with a strong record at home in competition with foreign industry that could siphon off their market share. They are likely to attempt to strengthen their institutional self-interests, regulatory powers and administrative capabilities, and to carry out policy as cost-effectively as possible, as a means to increase the ability to have influence and to promote general welfare.

The major goal of a regional hegemon that also has a strong position in foreign markets is to maintain its dominant position and to prevent rival coalitions from challenging its leadership at home, and to ensure that foreign markets remain open in order to allow it to compete on a level playing field in those markets. It is not common that a coalition of actors behind a certain technology gains a globally dominant position and is successful in maintaining global superiority over decades in a high-technology sector of vital economic and industrial importance. However, the US GPS coalition has been able to enjoy such a position. Satellite navigation systems in other regions depend on the GPS infrastructure and the United States should be expected to defend its global superiority. In addition, we should expect the European Union to protect its unchallenged dominance at home and leading position worldwide in wireless communications and to mount a challenge to the United States in satellite navigation in order to stimulate competition at international level and maximize welfare and independence at home.

It is plausible to argue that the EU strategy amounts to a sincere effort to strengthen Europe's strategic independence and political control over a critical infrastructure as a response to the need to reduce the transatlantic military gap and to American reluctance to share control over its own satellite navigation system. The promotion of an operationally independent European capability in satellite navigation could provide an instrument for strengthening the European Union as an international security actor (Ginsberg, 2003). While US policy for satellite navigation represents an accidental spin-off from security-oriented policy, it has gradually evolved toward a more explicit industrial policy in light of mounting international competition and lucrative future world markets. The EU policy for wireless Internet and the US policy for satellite navigation have been to promote the acceptance and use of W–CDMA and GPS as the dominant world standards, respectively. The relative industrial-economic positions of Europe and the United States and the associated policy realities of global competition must be included in the analysis in order to better understand variation in industrial strategies for high-technology industries.

Satellite navigation and transatlantic relations

Policy-makers and industrialists in Europe and the United States view GNSS as strategic information and communications infrastructures. The European satellite navigation and positioning programme, Galileo, is the first pan-European public-private partnership and the first project conducted jointly by the EU and the European Space Agency (ESA). Galileo, a civilian programme under civilian control, will strengthen European sovereignty in safety-critical applications and reduce the dependence on third parties for telematics and transport infrastructure control and management (European Commission, 2001b and 2002a). It will deliver numerous mass-market services (personal communication, navigation and localization; vehicle systems etc.), professional services (oil and gas exploration, mining, timing, fleet management, surveillance, environment, land and precision survey, construction, space, etc.), and safety-of-life services (aviation, rail, maritime, emergency, surveillance, etc.). The European Union and the US administration are engaged in transatlantic discussions on how to ensure the implementation of interoperability between Galileo and GPS and to reap the benefits of their combined use in order to allow operators to use both systems with a single receiver. The European Commission stresses that Galileo and GPS will be complementary but separate infrastructure systems and that together they will increase the total size of the global satellite navigation and positioning market (Figure 5.1).

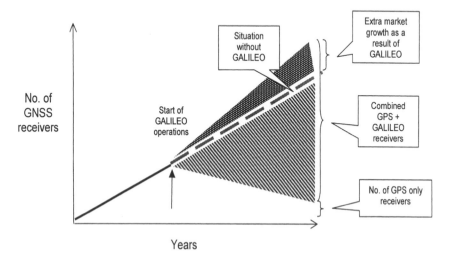

Figure 5.1   Market growth opportunity for Galileo
Source: European Commission, 2002b.

Funding and objectives: the policy debate
In mid-March 2002, the European heads of state and governments reaffirmed the strategic importance of the Galileo project and gave it unanimous backing at the European Council meeting in Barcelona. In late March, the EU Transport Council voted to support and release financing for the development phase of Galileo (Euro 450 million from the EU Trans-European Network budget) in addition to the complementary funding agreed by European ministers for research and space affairs at the ESA Council Meeting in Edinburgh in November 2001. The transport ministers subsequently adopted regulations for establishing the Joint Undertaking, which will undertake the management of the Galileo programme in cooperation with the ESA, and tasked the European Commission to set it up without delay (Council 2002). The first satellites were expected to be launched in 2005 and the system to be fully operational in 2008 but it is likely they will be delayed.

The EU agreement on Galileo in spring 2002 followed debates in and among national governments within Europe and between Europe and the US administration.[2] Some government departments in Germany, the Nether-lands and the UK (and also in Austria, Denmark and Sweden), particularly the Treasury departments (and others such as the UK Department of Transport, Local Government and the Regions), wanted public investments to be kept to a minimum and assurances that Galileo would be commercially driven, with the private sector bearing its share of the development costs at an early stage. They envisaged that private-sector investments would amount to around two-thirds of the programme cost during the deployment phase (2006–7), with major revenue streams expected to come from commercial and professional services and royalties on chip sales. In addition, some ministries of defence in the European NATO-member countries, not least the UK Ministry of Defence, did not want to upset the special relationship with the Pentagon and the American intelligence community.

European ministers of research, industry and space affairs were more enthusiastic toward the Galileo programme and eventually obtained support from the heads of government even in reluctant governments. In late February 2002, the German minister for transport announced that the German government would approve the allocation of €155 million to the funding of trans-European networks, which resulted in a majority block being formed and eventually unanimous approval of funding for Galileo's development phase (2002–5). However, ESA ministers had problems getting their act together. They had oversubscribed the ESA GalileoSat programme to the amount of €730 million, about 30 per cent beyond the required €550 million, and a disagreement emerged about the distribution of the work activities that would be allocated to industrial players in each country. Ordinarily, part of the bargaining game in such a large R&D project is to threaten to withdraw or reduce contributions unless the return of invested money and programme-development costs meet expectations. Such 'negative' distributive bargaining was not, however, an issue with Galileo, because of its strategic importance and potential economic-industrial benefits. The German government argued that the ESA coordinated procedure for mandatory space programmes would contribute to European GDP, benefiting the large German economy in a context where there was already a significant willingness in funding the Galileo programme. The country that invests most funds also strengthens its role in terms of contract distribution and industrial leadership. Other countries, in particular Italy, but also the UK, France and Spain, did not agree. Germany resisted cuts in its proportion of the budget and a proposal according to which 70 per cent of the ESA financing would be allocated to Germany, France, Italy and Britain, to be divided into four equal parts or 17.5 per cent each (*Space News* 2002).

The political-distributional bargaining on the repartition of financing (and contracts) between ESA Member States – which is complicated by a policy of geographic 'just return' and the fact that the total membership of the EU and ESA amounted to 18 countries – continued throughout 2002 and into 2003.

The ESA and the European Union were not able to sign the necessary consti-
tuting acts for establishing the Galileo Joint Undertaking, which is intended
to run the development phase (2002–5) and to ensure the unity of the administration and financial control of the Galileo programme. It will supervise the
development of the space and ground segments to be carried out by the ESA,
foster the development of applications and services, gather the necessary public and private funding, ensure an optimum integration between Galileo and
the first-generation European satellite navigation project (EGNOS), and
prepare for the management of the deployment and operational phases (to be
managed by a private-sector company). While the launch of the Galileo satellite navigation system is listed as one of the main priorities for supporting the
European information society (European Commission, 2002h), the strategic
importance of the Galileo programme also led to controversies regarding
where the Joint Undertaking should be located. The Italian government
wanted it to be located in the Tiburtina Valley in the greater Rome area where
some major satellite players are headquartered. The European Commission
and the ESA stressed that the delay in launching the development of Galileo
represented a serious setback. Industrial teams throughout Europe were wait-
ing for the decision and Galileo needed to be operational by 2008 in order to
reap benefits launching high-capability services years before the modernization of the American GPS ground and space infrastructure, which faced possible delays due to the changeover in presidential administrations and
competition for public funding from other defence programmes.

  In September 2002, the European Commission published a report on the
status and progress of the Galileo programme. The EU Transport Council
adopted its conclusions in early December and reiterated the need for a
transatlantic agreement in order to achieve interoperability between Galileo
and GPS at user level and compatibility at system level. Moreover, it asked
the Commission to continue negotiations with the Russian Federation to
strengthen collaboration and ensure interoperability between Galileo and
Glonass, invited the Commission to prepare a proposal for negotiations with
the People's Republic of China, and supported collaboration with other third
countries (European Commission, 2002g). The Commission also signaled its
intention to present a proposal to establish an operational Galileo Security
Authority to further institutionalize the work on security considerations
(such as encryption policy and technology) and negotiations with third countries (for example, frequency-sharing arrangements). In late 2002, the European Union adopted the financial regulation of the Joint Undertaking, and
the rules of procedure of the Galileo Joint Undertaking Supervisory Board
(composed of representatives of the EU Member States), which will supervise the Joint Undertaking together with the ESA Programme Board. It also
authorized the provisional administrative steps to prepare the operation of
the Joint Undertaking and the concession contract (the contents and scope of
which were to be prepared in parallel with the concession competition

among candidate concession holders – drawn from system and operations suppliers, banks and equity shareholders), which at the time of writing had a deadline for submitting final bids set for September 2004 and a decision on a winner before the end of 2004.

Key to the future: the perspective of industry
Galileo is the spearhead project for the evolving European strategy for the space sector and a technology-based economy. It is expected to be of significant importance for the European aeronautics and space industries and is expected to have positive implications for the wireless communications, information technology and electronics sectors (European Commission, 1999a, 2000, 2001c). The European space industry, headed by Galileo Industries (Astrium, Alenia Spazio and Alcatel Space), which hoped to become the Galileo prime contractor and which won the first development contract in July 2002, has been the strongest proponent of the Galileo project. Politically, the Galileo Industries depicted the project as a significant moment in the history of the European Union. Before the EU decision in March 2002, industrial leaders representing the major companies and trade organizations (including the European aerospace and defence company, EADS) reprised the vital importance of the Galileo infrastructure programme for the development of key high-technology markets, the creation of more than 100,000 jobs, the promotion of European know-how and products around the world, and European industrial progress in strategic future markets related to mobility in the information society (Blank 2002; *Galileo's World*, 2002). The European aerospace industry, along with the European Commission and other strong promoters of Galileo, stressed that a decision was urgently required and supported the perception among many policymakers in Europe that the United States intended to protect its economic and commercial interests.

European industry forwarded concerns to the EU and national governments that US companies would most likely be given privileged access to technical specifications and planned modifications, thus putting European firms at a competitive disadvantage. The US administration tried to dissuade foreign governments and industries from investing in their own systems to retain its monopoly, protect past investments, and support the entrenched position of its domestic industry. In this context, industry argued that public support to develop a European satellite navigation capability was a strategic necessity and that without an active European participation in future GNSS markets the European space industry could be eliminated as a supplier of future international system(s). Participation in the world satellite navigation markets would permit European industry to develop technological capabilities and long-term commercial and industrial leverage. The strong global position of the US GPS industry, and the relatively limited expected impact of retaliatory measures by other countries on European private-sector actors (due to their relatively weak presence in overseas markets) if the European Union actively supported Galileo, offered European industry an opportunity to ask for substantial public support from the European Union institutions. The European space industry further facilitated a momentum behind Galileo in that the major companies were able to organize themselves at the industrial and political level. In addition to the Galileo Industries consortium, European industry is represented in the political decision-making process through the Organization of European GNSS industry, OREGIN (the focal point for the Galileo user segment), and Galileo Services (Galileo downstream technology, services and applications development).

Transatlantic bargaining? The US perspective
The US policy for GPS as a dual-use infrastructure is aimed at strengthening and maintaining national security, encouraging private-sector investment in and use of GPS technologies and services, promoting safety and efficiency in transportation and other sectors, fostering international cooperation in using GPS for peaceful purposes, and advancing scientific and technical capabilities. The US Department of State had the task, as of US GPS policy of 1996, to pursue cooperation with other nations to promote GPS as a world standard. In 1998, for example, the US government signed a joint statement on GPS cooperation with Japan, which was followed by cooperation initiated in 2002 between GPS and the Japanese regional constellation called Quasi-Zenith Satellite System (QZSS). It also conducted talks with Europe and the Russian Federation. The US policy for GPS is today jointly controlled by the Interagency GPS Executive Board at the Department of Commerce, with the objective of increasing the acceptance and use of GPS and promoting GPS as a world standard (Braibanti and Kim, 2002).

The US government had an incentive to maintain its dominance in satellite navigation for reasons of industrial and trade policy, as well as national security, and repeatedly aired concerns about some aspects of the EU's plans for Galileo. Initially, the GPS infrastructure was intended to become a so-called force-enhancer that would reinforce the combat effectiveness of US (and NATO) forces. The US Department of State stressed that the European Union should not develop controlled-access services, user fees and regulatory measures to generate revenue streams since that would hardly be compatible with open markets and the realization of a seamless global navigation satellite system (West 1999). In 1998 and 1999, it presented basic principles for cooperation and a draft transatlantic agreement to the European Commission demanding that Europe support market-driven competition and freedom of choice for end users, ensure that manufacturers would have equal access to technical specifications for receiver production, not impose any direct user fees for safety-critical services, not mandate the use of their systems, and that any disputes should be settled through existing trade agreements and organizations (WTO). The US government stressed the need for protection of national security interests and informed the European Union that a transatlantic framework agreement needed to be in place before technical discussions.

In the autumn of 2000, the US government presented to the European Union, a new framework agreement which reiterated the need for non-discrimination and free trade and demanded that no overlay of military GPS band would be allowed and that consultations would be required before introducing any new standard or regulation for satellite navigation. The proposed agreement was followed by a counterproposal in May 2001 from the European Commission. Hawks in the US Department of Defense became increasingly active and framed the issue as a central concern for NATO and US national security. In early December 2001, shortly before EU meetings on Galileo, the US Deputy Secretary of Defense Paul Wolfowitz expressed concerns to the EU defence ministers about security ramifications for future NATO operations. Wolfowitz claimed that the Galileo signals could jeopardize the military GPS signals and that Galileo could be used for military purposes. The military-only signal, defined within the NAVWAR project and the future GPS III programme, allowing the Department of Defense to maintain an edge in precision weapons targeting not available to other parties. Wolfowitz indicated that civilian authorities in Europe should not manage the Galileo project, and that European NATO countries and defence ministers must exert pressure on their governments in Europe with the objective of allowing military authorities to discuss strategic issues.

The Clinton Administration and particularly the Bush Administration lobbied the EU institutions and national ministries, saying that logic and economics suggested that there was no real need for a second satellite navigation and positioning system: 'The United States Government sees no compelling need for Galileo, because GPS is expected to meet the needs of users around the world for the foreseeable future' (US Department of State, 2002a and 2002b). In addition, the money that had to be invested in the Galileo project could be spent on developing other badly needed European capabilities. 'Given the serious US–European military capabilities gap and limited European resources to close it, many have believed that Europe would be better served by spending the large resources involved on Galileo (at least $3 billion) for other war-fighting purposes, such as intelligence satellites' (Bialos 2002).

When these lobbying efforts failed to sway an increasingly determined and unitary EU actor, the US government decided to raise the debate within NATO and play on the Atlanticist orientation of several EU government departments. The willingness of many supporters of Galileo to consider autonomous military capabilities contributed to tensions with the Bush Administration, and particularly its more conservative camps, about the emergence of high-capability strategic assets potentially outside the immediate control of NATO. American NATO officials, the Department of Defense and the Department of State continued expressing their view that their European allies should not develop a system that would interfere with the civil and military GPS signals.

The US government did not want a European-controlled system that would challenge its global commercial and military monopoly and preferred European use of GPS. It therefore stressed that the European Union must accept its proposal for a transatlantic agreement. For some this was an untenable position after the European Union secured funding for Galileo in the spring of 2002. 'The reality, however, is that this "cart before the horse" approach, appropriate at the time, is now counterproductive. We now need to deeply engage with Europe to develop ways to work together, help shape what Europe creates and ultimately create a single system for end users', said the former head of the Department of State delegation to transatlantic talks on GPS-Galileo (Bialos, 2002).

European efforts to reach an agreement on public funding in 2001 and 2002 prompted renewed efforts by the US government to bring pressure to bear on European governments. Would the European Union respond in an acceptable manner to the basic principles of cooperation outlined by the US government? Would Europe introduce regulations and standards that mandated the use of Galileo? Would Galileo take on a strategic military role? How would Europe protect sensitive encryption technology and prevent hostile misuse of Galileo?

Satellite navigation and positioning is central to US and NATO military operations and weapons systems (command, control and consultation services, including navigation and precision strike). Its importance will become increasingly indispensable for missions and tasks in support of NATO operations. Transatlantic discussions need to resolve fundamental issues such as how to meet potential threats to the physical infrastructure and operations of Galileo and GPS and how to restrict uncontrolled and hostile proliferation of Galileo and GPS signal transmission and associated data (Lembke 2002b). The European Commission had considered overlaying the encrypted Galileo Public Regulated Service (PRS) directly on top of the GPS M-Code (the encrypted future military GPS capability). The Galileo PRS – a service that is encrypted and resistant to jamming and interference, which will be under the control of national security authorities of EU and ESA Member States – is intended for applications devoted to civil protection, national security and law enforcement that demand a high level of continuity of service. American officials voiced concerns about the co-sharing of frequencies between Galileo and the military GPS M-Code, which in their view constituted a strategic problem in that it is not 'dual-service compatible' and therefore unacceptable. 'The stakes are high, and I am not talking about dollars or euros. I am talking about our nation's security and the well being of the men and women in uniform we send in harm's way. Therefore, the sooner we can wrestle these technical issues to the ground, the better', said Robert G. Bell, NATO assistant secretary general for defence support (Bell, 2002). Transatlantic technical discussions on the interoperability and compatibility of European and American satellite navigation systems could thus result in a transatlantic regime agreement: 'Simply put, we need to respect Europe's decision – based on its own calculus of interests – to develop Galileo and recognize and deal with the new reality of European participation in global navigation. Galileo's development should usher in a new period of sober assessment of how the US and its trans-Atlantic partners can work together to create a win-win for consumers and our mutual security' (Bialos, 2002).

In 2003, the US objectives for transatlantic cooperation consisted of four overall goals: protecting national security interests (no interference with Department of Defense and NATO denial capabilities, equal access to the specifications and encryption algorithms for controlled-access services as well as to encryption regimes, no overlay of planned military signals, no discussions outside of NATO regarding any military use of Galileo); protecting investments in GPS infrastructure and the interests of its users (no degradation of service, freedom of choice for users, free-market competition, interoperability and backward compatibility); ensuring a commercial level playing in the global marketplace (including national treatment and most-favoured nation-like obligations in the transatlantic marketplace); and maximizing the benefits of combined GPS-Galileo services. In the field of regulations and standards, the US government is pushing for the need to ensure that any new standard must be technology-neutral and that agreements must be binding for the whole of Europe and its various organizations in the area of satellite navigation. Even though there was no real transatlantic progress on the issue of M-code overlay in the field of security during 2002, technical working groups were established to discuss compatibility and interoperability in non-military areas.

International resolutions and procedures adopted throughout 2003 have rendered the European Union an international player on an equal footing with the United States in negotiations on interoperability and frequency sharing, and have encouraged transatlantic negotiations with the objective of implementing a globally integrated satellite navigation infrastructure. In the spring of 2004, the European Union and the United States reached an agreement on technical issues and supported, for example, the idea of coexistence and interoperability (Galileo, and the next-generation GPS infrastructure, GPS 3), and that of non-discrimination in goods and services. In addition, they are fostering international partnerships on hardware development and service provision, adopting a seemingly more open approach toward the idea of internationalizing bids and programmes, and supporting deeper transatlantic industrial cooperation. European and American companies that have an interest in the development of both Galileo and GPS (such as Alcatel Space, Alenia Spazio, Thales, Boeing, and Lockheed Martin) have lobbied public actors on both sides of the Atlantic Ocean in support of greater transatlantic cooperation. Moreover, the European Union, for example, continues to reach bilateral agreements – such as with Canada, Australia, the

People's Republic of China, and the State of Israel – to generate international industrial, technological and financial cooperation.

Furthermore, the governance regime of the Galileo programme has been undergoing important changes. The procedure to select the concession holder of the Galileo satellite navigation system for the deployment and operational phase – the operative company (private consortium) that will manage these phases – was initiated in the autumn of 2003. The concession holder will be embedded in the legal and institutional framework for the overall management of Galileo and will be overseen by an EU public body (the Supervisory Authority) that will act as a licensing authority, a technological observatory, a custodian of radio frequencies, and a manager of EU spending allocated to the programme, which will remain administered and controlled by the civilian sector. (National defence ministries and military space investment have played a marginal role.)

The national economy and national security depend increasingly on satellite navigation for critical civilian infrastructures, applications and services as well as for military command-and-control capabilities (the creation of intelligence platforms that integrate space-based, air, land and sea capabilities). While the rationale for transatlantic and international cooperation has become stronger, the competitive race for de facto world standards between corporations (and between governments for industrial policy and security reasons) – and the associated revenues from governmental and commercial services and intellectual property – will continue to play a pivotal role. The EU and the US signed a long-awaited cooperation accord for satellite navigation at the US–EU Summit in Ireland in late June 2004, which called for full interoperability of civilian signals, and non-interference of the encrypted signals, between the EU and the US systems, and which supported equitable access to each other's markets, while working groups will continue to discuss a number of transatlantic trade and security issues.

Launching Galileo: a more assertive Europe
Galileo's proponents (the European Commission, the European heads of state and governments, the ESA, and European aeronautics, space and defence electronics companies) envisage Galileo as crucial for autonomy of Europe in defence matters in an era where vital economic, social and strategic functions increasingly rely on satellite navigation. The accuracy of GPS in precision bombing and satellite imagery – and the lack of access to and control over such capabilities – helped European governments and the European Commission to understand that Galileo is an important infrastructure for the EU Common Foreign and Security Policy. As the European Commission noted, 'If the EU finds it necessary to undertake a security mission that the United States does not consider to be in its interests, the European Union will be impotent unless it has the satellite navigation technology that is now indispensable. Although designed for civilian applications,

Galileo will also give the European Union a military capability' (European Commission, 2002b).

The European political and industrial community that rallied behind Galileo argued that Europe must exert a common political will in matters of high technology to interact with the Unites States on a more equal basis. If the US government would have to rely on a global satellite navigation system operated by allies in Europe, it would likewise develop a separate system. Some also questioned why the US government should have a monopoly over the control of weapons systems – and its GPS industry over commercial services and applications – based on satellite navigation and positioning, thus reinforcing the pre-eminence of American world power and the uneven use of global resources, including space-based communications capabilities in gathering economic intelligence through technical agencies. Galileo, the European Commission argued, was an important capability to liberate the continent from dependence on the American monopoly over satellite navigation in global markets and on its unilateral control of a global utility. The US government's explicit GPS strategy has been aimed at asserting market leadership and hegemonic control. The European Commission and many European governments stress that it is the choice of Europe to decide what constitutes a 'compelling need' and that there is a real need for independent control over satellite navigation capabilities.

The underlying industrial logic behind supporting Galileo is that demands on the European transport infrastructure will double by 2020, that Europe cannot build infrastructure fast enough to keep pace, and that the existing infrastructure must therefore be used more efficiently. According to the European Commission, a system under European control would generate more efficiency and benefits to European sovereignty and general economic progress (European Commission, 2002c). Accordingly, Europe should provide its own civil system since it cannot be dependent upon a third party and since there is also much to gain from two interoperable but separate GNSS infrastructures (new technology, global competition, enhanced performance and availability, additional value-added services). Europe also understands the US strategic objective to protect its monopoly in global satellite navigation markets, which major American aerospace companies expect to become increasingly lucrative. This potential market and export sales for commercial and military equipment incorporating satellite navigation and positioning have been central motives for both American and European public- and private-sector actors.

Wireless technology in the transatlantic marketplace

Europe in the lead
At the end of the 1990s, Europe enjoyed world leadership in digital wireless cellular communications, while a large portion of the infrastructure in the US

was based on analog technology (although the deployment of digital infrastructure experienced substantial growth). The US wireless industry and the
Council of Economic Advisors (CEA) viewed the third generation of wireless
(3G) as a driving force for American economic growth and technological
prowess. The US wireless carriers employed 150,000 people and generated
US$44 billion in annual revenue at the end of the 1990s (CEA, 2000). Global
economic stagnation, overcapacity, low levels of demand and business
investment, high costs of 3G licences, indebtedness and deteriorating credit
ratings have hampered growth in the telecommunications sector, but the
potential of advanced wireless services is significant (Friis, 2002). Table 5.1
presents an estimation of wireless penetration and subscribers by region
1997–2004.

Table 5.1   Estimated wireless penetration and subscribers by region

Penetration (%)	1997	1999	2001	2002	2003	2004
North America	20.1	30.7	46.9	55.5	63.9	72.1
Western Europe	14.1	38.4	69.5	76.8	81.0	83.1
South East Asia	2.4	5.4	9.1	10.8	12.4	14.0
Rest of World	1.1	2.8	6.6	9.1	12.0	15.2
Total	3.5	7.7	13.7	16.4	19.0	21.5

Subscribers (millions)	1997	1999	2001	2002	2003	2004
North America	59.9	93.4	145.8	174.3	202.7	228.6
Western Europe	54.6	149.2	270.9	300.0	317.1	326.1
South East Asia	66.4	152.9	265.1	318.8	370.6	425.4
Rest of World	27.0	71.3	171.1	239.5	323.3	410.6
Total	207.9	466.8	852.9	1032.6	1213.7	1390.8

Source: Wireless Strategy Analytics (2001).

A coordinated pan-European approach toward digital wireless technology
and markets has been essential for securing critical mass, economies of scale
in terminal and infrastructure equipment, network economies in services,
and world leadership in global markets (European Commission, 1999b and
1999c; Council, 1999). Network externalities and compatibility standards
have become increasingly important for policy-making (Besen and Johnson,
1986; Abbott and Snidal, 2001; Werle, 2001; Lembke, 2002c). European
policy-makers and industrialists realized that it would take time to introduce
the new era of wireless multimedia. They decided to pursue a strategy that
combined support for further market integration in Europe and for alliance
building with standards and industrial actors in Asia, North America and
elsewhere. Ericsson and Nokia stressed the importance of the Asian market

and gained the support of Japanese industry (NTT DoCoMo, NEC, Fujitsu, Matsushita/Panasonic and Mitsubishi Electric) and wireless operators in the broader Asia-Pacific region. This approach, which aligned Europe with developments and strategies in the Asia-Pacific region, was supported because of the prospect of lucrative Asian markets. The benefits of a larger global market were greater for internationally oriented firms with strong presence in overseas markets than the risks and costs of future import competition and declining market shares at home (Lembke, 2002a).

Playing catch-up: the standardization initiative of US industry
Industrialists, legislators and administration officials in the US launched a campaign against European practices in the field of wireless standardization and regulation after the decision on the basic concept of the future Europe radio interface technology (wideband code division multiple access, W-CDMA) in early 1998. On the industrial side, Qualcomm headed the lobbying (with support from Lucent Technologies and Northern Telecom, Nortel), which had substantial investments in its own (non-wideband) CDMA2000 system that they wanted to protect. The development of wireless technology was subjected to an international intellectual property rights (IPR) blocking situation that was stalling international standards activities, primarily between Qualcomm and Ericsson – the world's biggest producer of mobile networks (mobile switching, base station controllers and other equipment for wireless networks). IPR has played a significant role in the development of the next-generation wireless technology infrastructure by structuring international and intra-industry competition and cooperation. Through royalty-bearing and reciprocal licence agreements, leading manufacturers leverage their preferred technology under their patent portfolios, which in turn allow suppliers in other regions of the world to develop, manufacture and sell infrastructure and subscriber equipment. Manufacturers can thereby increase the global footprint of the technology and market size as well as transform the international division of labour.

The European approach was guided by the quest for deeper European integration and by the 'collaborative competition model' which supported harmonization, open systems and *ex ante* or 'anticipatory' standardization resulting in publicly available standards, whereas the US 'market determination model' favoured divergence, proprietary systems and *a posteriori* standardization. The EU institutions, the European Telecommunications Standards Institute (ETSI), and the European wireless industry were concerned about licensing and IPR strategies that threatened to turn standardization and technical issues into battlegrounds for competing commercial interests. They were likewise concerned about what they perceived as a 'misinformation campaign' on Capitol Hill that could plunge the US and the EU into a transatlantic dispute. (The US government was likewise concerned about what it perceived as misinformation and myths about the GPS navigation infrastructure.)

In late 1997, the ETSI Director-General asked Qualcomm whether it claimed any IPR essential to the radio access technology developed through the ETSI by European, Asian and North American companies. Would Qualcomm be prepared to grant licences for the patent rights if it claimed to own essential IPR in accordance with the terms and conditions set out in ETSI IPR policy? Qualcomm responded that it owned IPR that were essential to the proposed radio technology, including the leading proposals supported by European wireless manufacturers and the allies they had gathered in the Asian and North American manufacturing industry (Qualcomm, 1998). The company stated that if W-CDMA were to remain as it stood, it would not agree to grant licences under its essential intellectual property according to ETSI IPR policy. It lobbied intensively on Capitol Hill, calling for convergence between its own proposal, CDMA 2000, and the ETSI proposed specification for W-CDMA. 'Qualcomm wished to force through a single standard that was not linked to GSM . . . because GSM was already well positioned in the market. In the end, this is the hard battle of global competitiveness and about being first to the marketplace.'[3]

Championing CDMA

The transatlantic disagreement deepened when the draft of the common EU regulatory position on 3G wireless communications emerged in Europe. At a hearing on 'Trade Relations with Europe and the New Transatlantic Economic Partnership' at the US House Subcommittee on Trade/the Committee on Ways and Means in July 1998, Qualcomm presented criticism of ETSI and European standardization. It claimed that the ETSI standardization and EU policy (1) created an unnecessary barrier to trade in violation of the WTO Technical barriers of Trade (TBT), (2) favoured a wireless technology manufactured by large European concerns, and (3) supported an exclusionary industrial policy by denying GSM's competitors entry into the European market. Therefore, Qualcomm argued, it was forced to fall back on its IPR to protect its current customers and its position in the next generation of wireless technology.

Qualcomm used its political contacts on Capitol Hill to push for its own preferred technology. Members of Congress sent letters to United States Trade Representative (USTR) Charlene Barshefsky accusing the European Union of pursuing an industrial policy that could leave American firms competitively disadvantaged in Europe and have broader ramifications for the transatlantic trading relationship (Matsui, 1998). Senator Ernest F. Hollings charged that European practices were protectionist and that competing technologies developed in the United States could be locked out of the European market, which resulted in an 'asymmetrical transatlantic relationship'. Hollings argued that since the American market remained open to technologies developed in Europe, the United States 'should ensure that there is a reciprocal trading relationship that would enable US companies to profit in Europe' (Hollings,

1998). Some Members of Congress went as far as suggesting to the USTR that the European approach to 3G wireless should be included in the National Trade Estimate Report as a Super 301 priority; that is, it should be judged unduly restrictive to trade and thus punishable by unilateral trade retaliation. After pressure from Congress and the American CDMA industry, the USTR responded that it was reviewing the consistency of the EU's measures with its WTO obligations and that it considered wireless standards as an issue of vital importance for US telecommunications manufacturers and service providers. As Barshefsky told Congress, 'Let me assure you that this Administration stands by previous assurances that the United States will use the WTO to open foreign markets to US telecommunications equipment and services' (Barshefsky, 1998).

In letters to the US Congress, the ETSI Director-General Karl Heinz Rosenbrock stressed that its standardization process was driven by the private sector (80 per cent of the funding) and was marked by openness, balance of interests, an appeals process and consensus, and, contrary to the claims of US industry, did not result in the creation of unnecessary barriers to trade between the United States and Europe (ETSI, 1998a and 1998b). The European leadership in wireless communications was the result of a balance of interests leading to collective benefits for market actors through collaborative competition: 'Just as the US government recognizes the importance to encourage long-term growth for enterprises and promote efficiency and economic competition through harmonization of standards, so does Europe' (ETSI, 1998a).

In December 1998, the Clinton Administration sent a letter to Martin Bangemann, EU Commissioner for telecommunications and industrial policy, signed by US Secretary of Commerce William N. Daley, USTR Ambassador Charlene Barshefsky, FCC Chairman William Kennard, and US Secretary of State Madeleine Albright. They continued voicing concerns throughout 1999 about the European regulatory process for 3G wireless, stressing that the United States wanted the procedures of any EU Member State to support neutral licensing in terms of technology, unlimited market access, and non-discriminatory treatment of American suppliers of wireless telecommunications services and equipment (USTR 1999a and 1999b). Bangemann replied to the US complaints, stressing that industry should drive the wireless standardization, innovation and commercialization process (European Commission, 1999c). He reminded the US government of its regulatory intervention in the development of digital television by adopting an exclusive standard in 1996 that had the same objective of interoperability. In addition, the US government and standards bodies had opted for a single radio standard for the first generation of (analog) wireless communications. The European Commission pointed out that the US had not respected the 1992 recommendation by the International Telecommunications Union (ITU) identifying spectrum for 3G wireless communications. It claimed that

US policy had led to different 3G system proposals and to a fragmentation of spectrum allocation at global level, which moreover potentially blocked new entrants from entering the US marketplace.

A central objective of the EU policy for wireless communications was to support interoperability and pan-European roaming as well as standardization based on an open multinational consensus-based approach in order to facilitate economies of scale in terminal equipment and network economies in services, throughout the EU territory and beyond, in accordance with market demand. The European Commission stated that it had no intention to impose backward compatibility between wireless systems, nor convergence of future wireless standards toward a single converged standard at European or global level. Under the EU legislative framework, standardization was entrusted to formally recognized organizations in a process that involved companies also from North America, Japan and other parts of the world. The European Commission supported the 'new' European standardization model, which supported competition on price and services and allowed competition between technologies as long as they constituted and were compatible with coherent standards (Lembke, 2001).

Diversity within US domestic industrial interests
Legislators in the US Congress continued lobbying the Clinton administration about the EU's approach to standards for digital wireless technology, claiming that the EU's adoption of an 'exclusive, mandatory standard for digital wireless technology' would exclude American technology from European markets and thus discriminate against American firms, workers and consumers (Levin, 1999; Conrad, Baucus and Robb, 1999; see also FCC, 1999). Senator Tom Daschle urged the USTR 'to consider the full range of negotiating tools in order to send the necessary message to the European Union that the United States will not tolerate any protectionist effort to shut out American digital wireless technology from competition in European markets' (Daschle, 1999).

While Qualcomm received substantial Administration and Congressional support in opposing the EU's regulatory regime, a number of complaints were made to the US government regarding the political activity of the CDMA industry on Capitol Hill. The Computer and Communications Industry Association (CCIA), for example, complained to Vonya McCann (US Coordinator and Deputy Assistant Secretary of International Communications and Information Policy at the US Department of State) about 'the apparent efforts by some manufacturers of wireless equipment to use the US Government to advance their firms' parochial interests in the international standards-setting process at the expense of others' (CCIA, 1998). The North American GSM Alliance LLC, the North American Interest Group of the GSM Association, and the GSM Alliance (a consortium of US and Canadian wireless carriers) urged lawmakers to stress the need for multiple standards and market competition at both domestic and global levels. In addition, the Universal Wireless Communications Consortium (UWCC), which promoted TDMA technology, called on the US administration to keep a hands-off approach with regard to the formal international standardization process and argued for a multiple global standards regime for 3G wireless communications (UWCC, 1998). It complained to the US Department of Commerce that the latter had favored CDMA technology in bilateral talks with China and elsewhere at the expense of other technologies to the point that it appeared as if it was the US government's technology of choice. 'The Administration's absence of any public focus on TDMA in regard to its China trade agenda is creating an unintended but potentially serious problem for UWCC members that employ over 70,000 employees and have over US$30 billion invested in TDMA' (UWCC, 1999).

Regional standard bodies from around the world were to submit proposals for 3G wireless standards to the ITU at the end of June 1998. The US Department of State led the process of selecting proposals in coordination with the FCC and the National Telecommunications and Information Administration of the Department of Commerce. Four proposals had been selected and would be circulated to industry representatives on the US National Committee for final review before being submitted to the ITU. Several US House representatives voiced their concerns to McCann at the Department of State and stressed that decreasing the number of proposed standards could stymie America's progress in the wireless telecommunications industry: 'Each of the American proposals has significant US industry support from both wireless carriers and equipment manufacturers. I know you can appreciate the years of cooperative industry work that led to the development of these four proposals, and I trust that the final US proposal will acknowledge this fact and refrain from favoring any one technology over another' (Hutchinson, 1998). In early 1999, the Chair of the US Subcommittee on Technology and Competitiveness, Susan Corralez-Diaz, sent a letter to President Clinton on behalf of the President's Export Council. She stressed the importance of aggressively promoting a multiple-standards regime in domestic and international organizations: 'It would be sharply counter to the interests of the US industry as a whole either to advance any particular US technology over another, or to fail to promote a multiple standards regime' (Corralez-Diaz, 1999). Conrad Burns, Chairman of the US Senate Subcommittee on Communications, and other members of Congress stated that there was no clear evidence of anti-competitive trade practices or market barriers in the European Union. They urged the Clinton Administration to promote an open, competitive global marketplace and timely provision of 3G wireless services in the United States and abroad and to resist delays in the consideration and approval of multiple wireless standards at home and abroad (Burns, 1999; Helms et al., 1999).

A compromise solution

In Europe, equipment manufacturers with interests in the Asian markets aired concerns to the European Commission about the US trade pressure on the Japanese governments and standards bodies, which threatened Europe's potential future leadership in lucrative Asian markets. Industry argued that if the Japanese government had to bend to the US pressures, this would have a number of serious and strategic implications. 'International standards for products, processes and networks are increasingly important to industry due to the quickening pace of technological innovation and the globalization of trade. Japan is key to capturing Asia, a market that by the year 2005 is expected to be larger than Europe and North America combined. Therefore the support of Japan for a future mobile communication standard is of critical importance'.[4]

The European manufacturers – notably Ericsson and Nokia – pointed out to the European Commission that it had to be prepared for a transatlantic trade war and that it should further strengthen the cooperation with the Japanese government. If the US succeeded in forcing harmonization ('a compromise standard') on Japan, these companies argued it would reduce the integrity and performance of the technology proposal in Europe, weakening the likelihood of gaining a stronghold in Asian markets developing a truly wireless multimedia infrastructure and society. Secondly, it would disrupt the close strategic cooperation between European and Japanese industry and standards bodies as well as impeding global economies of scale. Thirdly, a compromise solution would challenge the overall European objective to strengthen its information and communications technology industry. The balance of economic and political power would shift to the US, diminishing the chance of European technology maintaining or increasing its global position, and potentially threatening thousands of jobs in Europe.

The European Commission discussed different options to ward off the American pressure, including setting up a task force within the ITU – with support from Japan – to work toward interoperable standards and a global infrastructure. It reckoned that such a move would keep Japan and Europe in one camp and promote the development of a common global standard while avoiding isolation of the US or further polarizing the other regional parties involved. The discussions that took place on 3G wireless standardization and trade in the Transatlantic Business Dialogue (TABD) were critical in reducing transatlantic tensions, as were the technical and standards activities in the Third Generation Partnership Project (3GPP), which consisted of formally recognized standards bodies from Europe, Japan, China, Korea and the United States, supported by industry groups and around 500 companies.[5]

In addition, the international political and industrial pressure exercised by pure-play wireless operators (with a strong international position in GSM markets and with investments in multiple technology infrastructures) on equipment manufacturers through the Operators' Harmonization Group

(OHG) was of pivotal importance. It argued that IPR should not be used by any company or group of companies to delay the introduction of next-generation services, withhold the use of the technology from achieving a harmonized international standard, restrict the import or export of equipment to or from any country, increase the cost of equipment or services beyond customary levels, or stifle innovation and the free flow of ideas. The OHG concluded that continued public IPR disputes were damaging to the global wireless industry (OHG, 1999a and 1999b).

The work on technical specifications for 3G W-CDMA wireless hardware and software continues through the 3GPP with the freezing of sets of specifications. They add further functionality as a result of ongoing standardization work (for example, a steady trend away from circuit switching – voice and low-speed data – toward packet switching – voice and medium-speed data – and with the option of new internet protocol technology – voice and high-speed data). These specifications represent an evolution of the GSM infrastructure and only the radio access technology is radically new. In addition, operational networks have been set up on a trial basis and there is already a real commercial service (called FOMA) in Japan. In early 2003, NTT DoCoMo announced that it intended to subsidize 3G-handset development cost in order to reduce the burden of domestic manufacturers and to spur the market, and it is aggressively seeking to increase its role in American and European markets. In January 2003, commercial W-CDMA service was initiated in Italy. While not specifically tied to 3G networks, a lot of stress in the United States (as well as elsewhere) has been placed on location-based services; obtaining a precise location for a mobile is useful both for security reasons (enabling the police to track down miscreants) and for commercial services (targeted advertising, providing information on restaurants, cinemas, etc, in the physical vicinity of the user). Furthermore, the Chinese Ministry of Information Industry and a coalition of manufacturers, with support of Siemens, are moving ahead with a homegrown 3G wireless standard, TD-SCDMA, as a way to strengthen domestic industry, as a hedging strategy and as a potential bargaining tool with foreign industry.

The relative international competitiveness of European industry may weaken and rival technologies and their coalitions may gain advantages as a result of the EU policy and technology strategy for wireless Internet. It is far from certain, however, that European companies, and adopters of their technology worldwide, will see their command of the global marketplace dramatically reduced and its position as a regional hegemon at home significantly weakened, even though East Asian and American firms are likely to become stronger in European and international markets. In the autumn of 2002, the penetration of wireless communications in Europe based on the GSM standard amounted to 75 per cent of the population (European Commission, 2002f), and the GSM technology is gradually becoming stronger in North America. Supporters of wireless expect a growing demand for data traffic and revenues as 3G becomes a commercial reality. According to the UMTS Forum, global service revenues from 3G networks will represent a market opportunity of US$320 billion by 2010 (US$118 billion of which will be generated in the Asia Pacific region with markets with low wireless-penetration rates, such as China and India, representing the greatest growth opportunities) – even though the minority of users will still use 2G – and around US$1 trillion over the whole decade (UMTS Forum, 2002).

Regulatory strategy and support
The European Union institutions have continued analysing the central financial, technical and regulatory challenges concerning the deployment of 3G wireless infrastructure and services as a means to support the creation of a competitive knowledge-based economy for Europe (European Commission, 2001a, 2002d and 2002f). The EU policy for wireless Internet emphasizes the need to support open platforms and architectural and application programme interface standards, hardware and software interoperability and consumer access to new services and applications. The European policy for standards has been modified to allow for competition between technologies (Lembke, 2001). The ambition of the European Commission is to ensure a stable regulatory environment that supports a competitive market and user choice regarding various technology platforms, including 3G wireless communications until this market reaches cruising speed. 'The main task of the EU institutions is to prepare a suitable regulatory environment which allows for the necessary degree of European harmonization and ensures the regulatory certainty on which the future 3G players can build their business cases' (European Commission, 2001a). It has asked national governments and regulatory agencies – and equipment manufacturers, network operators and service providers – to consider reforms of spectrum assignment practices, licence conditions and methods and legal coverage requirements, and to consider establishing more flexible network-sharing conditions. As a response to the Barcelona European Council in March 2002 and the Seville European Council in June 2002 of European heads of state and government, the European Commission launched a public consultation process on remaining barriers to the full deployment 3G wireless infrastructure and achievement of widespread access to new services and applications. The so-called EU 'eEurope' Action Plan 2005, a follow-up document to eEurope Action Plan 2002 which was adopted by the European Commission in May 2002 and which will run from 2003 to 2005, intends to accelerate the deployment of 3G wireless infrastructures.

The industrial landscape is different in the United States, which has coloured the behaviour of the government and regulatory agencies. American manufacturers produce equipment for several second-generation terrestrial wireless standards, and network operators have invested in and defend different technology platforms. In the autumn of 2000, then President Clinton released a memorandum directing the FCC and Department of Commerce, which have shared responsibility and jurisdiction for the management of radio frequency spectrum, to lead a government-industry effort to ensure the timely deployment of 3G services and to complete assignments of licences for spectrum by the autumn of 2002. In the summer of 2002, shortly after an interagency Spectrum Policy Task Force was created to study spectrum policy, the Bush Administration reached a deal with the Department of Defense to make spectrum available for commercial services that the latter had controlled. In late 2002, the Task Force made its final recommendations on advanced wireless services, including 3G, as part of the government's ambitions to pave the ground for market competition among multiple 3G standards and to support the future competitiveness of US industry.

Conclusion

The American and European approaches to satellite navigation and third-generation wireless communications represent offensive political-economic approaches with the objective of gaining access to lucrative export markets, enhancing overall competitiveness in high-technology industries, promoting job creation, stimulating positive macro-economic externalities and user benefits, and strengthening policy capacities and global economic, political and strategic positions. It illustrates the role of governments in structuring the context of global competition in high-technology industries and, arguably, a possible trend toward a new form of critical industry support for high technology in the transatlantic marketplace. By extending the global footprint of its preferred technologies, industry seeks to maximize economies of scale in equipment and network economies in services. This chapter contends that the variation and similarities in behaviour and strategies across sectors and the Atlantic are largely the result of relative international competitiveness.

In the field of satellite navigation, the US significantly benefits from a position of unchallenged dominance in terms of job creation, scientific and technological progress, and market shares in civilian and defence markets for equipment and services. A European competitor risks the future benefits accruing from this monopoly and expected lucrative markets. The European Union has decided to counterbalance the position of the US GPS coalition and technology as a global hegemon and the institutional deadlock of GPS in European markets that are expected to increasingly rely on satellite navigation and positioning. Even though it could be the case that this major European investment will not be as successful in commercial and security terms as is hoped, the US GPS interests will likely see its global superiority increasingly challenged. Both the US government and the European Union teamed up with Japan, in the field of satellite navigation and wireless communications respectively, in order to strengthen the coalition behind the commercial and technology strategies of leading domestic industrial actors at home. It is difficult, however, to achieve and maintain a position as regional industrial hegemon at home and even harder to do so on a global scale in high-technology sectors of vital and growing importance.

The US policy for wireless communications eventually supported multiple standards as being conducive to domestic and global competition and innovation, thus echoing the European philosophy in the field of satellite navigation. The global orientation of the US and particularly the European approach in the wireless sector are largely the result of the pressure from those internationally oriented equipment manufacturers, and pure-play wireless operators who had invested in more than one wireless technology, which had commercial and research presence in overseas markets, and therefore were sensitive to the behaviour of foreign governments and industrial actors. The United States faced a more complicated situation because of investments in and competition between several wireless technologies. This situation is less the result of deep-rooted historical, structural and cultural systems of political economy and models of industrial policy than of relative international competitiveness and lobbying between different interests. If the situation had been the reverse, it is more plausible to expect that the US would have challenged a European satellite navigation system that enjoyed a global monopoly. The US would less likely have supported market competition between various wireless standards if it would jeopardize the position of a technology platform which enjoyed a commanding international leadership and a position as regional hegemon in the United States. This comparative analysis suggests that a more nuanced perspective on new forms of high-technology infrastructure support can generate valuable insights into the logic of the transatlantic marketplace.

Notes

1 The author is grateful for the financial support of the Swedish Institute of International Affairs.
2 The European airlines community voiced a number of concerns over the European plans to fund the first generation of satellite navigation and positioning in Europe – the European Geostationary Overlay System (EGNOS). The Association of the European Airlines (AEA) complained about cost allocation and cost recovery. It argued that EGNOS constituted a wrong business investment from a European airspace user's point of view since it did not provide any tangible operational benefits to commercial airlines. In addition, significant investments of taxpayers' money in an overlay system to GPS (EGNOS) would increase Europe's dependency on GPS and would not remove the institutional deadlock of the use of GPS in Europe. Rather, Europe needed to leapfrog in order to reach and potentially surpass the American dominance in satellite navigation. In January 2002, the European Commission's Directorate for Transport and Energy wrote to the

International Air Transport Association (IATA) saying that the civil aviation community would not be discriminated against and would only be asked to pay its fair share of the cost of the Galileo programme, which was well received by the IATA. In a letter to the EU Commissioner for Transport and Energy, Loyola de Palacio, the IATA indicated its support for the Galileo programme: 'I would like to confirm, once again, that the international airlines community welcomes the Galileo initiative on the basis that it will play a prominent role in meeting the needs of civil aviation for a worldwide, safe and cost-effective GNSS solution covering all phases of flight' (Jeanniot, 2002).

3 Author interview with European Commission official, June 1999.

4 Ibid.

5 In the framework of the TABD, standardization and regulatory policy regarding 3G was discussed under the Electronics, Electrical, Information Technology and Telecommunications Sectors (EETSI) group. A number of principles with respect to 3G mobile infrastructure and policy were agreed in late 1998. Government regulation should be kept to a minimum, interoperability of networks and standards should be ensured, market forces should drive the process, and frequency and licensing procedures should be consistent with ITU recommendations (TABD 1999b, 1999c). EETSI held a specially convened meeting in Washington in February 1999 on the issue of further cooperation and dialog on 3G wireless standards and regulatory policy. 'All participants in our meeting strongly agreed that the United States should not on present grounds initiate a Super 301 action. This is in the interest of avoiding government action counterproductive to Trans-Atlantic progress on 3G wireless issues' (TABD, 1999a). Motorola had been arguing against any Super 301 action, that is, to define it as unduly restrictive to trade and thus politically punishable by unilateral trade retaliation.

References

Abbott, K. W. and D. Snidal (2001), 'International "Standards" and International Governance', *European Journal of Public Policy* 8:1, 345–70.

AEA, Association of European Airlines (1999), *Global Navigation Satellite Systems: A European User Point of View*, Position Paper.

Barshefsky, C. (1998), Letter to Congressman R. Matsui, 14 September.

Bell, Robert G. (2002), 'Solving The Technical Issues of Galileo, GPS', excerpt from conference in Brussels on 19 June, published in *Spacenews*, 8 July.

Besen, S. M. and L. Johnson (1986), *Compatibility Standards, Competition, and Innovation in the Broadcasting Industry*, Washington DC: RAND Corporation.

Bialos, J. P. (2002), 'Togetherness on Galileo', *Space News*, 6 May.

Bingham, R. D. (1998), *Industrial Policy American Style: From Hamilton to HDTV*, Armonk, NY: M. E. Sharpe.

Blank, O. (2002), Director-General of the European Information, Communications and Consumer Electronics Technology Industry Association, EICTA, letter to the EU Commissioner for Transport and Energy and Vice President, Loyola de Palacio, 25 February.

Borrus, M. and J. Zysman (1997), 'Globalization with Borders: The Rise of Wintelism as the Future of Global Competition', *Industry and Innovation* 4:2, 141–66.

Braibanti, R. and J. Y. Kim (2002), *GPS-Galileo Negotiations: Commercial Issues at*

Stake, Briefing to the US GPS Industry Council, Sunnyvale, California, 21 March.

Burns, C. (1999), letter to USTR Ambassador C. Barshefsky, 17 March.

Computer and Communications Industry Association (CCIA) (1998), letter to Ambassador McCann, Department of State, 18 June.

Conrad, K., M. Baucus and C. Robb (1999), letter to USTR Ambassador C. Barshefsky, 9 February.

Corralez-Diaz, S. (1999), letter to President Clinton on Behalf of the President's Export Council, 11 January.

Council of Economic Advisers (CEA) (2000), *The Economic Impact of Third Generation Wireless Technology*, October.

Council of the European Union (1999), 'Council Decision on the Coordinated Introduction of Third Generation Mobile and Wireless Communications System (UMTS) in the Community', 128/1999/EEC, Brussels, January.

—— (2002), 'Council Regulation (EC) No. 876/2002 of 21 May 2002 Setting Up the Galileo Joint Undertaking', Official Journal of the European Communities, 28 May.

Daschle, T. (1999), letter to USTR Ambassador Barshefsky, 25 February.

Egan, M. (2001), 'Mutual Recognition and Standard Setting: Public and Private Strategies for Governing Markets', in M. A. Pollack and G. C. Shaffer (eds), *Transatlantic Governance in the Global Economy*, Lanham, MA: Rowman and Littlefield.

ETSI, European Telecommunication Standards Institute (1998a), letter to Chairwoman Morella, US House Subcommittee on Technology, 19 June.

—— (1998b), letter to Chairman Crane, US House Subcommittee on Trade, Committee on Ways and Means, 18 August.

European Commission (1999a), 'Galileo: Involving Europe in a New Generation of Satellite Navigation Services', COM 54, Brussels, 10 February.

—— (1999b), 'Note by the European Commission to the United States Government on the Introduction of a Third Generation Mobile and Wireless Communications System (UMTS) in the Community', Brussels, 12 January.

—— (1999c), letters to W. Daley, Secretary of Commerce and Ambassador C. Barshefsky, USTR, from Commissioner Van Miert, 22 July.

—— (2000), 'Commission Communication to the European Parliament and the Council on Galileo', COM 750, Brussels, 22 November.

—— (2001a), 'The Introduction of Third Generation Mobile Communications in the European Union: State of Play and the Way Forward', COM 141, Brussels, 20 March.

—— (2001b), 'Assessment of the Galileo: Cost-Benefit Analysis', SEC 985, 18 June.

—— (2001c), 'Towards a European Space Policy', COM 718, Brussels, 7 December.

—— (2002a), 'Galileo: An Imperative for Europe', Information Note, 18 January.

—— (2002b), 'The European Dependence on US-GPS and the Galileo Initiative', Technical Note, 14 February.

—— (2002c), 'Galileo: Yes, At Last', Press Release, IP/02/478, Brussels, 26 March.

—— (2002d), eEurope 2005: An Information Society for All. An Action Plan presented for the European Seville Council on June 21–22 (COM) 263, Brussels, 28 May.

—— (2002e), Towards the Full Roll-Out of Third Generation Mobile Communications, Brussels, COM (2002) 301, 11 June.

—— (2002f), Barriers to Widespread Access to New Services and Applications of The

Information Society Through Open Platforms in Digital Television and Third Generation Mobile Communications, Commission Staff Working Document, Brussels.

—— (2002g), State of Progress of the Galileo programme, COM (2002) 518, Brussels, 24 September.

—— (2002h), Towards a Knowledge-based Europe: The European Union and the Information Society, Manuscript for information brochure, October.

FCC, Federal Communications Commission (1999), *US and EU Telecommunications Policy*, FCC Commissioner Ness, Speech, European Institute, Washington DC, 12 January.

Friis, J. (2002), 'Third Generation – Now a Reality', *Wireless Technology Report*, Spring.

Galileo's World (2002), 'Europe Needs Galileo', *Industrial Position*, 21 March.

Ginsberg, Roy H. (2003), *Ten Years of European Union Foreign Policy: Baptism, Confirmation, Validation* (Berlin: Heinrich Böll Foundation).

Gourevitch, Peter A. (1986), *Politics in Hard Times* (Ithaca, NY: Cornell University Press).

Grossman, G. M. and Helpman, E. (1994), 'Protection for Sale', *The American Economic Review* 84, 833–50.

Hart, J. and S. Kim (2002a), 'The Global Political Economy of Wintelism: A New Mode of Power and Governance in the Global Computer Industry', in J. N. Rosenau and J. P. Singh (eds), *Information Technologies and Global Politics: The Changing Scope of Power and Governance*, Albany, NY: Sstate University of New York Press.

(2002b), 'Explaining the Resurgence of US Competitiveness: The Rise of Wintelism', *The Information Society*, 18, February, 1–12.

Helms, J., T. Lott, R. Selby, M. Dewine et al. (1999), letter to President Clinton, 4 March.

Hocking, B. and S. McGuire (2002), 'Government-business strategies in EU–US Economic Relations: The Lessons of the Foreign Sales Corporations issue', *Journal of Common Market Studies* 40:3, September, 449–70.

Hollings, E. F. (1998), The US Senate Committee on Commerce, Science, and Transportation, letter to USTR Ambassador C. Barshefsky, 13 August.

Hutchinson, K. B., D. Armey and S. Johnson (1998), letter to Ambassador V. McCann, US Department of State, 29 June.

Jeanniot, P. J., (2002), *Letter to EU Transport Commissioner and Vice President L. de Palacio*, 28 January.

Kim, J. Y. (2002), Interagency GPS Executive Board, 'The Global Positioning System: A Worldwide Information Utility', Presentation at NAVSAT 2002, Nice, France, 12 November.

Lembke, J. (2001), 'Harmonization and Globalization: UMTS and the Single Market', *INFO: The Journal of Policy, Regulation and Strategy for Telecommunications, Information and Media* 3:1, 15–26

—— (2002a), 'Global Competition and Strategies in the Information and Communications Technology Industry: A Liberal Strategic Approach', *Business and Politics* 4:1, 41–69.

—— (2002b), 'EU Critical Infrastructure and Security Policy: Capabilities, Strategies and Vulnerabilities', *Current Politics and Economics in Europe* 11:2, 99–129.

—— (2002c), *Competition for Technological Leadership: EU High Technology Policy*,

Cheltenham, UK, and Northampton, US: Edward Elgar Publishing.

Levin, S. M. (1999), Subcommittee on Trade of the Committee on Ways and Means, letter to USTR Ambassador C. Barshefsky, 24 February.

Matsui, Robert (1998), letter to USTR Ambassador C. Barshefsky, Summer.

Milner, H. V. (1988), *Resisting Protectionism: Global Industries and the Politics of International Trade*, Princeton, NJ: Princeton University Press.

—— and Yoffie, D. B. (1989), 'Between Free Trade and Protectionism: Strategic Trade Policy and a Theory of Corporate Trade Demands', in B. J. Cohen and C. Lipson (eds), *Issues and Agents in International Political Economy*, Cambridge, MA and London: MIT Press.

Nester, W. R. (1997), *American Industrial Policy: Free or Managed Markets*, New York: St Martin's Press.

OHG, Operators' Harmonization Group (1999a), 'Open Letter to the ITU on Third Generation Intellectual Property Rights (IPR) on IMT-2000 Radio Transmission Technologies', Beijing, 15 January.

—— (1999b), 'Open Letter to the ITU and Standards Development Organizations', Tokyo, 29 April.

Qualcomm (1998), Letter to K. H. Rosenbrock, Director-General of the European Telecommunications Standards Institute, 21 April.

Smith, M. (2001), 'The United States, the European Union and the New Transatlantic Marketplace: public strategy and private interests', in E. Philippart and P. Winand (eds), *Ever Closer Partnership: Policy-Making in US–EU Relations*, Brussels: P.I.E.

Space News (2002), 'Chairman Tackles Controversial Issues', interview with S. Witting, Chairman of the German Aerospace Centre, 29 July.

Transatlantic Business Dialogue (TABD) (1999a), *Statement of Conclusions and Recommendations*, TABD EETIS group, Washington DC, 17 February.

—— (1999b), *TABD Mid-Annual Report*, Washington DC, June.

—— (1999c), *TABD Statement of Conclusions from the 1998 Conference in Charlotte*, November.

UMTS Forum (2002), *The UMTS 3G Market Forecasts: Post September 11, 2001*, Report 18, February.

US Department of State, Office of the Spokesman (2002a), 'US Global Positioning System and European Galileo System', Media Note, 7 March.

——, Office of the Spokesman (2002b), 'GPS-Galileo', Taken Question from Daily Briefing of 8 March, 11 March.

US Trade Representative (USTR) (1998), Letter to Commissioner M. Bangemann, M. K. Albright, C. Barshefsky, W. M. Daley and W. E. Kennard, 19 December.

—— (1999a), Letter to Commissioner K. Van Miert, W. Daley and C. Barshefsky, 2 July.

—— (1999b), Letter to Commissioner Erkki Liikanen, W. Daley, C. Barshefsky and W. E. Kennard, 13 October.

UWCC, Universal Wireless Communications Consortium (1998), 'Universal Wireless Communications Consortium (UWCC) Announces UWC-136, the TDMA IS-136 Solution for Third Generation', *Press Release*, 23 February.

—— (1999), Letter to Secretary of Commerce W. M. Daley, 22 April.

West, M. B. (1999), 'US Committed to Maintaining Free GPS Service', *CNES Magazine*, 6, 28–9.

Werle, R. (2001), 'Institutional Aspects of Standardization: Jurisdictional Conflicts and the Choice of Standardization Organizations', *European Journal of Public Policy*, 8:1, 392–410.

Wireless Strategy Analytics (2001), '2.5G and 3G Wireless Applications', Presentation Material, Boston, MA.

New issue-areas in the transatlantic relationship: e-commerce and the Safe Harbor arrangement

Introduction

In the recent past, scholars have sought to understand better the evolving EU–US relationship, both in its own right, and as an important example of emerging forms of international governance.[1] Particular attention has been paid to the important role that transnational actors have begun to play in this relationship. Business, consumer, labour and environmental interests have been given a formal voice in EU–US relations through the creation of various dialogues. This literature has found that business interests play by far the most important role in this process, through the Transatlantic Business Dialogue (TABD) (Cowles, 2001; Bignami and Charnowitz, 2001; Knauss and Trubek, 2001). The Transatlantic Consumer Dialogue (TACD) is seen as playing a subsidiary role, while the Transatlantic Environmental Dialogue (TEAD) and Transatlantic Labour Dialogue (TALD) are respectively suspended and moribund.

This body of work has provided an excellent starting point for our understanding of transatlantic relations, and the role that transnational actors play within them. However, by focusing on the implication of transnational actors for the transatlantic relationship, it has in part neglected the reverse relationship – the implications of the transatlantic relationship (and its dialogues) for transnational actors. Further, general conclusions about which interest group is stronger or weaker overall in the process may be misleading; different actors may play more or less substantial roles in specific policy areas. Even if the TABD may have substantially more influence than other interests in a global sense, it may play a less prominent role in certain policy areas than others.

In this chapter, I seek to examine the role that transnational actors have played in a specific policy area; the protection of privacy in e-commerce. E-commerce is an increasingly important issue area in the transatlantic relationship, as its economic weight increases, and as its cross-national implications lead to increased regulatory interdependence between the EU and the US (Farrell, 2003). Perhaps the most salient transatlantic issue within e-commerce has been privacy. Differences between the EU and the US in the area of privacy protection threatened to lead to a grave dispute, after the EU introduced legislation that potentially had consequences for US e-commerce firms. Negotiations between the EU and US between autumn 1998 and mid-2000 culminated in the so-called 'Safe Harbor' arrangement, whereby the two sides sought to resolve their differences through a novel institution involving both public and private enforcement.[2] The Safe Harbor negotiations are an important test case for how the transatlantic relationship may deal with the novel regulatory challenges posed by e-commerce. Indeed, it has been cited as an example for how these challenges may be resolved in future (White House, 2000).

The history of the Safe Harbor negotiations provides sometimes surprising insights into the relationship between transnational actors and the EU–US relationship in a key policy area. While business sought to influence negotiations – often with some success – it typically did not do so through the TABD, instead relying for the most part on direct bilateral contacts. In contrast, consumer interests took direct advantage of the opportunities offered by the TACD to gain access to US-policy makers who otherwise would have had little interest in meeting with them. While they opposed the arrangement that was reached, important consumer groups felt that they had gained substantial concessions, which would provide them with important leverage in future disputes. Further, the existence of TACD not only had important implications for their access to policy-makers, but created the basis for a coherent voice representing consumer interests not only in the Transatlantic relationship, but in the US too, where consumer groups had previously been bitterly divided among each other.

This chapter begins with a brief account of the transatlantic differences over privacy that led to negotiations, and of the negotiations themselves. I then go on to describe the two key actors, TABD and TACD, and the specific implications of the transatlantic relationship for the power of these actors to achieve desired results in the arena of privacy policy. My discussion focuses on how the transatlantic relationship has affected interest politics within the US; it was in the US polity that the political questions surrounding privacy and the EU's demands played out. I conclude by examining the more general implications that this may have for study of the transatlantic relationship.

Transatlantic disputes over privacy

Regulation of privacy has taken very different trajectories in the EU and US. In both political systems, privacy became a topical policy issue in the early 1970s, when political actors started to become aware of the potential of new technologies for invading the privacy of individuals. Initial worries concentrated on the potential for abuse of centralized databases, especially by governments.[3] Accordingly, legislation was introduced in many advanced industrial democracies to forestall the abuse of such databases. In European states, this led over time to the creation of extensive global protections for the privacy of individuals, with regard to both the government and other actors. In the US, in contrast, while individuals were protected against certain incursions into their privacy by the government, legal protection for privacy in many other areas of social life was sporadic to non-existent. While this in part reflected fundamental differences in values (such as, for example, the extraordinary weight given to freedom of expression in US constitutional discourse), it also reflected the ability of US business to stymie legislative change that might hamper its own operation (Kobrin, 2002). While self-regulatory schemes purported to protect privacy in areas such as direct marketing, these schemes were undemanding and often ignored in practice. They may perhaps better be understood as attempts by firms to provide a patina of legitimacy for their activities and forestall criticism and legislation than as serious efforts to protect consumer privacy (Froomkin, 2000).

These two approaches to privacy came into conflict as a result of two coinciding sets of pressures; the increasing porousness of national borders to information exchange, and the desire of European legislators to prevent this porousness from undermining European citizens' privacy rights. As the European Union sought to further the integration of its Member States' economies, it had found it necessary to create overarching legislation at the European Union level, in order to prevent blockages of data flows between its Member States. The Data Protection Directive (in its rather long-winded official title, the 'Directive on the Protection of Individuals With Regard to the Processing of Personal Data and on the Free Movement of Such Data') was thus primarily intended to alleviate incompatibilities between the national laws of EU Member States (European Commission, 1995). However, it also imposed quite strong restrictions on the export of EU citizens' personal data to jurisdictions outside the EU. Such export was forbidden unless either the third-party jurisdiction in question had been recognized by the EU as providing 'adequate' protection, or other restrictive requirements set out in the Directive, were satisfied. The rationale for this was quite clear: information and communication technology would otherwise allow firms to evade the force of the Directive by exporting data outside the EU and processing it there.

The Directive, which came into force in late 1998, had serious implications for US multinationals and e-commerce firms. In contrast to most other member countries of the Organization for Economic Cooperation and Development, the US had no overarching set of laws protecting privacy, and instead relied on a mixture of sectoral laws and self-regulatory schemes. Most commentators agreed that it was highly unlikely that the EU would recognize the US as an 'adequate' jurisdiction, so that US firms wishing to import data on their customers or employees in the European Union would at best face substantial uncertainties. At worst, these firms might have their data flows blocked, and/or legal penalties imposed on them. US e-commerce firms in particular were aghast at the Directive. US policy had sought to leave e-commerce largely unregulated, on the principle that it was in such a state of flux that government efforts to regulate would likely do more harm than good. This light hand accorded well with the interests and expressed desires of e-commerce firms, which had considerable influence over administration officials under the Clinton administration. When the European Union proposed to regulate privacy – and effectively to seek to determine the behaviour of US-based firms – many of these firms saw this as the thin end of a regulatory wedge. Further, some believed, with more fervour than accuracy, that the Data Protection Directive's extraterritorial ambitions was intended as retaliation against the Helms-Burton measures that asserted extra-territorial jurisdiction over European firms.

The initial reaction of the US administration was to try to persuade or, if necessary, force the EU to back down on their threats of data blockages that might affect US firms. Ira Magaziner, the US administration's e-commerce 'czar', sought to create divisions among European states, and threatened WTO action against the EU as a final resort. Both blandishments and threats proved ineffective; EU officials believed that they could not back down without effectively undermining the implementation of the Directive.

Early EU–US discussions

Informal discussions began between the EU and the US in late 1997, but were hampered by the lack of an obvious coordinator for privacy policy within the US administration. Privacy touched not only on e-commerce but on broader-issue areas that had traditionally been the bailiwick of the Federal Trade Commission, the Department of Commerce, and the Department of the Treasury. In the EU, the European Commission's Directorate-General for the Internal Market (DG Internal Market) was the designated interlocutor; privacy had emerged as a policy issue in the context of market integration. There was no formal cross-Directorate-General committee as such, although DG Internal Market did engage in informal discussions with other DGs in the course of formulating its position.

While both Magaziner and Commissioner Mozelle Thompson of the Federal Trade Commission engaged in informal discussions with European officials, they were not designated representatives of the US as such. The US Trade Representative (USTR), despite its considerable experience in transatlantic disputes, expressed little interest in taking a lead role in the emerging conflict, which, although it potentially had serious consequences for transatlantic trade in services, was not itself a traditional dispute over trade.

After discussions within the administration, the Commerce Department, and in particular Ambassador David Aaron, the Department's Undersecretary for International Trade, emerged as the lead negotiators, reporting back to an inter-departmental committee headed by the White House's Office of

Management and Budget (OMB). The Department of Commerce had already developed significant expertise in the area of privacy and self-regulation. Further, it was deeply involved in the transatlantic relationship, and was highly aware of the sensitivities of European officials and politicians. Even while Commerce was highly responsive to the interests of US firms, it was also more adept than certain others within the administration at representing those interests in the transatlantic context, and potentially in finding areas of common ground with European negotiators.

Negotiations proper started in early 1998, some several months before the Directive was due to take effect. Initially, they proved highly frustrating for both sides. On the one hand, European negotiators demanded that the US introduce a system of privacy protection along European lines, with strong laws with comprehensive coverage, which would be backed up by specialized officials, along the lines of the system of data-protection commissioners existing in Europe. As described by a European negotiator; 'we had on our side a relatively strict set of rules which meant that transfers to the US risked being illegal – they either had to be stopped or their protection had to be increased. There was a problem there that needed to be solved, and certainly the simplest way of solving it was to say hey US, what about adopting something similar.'[4] On the other hand, US officials refused to countenance suggestions of broad-scale legal reform within the US because 'within the US government there was a fair amount of sentiment that we weren't going to be pushed around by the Europeans, and too bad if they had this law, we weren't going to have to oblige them'.[5] Instead, US negotiators sought to win European recognition of the existing patchwork of laws and self-regulation as adequate. The strong – and almost entirely incompatible – positions taken by the two sides led to considerable pessimism among negotiators that any substantial agreement might be possible.

The Safe Harbor arrangement

The breakthrough came with a suggestion by Ambassador Aaron that the EU did not have to recognize the US system as a whole; rather, it might accord recognition to a subset of firms that had voluntarily agreed to adhere to a given set of privacy standards.[6] These firms would then have 'safe harbor' from EU enforcement action as long as they obeyed these principles. While initially cautious, European Commission officials were intrigued enough by this suggestion to continue negotiations – and to discuss in more detail what these principles might involve. A first draft of these principles was announced in a draft letter from Ambassador Aaron to US industry in November 1998, as summarized here:

1 *Notice* – organizations must inform individuals about what type of personal information were collected, how it was collected, whom it was disclosed to, and the choices individuals had for limiting this disclosure.

2 *Choice* – organizations must give individuals the opportunity to opt out when information is used for purposes unrelated to the use for which they originally disclosed it. Individuals must be given opt-in choice with regard to certain sorts of sensitive information.

3 *Onward transfer* – Individuals must be able to choose whether and how a third party uses the information they provide. When information is transferred to third parties, these parties must provide at least the same level of privacy protection originally chosen.

4 *Security* – Organizations must take reasonable measures to assure the reliability of information, and prevent loss or misuse.

5 *Data integrity* – Personal data must be kept accurate, complete, current, and used only for the purposes for which it is gathered.

6 *Access* – Individuals must have reasonable access to data about themselves, and be able to correct it when it is inaccurate, subject to the sensitivity of the information and its dependent uses.

7 *Enforcement* – There must be mechanisms for assuring compliance with the principles, recourse for individuals, and consequences for the organization when the principles are not followed. Enforcement could take place through compliance with private-sector privacy programmes, through compliance with legal or regulatory authorities, or by committing to cooperate with the data-protection authorities in Europe.

Aaron and other US officials hoped that these principles would be swiftly accepted by the EU, and thus resolve the nascent dispute. However, EU Member States proved far more suspicious of the proposed arrangement than US negotiators had anticipated. Some (most notably France and Germany) were overtly hostile to the strong reliance on self-regulation implied by the enforcement principle, while others were dubious about the specifics of the principles, and the extent to which they provided a level of privacy protection that was adequate according to the Directive. Further, the Member States' Data Protection Authorities were hostile to the proposal; even though they had no official veto power, they did have a consultative role which they used to express their (largely negative) opinion of it. In consequence of the Member States' difficulties with the proposed arrangement, the Commission and the US Department of Commerce embarked on an extended set of negotiations over the principles.

Negotiations over Safe Harbor

Negotiations focused on the principles that Aaron had suggested; the EU sought to make these principles tighter, and to bring them more closely in line with its interpretation of the Directive. Perhaps the most difficult of the seven principles to agree upon was access. Initially, the EU sought to ensure that individuals could have almost unlimited access to information that firms held about them. The United States counter-proposed that access should be 'reasonable', in order to prevent access from being exercised for frivolous or malicious purposes, or in circumstances where the cost to firms of providing information would be out of proportion with the benefit to the individual. The Europeans, for their part, believed that the term 'reasonable' was too vague to be useful in this context: firms might deny access on grounds that they themselves found reasonable, but which were specious or unconvincing in a broader sense of the term. Further, EU negotiators had identified access as a key principle to the success of self-enforcement: in the absence of the broad safeguards which European consumers had when dealing with European companies, access provided a means for consumers to be sure that firms were actually doing what they were saying. Eventually, a compromise was reached whereby access had to be granted except when the costs of providing it would be 'disproportionate', a formulation which provided a higher degree of specificity in the eyes of the EU.

The principle of choice posed difficulties for other reasons: following the lead of the Data Protection Directive, the EU wished to distinguish between certain categories of sensitive data, where individuals would have to opt in explicitly to uses of the data other than those for which the data had originally been collected, and other categories of data, where the ability to opt out would be sufficient. While the US accepted this basic principle (and indeed had domestic legislation which already required opt-in for certain kinds of data, such as medical data), there were pronounced disagreements between the two sides as to which categories of data could be considered sensitive. In particular, there was a philosophical disagreement over data on racial or ethnic origin, highly sensitive in Europe, because of memories of National Socialism, but commonly used and available in the US. In the final version of the principles, the US agreed to accept the European position despite its reservations, and included data on ethnic and racial origin as a 'sensitive' category requiring opt-in.

Onward transfer of data also presented problems. The European Union sought to prevent onward transfer from becoming a loop-hole through which firms in the Safe Harbor could send data to other firms not bound by the Safe Harbor. However, the US wanted to ensure that firms in Safe Harbor should not be held liable for the behaviour of third parties, when they themselves had made good-faith efforts to ensure that the data would be treated properly. Negotiations were also complicated by the ongoing domestic US discussion of financial privacy in the context of the 1999 Gramm-Leach-Bliley bill on financial services, where there was vigorous debate about whether financial firms would, or would not, be able to share data with their affiliates. The US deliberately slow-pedalled their negotiations with the EU over onward transfer, for fear that any agreement that was reached would be seen as establishing a precedent for current debates in Congress. The final form of the principle marked a compromise whereby organizations would only be able to transfer personal information to third parties which also subscribed to the principles, were bound by the Directive or another adequacy finding, or had entered into a written agreement with the original firm undertaking to give the data the same level of protection as under the principles. As long as these strictures were abided by, organizations would not be held liable for the misuse of data by third parties to which they had passed it on.

Finally, there was the principle of enforcement, which became the most difficult negotiating point toward the end of the negotiations. Much of the difficulty centered on the unwillingness of EU Member States to accept that self-enforcement could provide an adequate form of privacy protection. Their scepticism was bolstered by their domestic Data Protection Commissioners, which, although they accepted that self-regulation could protect privacy in principle, were in practice unconvinced by the arrangements existing in the United States. In particular, Commissioners pointed to the fact that individuals were not able to complain directly to the FTC and have a guaranteed investigation of their claims, in contrast to arrangements in Europe. At times there was a clear disconnect between Commission negotiators, who had accepted that self-regulation could work in the US at a relatively early stage, and officials in the Member States and data-protection commissioners, many of whom remained resolutely unpersuaded.

This disparity sometimes led the EU negotiators to weave back and forth on the issue of enforcement, as they sought to reconcile the near-impossible contradictions of keeping the Member States on board while presenting negotiating positions which the Americans might possibly accept. The breakthrough moment when this disconnection disappeared came in a meeting in mid-January, when Member-State representatives were invited to Washington DC for three days of presentations from US government officials and private-sector bodies to explain how the enforcement aspects of Safe Harbor would work. Officials on both the EU and the US sides credit this meeting with having effected a sea-change in Member-State positions. The opportunity to question bodies such as BBBOnline and TrustE directly allowed some Member States to move from a position where they a priori rejected self-regulation as a means to enforcement, to one where they were prepared to engage with the specific strengths and weaknesses of this approach.

A second set of issues revolved around the different sorts of enforcement that might be possible under Safe Harbor. Under the principles, enforcement must involve independent recourse mechanisms which may be provided through private-sector-developed privacy programmes, through compliance with legal or regulatory authorities which provide for the handling of individual complaints and dispute resolution, or through direct cooperation with European Union data-protection authorities or their representatives. The second of these was a dead letter in the absence of appropriate legal authorities in the US, while the last was problematic. Cooperation with EU data-protection authorities was more suitable than other recourse mechanisms for certain sorts of data, such as employment and human-resources data (for which it was required). However, EU data-protection authorities, which have relatively limited resources, had no desire to deal with a deluge of US companies, each requiring specific agreements. US firms, for their part, were worried about the divergences of approach between different national data-protection authorities, which potentially gave rise to serious uncertainties. In the end, an arrangement was worked out whereby organizations could commit to work with the data-protection authorities through so declaring to the Department of Commerce. The authorities themselves would form an informal panel at the European level to harmonize their approach, and would deal with complaints through three member panels, including one member from the jurisdiction where the alleged problem had occurred.

The negotiations did not only look at the seven principles. Aaron's initial announcement had suggested that these principles would be accompanied by additional guidance for firms as to how they should be applied in specific circumstances. This guidance, which was issued on 19 April 1999 for public comment, along with redrafted versions of the principles, took the form of Frequently Asked Questions (FAQs). This was another of Aaron's innovations, borrowing from Web terminology, but the FAQs themselves became the subject of extensive negotiations on two levels. First, there were different views as to the precise status that these FAQs should have; they could offer guidance pure and simple, they could offer authoritative guidance, or they could be binding. If they only offered guidance, without any guarantees as to its authoritativeness, however, their usefulness to those seeking to apply the principles would be uncertain. On the other end of the spectrum, if they were binding, they would provide a high degree of certainty, but would by the same token be impossible to revise to meet new needs without extensive renegotiation.

In the end, the negotiators agreed that the FAQs should provide authoritative guidance, a formulation which, it was hoped, would provide certainty to businesses seeking to apply them, while maintaining the possibility of future flexibility and redrafting.[7] Second, as the FAQs became important, much of the negotiations focused on their content as well as on the content of the principles themselves, sometimes leading to heated debate. On many issues, European negotiators suspected that the US side was seeking to whittle away the commitments that had been made in the principles themselves, through seeking out carve-outs, special exceptions, and interpretations which maximized the flexibility of US firms. The US, for its part, felt that the Europeans often failed to acknowledge the wide leeway in interpretation and application that European firms sometimes enjoyed under the supposedly strict standards of the Data Protection Directive, and were determined that US firms should have some measure of equivalence on the level of practical application as well as theoretical principle.

The EU and United States announced on 17 March 2000 that they had reached a tentative conclusion to their Safe Harbor dialogue, and that they sought to conclude their dialogue by the end of the month. This announcement was followed by a meeting of the EU Council of Ministers' Section 31 Committee, which unanimously endorsed the arrangement on 31 May. Under the comitology procedure, the European Parliament was then entitled to exercise procedural oversight of the agreement: a draft report on the arrangement was prepared by Member of the European Parliament Elena Paciotti for the Parliament's Committee on Citizens' Freedom and Rights, Justice and Home Affairs.[8] This report delivered a negative assessment of the substance of the arrangement, citing the doubts of data-protection commissioners. Despite Commission pressure, the Parliament voted against the arrangement on the basis of this report. But the Commission took the view that the Parliament had exceeded its powers in so doing: its oversight in the matter was limited to purely procedural issues, and did not include the power to demand substantive changes.[9] Accordingly, the Safe Harbor arrangement came into practical effect from 1 November 2000.[10]

In the period since Safe Harbor has come into operation, some 300 companies have formally agreed to adhere to the Safe Harbor principles. While not a failure, it is safe to say that this is a far lower number than negotiators for both the EU and US initially anticipated. Further, there remain considerable uncertainties about the implementation of Safe Harbor; while a number of complaints have been made under the procedure, no formal action has been taken against any company for breach of its Safe Harbor requirements, even though Commission research suggests that there is evidence that a large number of Safe Harbor companies have failed to comply with the rules. Where the Safe Harbor may be having a more important effect is through its indirect influence on the standards of self-regulatory organizations (Farrell, 2003). One important self-regulatory organization (BBBOnline) has adopted the standards set out in Safe Harbor as the baseline for its own privacy standards. This was an intended effect on the part of EU negotiators, who hoped and anticipated that Safe Harbor might influence the behaviour of self-regulatory actors within the US, and thus pave the way over time for comprehensive legislative protection of privacy in the US (Farrell, 2003).

The relative power of non-state actors in the transatlantic relationship

Until recently, the relationship between the EU and the US was dominated by traditional transgovernmental relations between diplomats and officials on both sides of the Atlantic. However, starting with the TABD, non-state actors have increasingly been accorded a significant role in transatlantic policy discussions. Of the four main dialogues aimed at involving non-state actors in transatlantic relations, two have withered on the vine. The TAED has suspended its activities *sine die*, due to difficulties in getting funding from the US administration, while the TALD appears to be inactive. The TABD and TACD remain active; while they do not have a direct role in transatlantic negotiations, they may have an important indirect role in setting the agenda, in bringing new items into policy discussions, and in mobilizing support for and against various proposals on both sides of the Atlantic.

The detailed history of how non-state actors have become increasingly engaged in the transatlantic relationship is discussed at length in the literature (Pollack and Shaffer, 2001; see also Steffenson, Chapter 8 in this volume). Briefly, the scholarly consensus is as follows. The TABD, which was the first of the dialogues to become established, plays a considerably more substantial role than any of the other three dialogues. Business has used the TABD to influence the transatlantic agenda quite successfully, in terms of the transatlantic policies adopted – and not adopted – by US and EU policy-makers and regulators (Cowles, 2001). The TABD has enjoyed greater resources, greater influence, and a higher profile than others. Those who represent consumer, environmental and labour interests have found themselves struggling to catch up, where they have not indeed given up the struggle altogether.

This broad assessment of the influence of various groups within the transatlantic relationship captures important truths. Business interests incontrovertibly have much more influence on policy-makers – especially in the US – than consumer, environmental or labour interests. Many of the advantages enjoyed by business are structural ones. For example, it is highly unlikely that consumer interests will ever enjoy the same influence over policy-makers as business interests; consumer organizations typically have far fewer resources to deploy in the political marketplace.

However, precisely by virtue of their structural advantages, business interests have less need to take advantage of the formal channels of influence offered within the transatlantic relationship than others might. This point should not be exaggerated; it is clear that the existence of the TABD has given business access to areas of policy-making (such as EU trade policy) that were previously relatively opaque (Cowles, 2001). Nonetheless, to the extent that business has already enjoyed substantial influence over policy-makers, the existence of the TABD provides only one more tool to affect policy outcomes, albeit a quite important one in certain areas. Other groups may enjoy less influence within the transatlantic relationship than business. But by the same token, these groups may be relatively uninfluential in domestic politics too, especially in the US, where non-business interests have had little influence on international commercial and trade policy. Thus, even if these groups enjoy less power in an absolute sense, they may find themselves advantaged in relative terms by the new channels of influence created as part of the transatlantic relationship.

This observation is especially pertinent to the relationship between the TABD and TACD, the two civil-society dialogues which are still active. The TABD clearly enjoys far more influence over EU–US relations than the TACD. Prominent policy-makers are rather more likely to attend TABD meetings – and to take proper account of their conclusions – than TACD meetings.

However, by the same token, the fact that the TACD has come to play a formal role in transatlantic relations at all is itself a modest victory. Transatlantic economic policy has largely been the preserve of the USTR and of the Commerce Department, both of which have traditionally been responsive to business to the virtual exclusion of consumer and other interests. The existence of TACD has given consumer groups a formal voice in transatlantic policy deliberations, which make them more difficult to ignore completely, and has allowed them to leverage their influence over European policy-makers into a greater influence over US policy-makers too.

How has this played out in the area of e-commerce? E-commerce and the new economy have become more important both for business interests (which have sought to forestall government regulation of e-commerce) and for consumer groups (which have sought to ensure that consumers have strong statutory rights and protections against abuse). Privacy and data-protection – where EU–US differences were at their starkest – provides evidence of both business and consumer efforts to influence the transatlantic agenda. As I argue below, it offers evidence that in one issue area at least, the transatlantic dialogue has offered new possibilities to consumer groups to organize and press their demands; they were able to influence outcomes in a manner that would have been far more difficult in the absence of these transatlantic structures. In contrast, business interests had far greater difficulty in agreeing on the specifics of privacy policy, and thus, after raising the transatlantic dispute as a possible concern, were content to use more traditional national-level means of lobbying rather than presenting detailed proposals through the formal channels of the TABD.

Business interests and privacy in the transatlantic relationship
The development of the transatlantic relationship in e-commerce was a priority for business interests very nearly from the beginnings of the TABD. Indeed, the birth of the TABD was almost exactly contemporaneous with the beginning efforts of policy-makers on both sides of the Atlantic to address e-commerce and its associated issues. The issue became relevant before the transatlantic 'early warning' system to identify potential disputes in the making had come into operation. Business interests initially had difficulty in focusing policy-makers' interest on the European Data Protection Directive, despite the Directive's clear implications for the regulation of privacy within e-commerce. European businesses had lobbied over the Directive itself, but were less concerned with its extraterritorial implications than its domestic ones. US businesses, for their part, had been relatively slow to seek to counteract the potential effects of the Directive for transatlantic flows of data.[11] Although their EU-based lobbyists had made vigorous efforts to mitigate the extraterritorial impact of the Directive (Regan, 1999) while it was being drafted, they were slow to organize a coherent campaign against its implementation. In part, this may be attributed to the lack of an

obvious point of contact within the administration on international issues of privacy regulation.

Business began to organize properly in the context of the TABD in 1997. The Rome meeting of the TABD, held in that year, presented a number of recommendations regarding e-commerce, with particular attention paid to the EU Data Protection Directive, and its international implications. At this point, business, especially in the US, was hostile toward the Directive, which it viewed as potentially disrupting transatlantic commerce. The Directive's extraterritorial reach was seen as probably incompatible with WTO rules, and as a barrier to trade.[12] Generally, the feeling among firms in the TABD was that the Directive presented a serious problem, and that the TABD should fight to ensure that it was not implemented in a maximalist fashion.[13] Accordingly, the TABD recommended in its mid-year report that the EU should not create a barrier to trade, and that contracts and self-regulatory tools be developed to provide adequate protection for privacy. Business leaders also used this meeting to present their concerns to US and EU officials more informally, bringing the issue to the attention of Undersecretary Aaron among others.[14] However, it was not until early in the following year, following discussions within the administration, and further representations by business, that the US government began actively to develop a coherent position on the Directive.

Over the course of late 1997 and early 1998, the position of firms within the TABD began to change. The Europeans had proven resistant to business pressures to water down the implementation of the Directive at the Rome TABD meeting (Cowles, 2001), and firms gradually began to realize that the EU was not prepared to back down. Furthermore, privacy and data protection began to become increasingly salient within the US as well as in the European Union, as advocate groups began to publicize the embarrassing lack of means for consumers to protect their privacy, especially in the area of e-commerce. Many firms moved from a position of outright resistance to the Directive to a modified understanding that some accommodation with Europe was inevitable, and perhaps not entirely detrimental to their interests.

Accordingly, by mid-1998, the TABD position had shifted in a modest but nonetheless important fashion; rather than criticizing the EU position per se, the TABD sought to ensure that any potential agreement reflected the interests of its members. Specifically, it proposed that the problem should be solved through both EU and US converging on a recognition of self-regulatory mechanisms as a solution to consumers' privacy concerns – business muted its criticisms of the Directive's effects on trade, and instead sought to create principles of self-regulation and have them accepted by government. In this context, industry initiatives such as the Online Privacy Alliance (OPA) drafted privacy principles that were intended directly to address the transatlantic debate as well as debates within the US domestic context. Unsurprisingly, these principles were undemanding in the extreme; however, they were cited in TABD publications as evidence of industry's efforts to create credible mechanisms of self-regulation.

As direct discussions between the EU and the US over Safe Harbor began to develop, TABD policy proposals became increasingly less relevant. This was for two reasons. First, it was far easier for firms to agree in general terms that the transatlantic impasse on privacy was a problem than to identify and agree upon credible solutions to it. Just as in the parallel Global Business Dialogue on E-Commerce (GBDe), the privacy principles that firms could agree on were a rather vague lowest common denominator. These were effectively incredible as a solution; it was impossible that the EU accept the principles proposed by groups such as the OPA without almost entirely negating the effect of the Directive. Second, while the majority of firms and industry groups were primarily interested in a solution to the transatlantic dispute, even if this solution involved some concessions to the EU, some (primarily US-based) firms feared that any agreement might have knock-on consequences for the privacy debate within the United States. This was a commonly expressed worry; in the words of a US negotiator; 'there . . . was a fair amount of concern from the private sector that anything we agreed with the Europeans would become the template for domestic legislation. And . . . a great deal of concern that either we would turn around and put it in legislation, or just by dint of it being out there it would create a problem'.[15]

European negotiators, while more insulated from US firms, perceived similar pressures as 'industry was afraid that the discussions on Safe Harbor would turn into some kind of Trojan horse – what would be agreed with the Europeans would automatically become the national standard'.[16]

The US financial-services industry was especially worried about the potential consequences of a Safe Harbor agreement within the US; it was seeking to steer legislation through Congress that would mandate a substantially lower set of privacy standards. As a result of the difficulty in reaching agreement on specifics, the TABD continued to issue statements that were generally supportive of EU–US efforts to address the outstanding problem, and to urge a swift resolution, but did not provide detailed recommendations as to how that might be achieved, beyond reiterating the virtues of self-regulation. Their position was not specified clearly enough to have a substantial effect on negotiators' positions. According to a US negotiator, 'TABD, the first year, the members, this was where the private sector wasn't so sure what they wanted to do with it, there was not firm support for the Safe Harbor negotiations the first year that they met that this was on the table. The second year it had evolved and I think that there was more support, and they were saying hurry up and finish this. But it didn't have much of an impact on the negotiations'.[17]

In the absence of a detailed TABD position, individual firms and industry groups sought to lobby both US and EU negotiators on an individual basis. Even though EU and US negotiators retained final say (Farrell, 2003), there were numerous opportunities for business actors to express their opinions to negotiators on both sides of the Atlantic. The Department of Commerce solicited formal comments from business at various stages of the negotiations, and also engaged in close contacts with concerned firms at both political and senior administrative levels. Furthermore, other departments and agencies within the administration had their own contacts with firms, and the opportunity to reflect the interests of their various constituencies through the OMB-led committee to which Commerce reported. Treasury, for example, was highly responsive to the demands of firms within the US financial sector. While the links between the US administration and industry groups were stronger than the links between the EU and affected firms, EU negotiators also met frequently with US industry associations on trips to Washington, and in Brussels.[18]

In summary, the TABD's role in the Safe Harbor negotiations primarily involved the identification of a potential problem, rather than the detailing of suggestions as to how this problem might be resolved. Without the TABD's initial prodding, the US administration might have taken longer to react to the Data Protection Directive, and perhaps might have acted in a different fashion. It is also likely that the TABD's support for efforts to resolve the dispute was helpful to Commerce in selling its case to sceptics within the administration, even if this support was stated in a rather vague and generic fashion. However, the TABD did not provide detailed input into the negotiations, because of difficulties in agreeing a position among its member firms. Instead, individual firms used more traditional – and direct – lines of communication with the negotiating parties and other parts of the US administration.

Consumer groups and privacy in the transatlantic relationship
The TACD is a younger organization than the TABD; it was formally launched in September 1998. Prior to the launch of the TACD, there had been relatively little coordination among US consumer groups, in part because of divisions stretching back to the introduction of the North American Free Trade Agreement (NAFTA). Some consumer groups had supported NAFTA, arguing that free trade was in consumers' interests; others had pointed to NAFTA's potential costs for labour and the environment. This disagreement had left a legacy of bitterness and distrust.

Not only did the TACD allow US and European consumer groups to coordinate their policy better; it also allowed US consumer groups to come together in a way that they had not done previously. Unlike the TABD, the TACD had relatively limited resources; it decided to concentrate these on three groups of issues – food-safety, e-commerce, and a catch-all group for all other issues. The strong emphasis on e-commerce was in large part a reaction to the priorities of the TACD's funders; the consumer-affairs directorate of the European Commission had a direct interest in creating a transatlantic consumer voice in debates over e-commerce. Initially, US consumer groups were less interested than their European counterparts in e-commerce-related issues, with the exception of a few smaller organizations with specialist expertise and interests in the area. Within the e-commerce working group, the proposed Safe Harbor arrangement quickly emerged as an important issue.[19] Indeed, the Electronic Privacy Information Center (EPIC), a founding member of TACD, was already an important voice in the debate over the Directive, which it saw as a possible means to bring US domestic privacy laws and practices up to international standards. A group of TACD founder members had issued a highly critical assessment of Safe Harbor before the TACD was properly up and running.

The TACD was thus active from its inception on Safe Harbor and data-protection issues. In contrast to the TABD, it continued to issue detailed and critical comments on the various drafts of the Safe Harbor principles and associated Frequently Asked Questions, making specific recommendations as to how the principles might be improved: 'as they continued to propose various iterations of the Safe Harbor documents, we continued to try to put pressure on them'.[20]

Its activism may be attributed to two major factors. First, consumer organizations found it considerably easier than business to agree on privacy principles. The TACD worked on a consensus basis, but given the wide variation in interest and expertise among consumer organizations, certain groups such as EPIC – which were better informed and more interested in a specific area than the average member – tended to take the lead. Other groups tended to defer to the lead groups except where they had a direct interest in the matter. Second, in contrast to business, consumer groups had a strong interest in presenting a collective position through the channels of the TACD. These groups often had relationships with agencies such as the FTC, or with members of Congress. However, they had little to no history of interaction with certain parts of the administration, including the Department of Commerce and the USTR. The TACD, when it came into existence, transformed this situation. For the first time, consumer groups had an official voice in the transatlantic relationship, which they could also leverage into increased access to decision-makers within the US.

The TACD has had three main effects. First, it has allowed consumer groups to move beyond their previous disputes and present a unified voice on issues that were important to them. This has considerably increased their legitimacy and effectiveness. Second, the existence of the TACD has given consumer groups a means to differentiate themselves from 'astroturf' groups set up by business. This is a not-inconsiderable problem in the radically pluralist system of the United States, where firms very frequently set up organizations that are nominally supposed to represent consumer interests, but which are in fact fully funded by business. Previously, policy-makers and members of Congress could justifiably complain that they found it difficult to distinguish between 'genuine' consumer groups, and front organizations – TACD gave the consumer group community a way to organize itself domestically within the US, as well as internationally. A TACD participant noted that:

> Now, we're in a new stage where [policy-makers are] beginning to say – oh, there does exist an NGO constituency. And we can tell which ones are authentic or not, because they have this organization which includes the real ones, and they can give us something that represents the consensus position of a lot of groups, so it's not just one group's opinion, we can rely upon the fact that this actually has a real constituency. This is not a trivial issue in my opinion. And they can tell when we meet together that we are unified when we talk about things: it's not as if people start bickering amongst each other when we meet the government'.[21]

Third, and perhaps most importantly, it provided consumer groups with direct access to policy-makers who were previously largely inaccessible. Quite simply, administration officials charged with international trade and commercial policy had little interest in speaking to consumer groups prior to the inception of TACD because 'commerce has always been strictly a ra-ra pro-business operation . . . We didn't have any entree into Commerce, none of us did . . . We knew that Aaron was negotiating this thing for the government but we didn't have any real good entree with them'.[22] Ambassador Aaron's first call for comments on Safe Harbor, for example, was addressed exclusively to 'industry representatives'.[23] Privacy-advocacy groups complained, with considerable justification, that the administration was uninterested in their perspective, but eager to solicit the views of firms.

The creation of TACD meant that policy-makers within the Department of Commerce had little choice but to respond to advocacy groups' arguments about Safe Harbor and other related issues. Officials from both Europe and the US attended TACD meetings, and found themselves having to defend their positions, respond to criticisms and otherwise engage with consumer advocates. A TACD member noted that, 'I like to think that because we started to get involved, there was an increase in transparency in what the Commerce Department did. They started to develop an email mailing list, and they started to announce these . . . briefings . . . and invite anybody from civil society – I think they counted business groups as being civil society as well'.[24]

Further, TACD members were able to secure meetings with high-level officials on specific matters much more easily than previously:

> we've had high level meetings . . . In the United States, the Federal Trade Commission or the Department of Commerce, or USTR or State, and we meet with real people that have influence. And what's good about it is that it's given us an opportunity to find a consumer-group position which is credible because it's a real process in which you develop formal positions. The first stage is that they were clueless as to what we were thinking, because they would insulate themselves from us. They wouldn't give us access, they wouldn't meet, they wouldn't accept invitations. We wouldn't know what was going on, we would be

clueless as to a lot of important deadlines for things. And even if we went, they wouldn't be able to distinguish my group from some business-funded front group, that purported to represent consumer interests or something like that.[25]

Where US groups had difficulty in persuading US officials of their case, they often received a more sympathetic hearing among European officials. This was so in the Safe Harbor negotiations, even though the lead Directorate General – Internal Market – was less open to consumer interests than were other parts of the Commission.[26] Indeed, the Commission often found the arguments of US consumer advocates useful in exposing domestic differences on privacy within the US that helped its negotiating position. The attention that the Commission paid to consumer advocates was sometimes quite uncomfortable for Commerce Department officials, who found it odd that consumer groups should have such influence on Commission thinking, which perhaps indeed they exaggerated in stating that 'for some reason the European Commission listens to consumer groups more than they listen to business, and [they] never figured out why that is'.[27] Despite this, US negotiators sometimes were forced to acknowledge the points made by TACD position papers, which they acknowledged as having a significant impact on the negotiations.[28] A TACD member concluded that, 'I think we had an effect ultimately . . . If you look at Aaron's original proposals, and you look at what was finally negotiated . . . I think you'll see that they substantially strengthened it in a number of areas . . . Now, granted the Commission wanted those improvements . . . but so did US and European consumer groups'.[29]

The final TACD assessment of Safe Harbor was a negative one, pointing to continuing problems in the principles, as well as the many lacunae in the enforcement process. Nonetheless, even if it is unsatisfactory in itself, TACD members view the Safe Harbor as an important intermediary victory, which may provide both a basis to criticize the continuing lack of comprehensive legislation to protect privacy in e-commerce, and a minimum baseline for new legislation:[30]

> We looked at it as a two-part thing. First of all, we looked at it from the international perspective; we wanted to help the European groups. Second of all . . . this was all before we were able to raise the issue of privacy to as high a level as it has been raised . . . if we ended up with a really bad Safe Harbor, an atrocious one like Aaron proposed at first, that would have undercut and undermined all the work we're trying to do here down the street at Congress . . . The Data Directive is high, Safe Harbor is middle, US privacy law is low except for a couple of narrow parts . . . It's above [the standard of] US law, and it gives us a new benchmark.[31]

The existence of the TACD had important implications for the ability of consumer groups to influence the Safe Harbor negotiations. First, and most simply, it provided these groups with a means to present an unified view on Safe Harbor, which carried weight as the 'official' view of the consumer movement. Second, it provided consumer groups with access to decision-makers who otherwise would have been highly unlikely to meet with them.

This is not to say that consumer groups carried more weight in the process than business groups, or that Safe Harbor was an unalloyed victory for them. Far from it. However, it is to say that the civil-society mechanisms of the transatlantic relationship allowed them access to levels of decision-making that they would not otherwise have enjoyed, and an outcome which, if not ideal from their perspective, provides them with a baseline to work up from in their future efforts to improve domestic and international protections for privacy.

Conclusions

In this chapter, I have argued that the existing literature on the transatlantic relationship, and the role that private actors play in it, has some important gaps. Specifically, by focusing on the implications of private actors for the transatlantic relationship, it fails to pay close attention to the implications of the transatlantic relationship for private actors. By documenting the role of the TABD and TACD in the negotiation of the Safe Harbor arrangement, I hope to have shown that the transatlantic relationship can have important – and differential – effects for the ability of these groups to shape policy outcomes. In the area of privacy and e-commerce, the TABD provided an important early warning of the risk of conflict between the EU and the US over privacy. However, the TABD then had difficulties in shaping the EU–US negotiation process in any but the most generic sense. While it supported efforts of both sides to find a solution quickly, it had little advice to offer about the specifics of what this solution should involve. While the individual members of TABD, together with other interested firms, lobbied negotiators, they typically did not do so through formal TABD statements, but rather through more traditional informal channels of influence. Thus, it can be seen that in this policy area at least, the existence of TABD was not crucial to business efforts to shape the negotiating process. Firms could and did use other means to influence outcomes.

In contrast, the TACD was crucial to consumer-group efforts to make their voices heard in the transatlantic process. Without the TACD, US consumer groups would have had little hope of gaining access to the Department of Commerce. Within the TACD, consumer groups not only had such access, but sometimes were able to leverage EU support so as better to achieve their policy goals (the opposite relationship also held) (Farrell, 2002). The TACD's detailed policy positions affected the final Safe Harbor outcome in important ways.

In conclusion, one may point to the emerging institutional structures surrounding the transatlantic relationship as an important example of how consumer groups may exercise some influence over the terms on which international commercial relations are conducted. It is important not to exaggerate this; clearly, consumer groups remain disadvantaged in comparison to business. But nonetheless, they play a real and adversarial role. Further, the TACD has been successful in identifying a common set of consumer interests across the Atlantic, and in representing these interests. In an important recent paper, Stephen Kobrin speaks of how emerging transnational social issues require 'the rudiments of a transnational social community', as well as effective institutions (Kobrin, 2002). The TACD, and indeed the TABD reflect nascent efforts by social actors to organize transnationally in order to address regulatory issues that are not confined to the borders of a single nation state. They are thus an interesting – and important – experiment along some of the lines that Kobrin suggests. It remains to be seen whether they will lead to any more general reorganization of the transatlantic social space over time.

Notes

1 See especially Pollack and Shaffer, 2001.
2 I discuss other aspects of the negotiation of Safe Harbor in Farrell, 2002, 2003.
3 For detailed discussion of the history of the privacy debate, see Bennett, 1992 and Mayer-Schönberger, 1997.
4 Interview with European negotiator, 15 January 2001.
5 Interview with US negotiator, 18 September 2000.
6 The course of the negotiations is documented in more detail in Farrell, 2003.
7 It remains to be seen whether the FAQs will be easily revisable in practice. Certainly, the negotiations over the FAQs were at times as difficult as the negotiations over the principles themselves.
8 The amended version of this report is document PE285.929, available at www .europarl.eu.int/meetdocs/committees/libe/20000621/libe20000621.htm.
9 Thus, while the Parliament's vote was embarrassing to the Commission, it was not sufficient to forestall the arrangement from taking effect. One should also note that the vote was relatively close, and that a substantial minority in the Parliament was in favour of the arrangement. Discussion with Pat Cox, President of the European Parliament, 13 September 2000.
10 Note that Safe Harbor is an arrangement, and not an agreement; technically, it is a recognition on the part of the European Commission that certain arrangements can be considered to be adequate under the Directive.
11 Interviews with US negotiators.
12 Interview with TABD official, 12 June 2000.
13 Ibid.
14 Interview with Ambassador David Aaron, 19 September 2000.
15 Interview with US negotiator, 18 September 2000.
16 Interview with European Commission official, 29 June 2000.
17 Interview with US negotiator, 18 September 2000.
18 Interview with European Commission negotiator, 11 January 2001.
19 One TACD member identifies Safe Harbor and the genetically modified food debate as the two major issues that the TACD faced in its early phase. Interview with TACD member, 25 September 2000.

20 Interview with TACD member, 25 September 2000.
21 Interview with TACD member, 18 September 2000.
22 Ibid.
23 For the full text of the letter, see www.ita.doc.gov/td/ecom/aaron114.html.
24 Interview with TACD member, 25 September 2000.
25 Interview with TACD member, 18 September 2000.
26 The Directorate General for Health and Consumer Protection, which was con-
    sumer organizations' traditional point of access to Commission decision-making,
    was only marginally involved in internal Commission deliberations over Safe
    Harbor until the last stages of discussion.
27 Interview with US negotiator, 18 September 2000.
28 Ibid.
29 Interview with TACD member, 25 September 2000.
30 Interviews with privacy advocates. See also the comments of Marc Rotenberg, exec-
    utive director of EPIC, available at www.epic.org/privacy/consumer/hr4678
    testimony_92402.html.
31 Interview with TACD member, 25 September 2000.

References

Bennett, C. J. (1992), *Regulating Privacy: Data Protection and Public Policy in Europe
    and the United States*, Ithaca, NY: Cornell University Press.
Bignami, F. and S. Charnovitz (2001) 'Transatlantic Civil Dialogues', in Pollack and
    Shaffer (eds), *Transatlantic Governance in the Global Economy* .
Cowles, M. G. (2001), 'The Transatlantic Business Dialogue: Transforming the New
    Transatlantic Dialogue', in Pollack and Shaffer (eds), *Transatlantic Governance in
    the Global Economy*.
European Commission (1995), 'Directive on the Protection of Individuals with
    Regard to the Processing of Personal Data and on the Free Movement of Such
    Data', 95/46/EC.
Farrell, H. (2002), 'Negotiating Privacy across Arenas: The EU–US "Safe Harbor"
    Discussions', in A. Héritier (ed.), *Common Goods: Reinventing European and
    International Governance*, Lanham, MD: Rowman and Littlefield.
_____ (2003), 'Constructing the International Foundations of E-commerce: The
    EU–US Safe Harbor Arrangement', *International Organization*, 57: 277–306.
Froomkin, A. M. (2000), 'The Death of Privacy?', *Stanford Law Review*, 52:
    1462–543.
Knauss, J. and D. Trubek (2001), 'The Transatlantic Labor Dialogue: Minimal Action
    in a Weak Structure', in Pollack and Shaffer (eds), *Transatlantic Governance in the
    Global Economy*.
Kobrin, S. J. (2002), 'The Trans-Atlantic Data Privacy Dispute: Territorial Jurisdiction
    and Global Governance', unpublished paper, Wharton School, University of Penn-
    sylvania.
Mayer-Schönberger, V. (1997), 'Generational Development of Data Protection in
    Europe', in P. E. Agre and M. Rotenberg (eds), *Technology and Privacy: The New
    Landscape*, Cambridge, MA: MIT Press.
Pollack, M. and G. Shaffer (eds) (2001), *Transatlantic Governance in the Global
    Economy*, Lanham, MD: Rowman and Littlefield.

Regan, P. M. (1999), 'American Business and the European Data Protection Directive: Lobbying Strategies and Tactics', in C. Bennett and R. Grant (eds), *Visions of Privacy: Policy Choices for the Digital Age*, Toronto: University of Toronto Press.

White House (2000), 'Fact Sheet: Data Privacy Accord with EU (Safe Harbor)', Washington DC: White House Office of the Press Secretary.

7   *Diahanna L. Post*[1]

Regulating biotech foods: government institutions and public reactions

Test after rigorous scientific test has proven these products [genetically modified food] to be safe. Sound science must trump passion. (US Secretary of Agriculture Dan Glickman)[2]

[Genetic engineering] takes mankind into realms that belong to God and to God alone . . . Even the best science cannot predict the unpredictable. (Prince Charles)[3]

Introduction

Food – genetically modified or otherwise – differs in many respects from the other sectors covered in this volume. Food is a basic part of our daily existence. It is bound up with cultural meanings and interpretations. Different cultures have quite different preferences for foods. Take for instance the British love of marmite, which most Americans detest, and the American love of peanut butter, which few other cultures seem to appreciate as much. Food technology has the same ambivalent reaction: Americans have eaten beef raised using growth hormones for years, but the same technology is banned throughout the European Union. As the quotations above illustrate, when it comes to explaining the differences in regulation of genetically modified food, there is no simple answer.

This chapter delves into why the issue of genetically modified food is so complex, why the public on both sides of the Atlantic appear to want different things, and why a formal resolution or compromise is so elusive. The focus of the chapter is on institutional reasons for the differing regulations, because this aspect has been under-studied relative to analyses of cultural, economic and social forces which have appeared in academic and popular-media accounts. The goal is to probe the assumptions underlying American and European regulatory structures and, rather than seeking to answer the question of the optimal regulatory structure for genetically modified foods, to give the reader the tools to ask 'how could it be otherwise?' This treatment responds to the complexity of the current situation, which is unlikely to witness either the disappearance of biotech crops in the United States or a sudden reversal of the European position for strict regulation.

The chapter is divided into four sections. The first section describes how genetically modified crops are regulated in the US and in the EU. Next, the appearance of biotech foods on the trade agenda and the trade impact of regulatory divergence are examined. The third section presents some possible explanations for why the regulatory structure differs so substantially across the Atlantic. Finally, two potential scenarios are explored for how the differences could play out. One is to bring the dispute before the WTO; the other is an attempt by the US to implement a tracking system for crops for European and worldwide markets.

Comparing regulatory frameworks

Although genetic modification of plants is not a new practice, manipulation at the level of DNA is. Since the late nineteenth century, scientists and farmers have been cross-breeding plants that each have desirable characteristics, such as disease resistance, in order to produce a crop that contains the characteristics of both plants. This conventional breeding process usually takes thousands of crossings and up to fifteen years to discover if the breeding successfully imparted the desired characteristics (Pollack, 2001). Genetic engineering of crops bypasses this tedious process by selecting a particular gene with desired characteristics – for instance, a gene from the Bt bacterium (*Bacillus thuringiensis*) that instructs plant cells to produce a toxin poisonous to some insects – and inserting that gene directly into plant cells. In addition, scientists also insert a 'marker' gene, by which they are able to tell whether a plant cell has successfully taken up the Bt gene.[4]

Most genetically modified (GM) crops on the market today, including soy, corn, cotton and canola (rape-seed), are modified to produce toxins that kill insect pests or make them resistant to weed-killing herbicides (Brown, 2001). Crops that are either still in experimental stages or not yet widely planted include those engineered to produce vitamins (such as 'golden' vitamin A-enhanced rice), vaccinations, and other nutritional and/or medical enhancements. Food crops that have been genetically engineered, such as corn, soy, and canola, are used in a wide variety of processed foods and oils.

The current frameworks for regulating genetically modified food in the European Union and the United States are derived from different answers to the question of why regulation is needed in this area. In the mid-1980s, both EU and US officials sought to address whether they already possessed sufficient legal authority to regulate biotechnology, or whether new legislation was needed.[5] Their answers shaped the subsequent form of regulations. In the EU, biotechnology came to be regarded as a unique and new form of agricultural technology, which required new legislative authority to regulate. As the European Commission Directorate General for the Environment argued,

'Biological barriers are by-passed and new organisms are created with novel properties not previously existing in nature' (European Commission, n.d., cited in Patterson and Josling, 2002). The European Council established new regulatory authority in the Deliberate Release Directive in 1990 and revised it in 2001 (European Council, 1990 and 2001). The Deliberate Release Directive is the primary legislation governing genetic engineering in the European Union.

In the United States, by contrast, the 1986 framework document for biotechnology regulation indicated that 'the recently developed methods [of genetic engineering] are an extension of traditional manipulations that can produce similar or identical products' (Office of Science and Technology Policy, 1986). In other words, genetic engineering was similar to other technologies and therefore it was not necessary to adopt new legislation to establish regulatory authority. The US framework document divides regulatory responsibility among three agencies: the US Department of Agriculture (USDA) oversees the safety of growing transgenic plants; the Environmental Protection Agency (EPA) evaluates microbial and plant pesticides; and the Food and Drug Administration (FDA) controls the safety of human consumption of biotechnologically derived food products. Each of these agencies possesses the authority to regulate under pre-existing statutes.[6]

The remainder of this section compares EU and US policies governing genetically modified foods in three areas: the authority to conduct field trials of modified crops; rules on marketing crops including labelling of food and the ability to trace food back through all stages of production, marketing, and ingestion; and feed for animals and seeds. Table 7.1 summarizes the policies governing each of these areas.

Field Trials

When a crop is deemed ready to move out of a controlled laboratory environment, researchers seek to conduct a field trial to see how that crop performs in the field. Because the field trial is the first time that a genetically engineered crop is released into the environment, regulators generally are concerned about protecting nearby conventional crops from pollen of genetically engineered plants as well as the potential for modified plants to mate with wild relatives and produce 'super-weeds'.

The European Deliberate Release Directive provides for a case-by-case review of risks to human health and the environment for each crop that is proposed for a field trial. Applicants who wish to conduct field tests of genetically modified organisms, or GMOs, are required to apply and submit a complete environmental-risk assessment – including identifying and evaluating any adverse effects of the crop to both human health and the environment – to the appropriate regulatory agency of the country where testing will occur. If the regulatory agency in the Member State approves the field trial, then it may proceed. Although this decision takes place entirely at the member-state level,

Table 7.1   Overview of EU and US policies toward genetically engineered food

Issue area	EU	US
Field trials	Permit issued on a case-by-case assessment	Permit issued on a case-by-case assessment, but most genetically modified crops are exempted from the permit procedures
Commercialization	Approval of the European Commission on a case-by-case basis; moratorium by environment ministers on any new approvals is in effect from 1999	Companies wishing to market crops petition to remove them from regulatory oversight unless they contain pesticides
Labelling	Currently mandatory to label products that contain genetically modified organisms; proposals to extend the range of products that must be labelled are under review	Voluntary guidelines for labelling foods as not produced through the use of biotechnology
Tracking	Mandatory 'traceability' system throughout the production and distribution chain for the purposes of monitoring environmental impacts and withdrawing unsafe products	Proposed 'process verification' system for the purposes of separating value-enhanced crops
Feed for animals	Labelled and subject to traceability system	Subject to same safety review as for any other use
Seeds	Labelled and subject to traceability system	Subject to same safety review as for conventional seeds

the Member State must also send notification to the European Commission of its decision, and the Commission in turn informs other Member States of the field trial. Additional precautions made mandatory in the 2001 revision of the directive also provide for monitoring of the long-term effects of interactions between genetically modified crops and the environment.

In the United States, the US Department of Agriculture regulates the field-testing of genetically engineered crops. In 1997, USDA relaxed its oversight over field tests and allowed certain modified crops to be field-tested without a permit (USDA, 1997). Such crops include those that do not produce pesticides such as *Bacillus thuringiensis* (Bt), and that are not related to noxious weeds. When crops meet these criteria, companies are requested to notify the USDA in advance about the conduct of the field test, and provide results afterward.

The EPA issues permits for field tests for plants that are engineered to produce their own pesticides, such as the Bt crops mentioned above (US EPA, 2001a, b, c). In the lenient regulatory atmosphere set by USDA, EPA's effort to assert jurisdiction over these plant pesticides was quite controversial, and in fact took several years to complete because of concerns that the agency was attempting to regulate the entire plant, and not just the pesticide within the plant. Under the regulations, EPA registers the pesticides under the Federal Insecticide, Fungicide, and Rodenticide Act and sets tolerances, or exempts the pesticides from tolerances under the Federal Food, Drug, and Cosmetic Act. Certain categories of 'low-risk' plants are exempted from oversight. EPA also requires that farmers planting Bt corn also plant a buffer zone of traditional corn to dilute the Bt corn pollen as a way of protecting monarch butterflies and other insects (Yoon, 2000).

But changes to the US regulatory requirements seem likely. In January, 2004, the USDA office of Animal and Plant Health Inspection Service initiated a potentially major overhaul of US rules, including a proposal to categorize field trials by the level of risk they pose (FCN, 2004a). One important component of the proposal was measures to reduce accidental contamination of conventional crops with GM varieties, a concern which had prompted previous efforts to tinker with the system (Office of Science and Technology Policy, 2002).

Commercialization

The thorniest issue in the US–EU controversy over genetically engineered crops concerns regulations governing large-scale planting and marketing of such crops. There are three aspects to commercialization: marketing modified crops and products containing modified crops; labelling of such products; and tracking modified crops throughout the food chain.

Marketing   The European Council Deliberate Release Directive requires that companies wishing to sell genetically modified crops notify the Member State where the product is to be marketed for the first time. The Member State has the power to reject the notification and terminate the marketing application. If, on the contrary, the Member State approves the application, the next step is to send the report of approval to the European Commission, which in turn forwards it to all other Member States. Approval for marketing requires that all Member States and the Commission agree. If another Member State or the Commission presents 'reasoned objections' (Article 15), then the Commission convenes a committee of Member-State representatives to decide the outcome. Approvals are made for a period of up to ten years; products approved under the 1990 Deliberate Release Directive are due for renewal of consent in 2006.

Under the Deliberate Release Directive one variety of genetically engineered corn and one of soybean have been authorized. Because the directive covers genetically engineered crops but not food derived from them, the European Parliament in 1997 adopted the Novel Foods Regulation (European Council, 1997) governing the marketing of food containing genetically engineered ingredients. Similar to requirements under the Deliberate Release Directive, under the Novel Foods Regulation companies must first apply to a Member State, which then communicates to the Commission and via the Commission to other Member States its assessment of the application. If there are objections among any Member States to the marketing of the product, the Novel Foods Regulation provides for consultations between the Commission and its scientific and regulatory committees. Ultimately, the Commission is supposed to make the final decision.

A streamlined approval process is outlined for products that are derived from genetically engineered ingredients but no longer contain the GMOs. These can be permitted as 'substantially equivalent' to their conventional counterparts. In these cases, authorization from the original Member State allows the marketing of this product, and the European Commission simply notifies other states of this fact. Several varieties of vegetable oils and a few other products have been accepted under this provision (ENDS, 2002c).

Despite the existence of these rules for approving the marketing of products containing genetically modified ingredients, since 1998 a moratorium has existed on the approval of any new GMOs. The moratorium was acknowledged openly in June 1999 by the environment ministers of the Member States (ENDS, 1999). The countries supporting the ban – including France, Austria, Luxembourg, Denmark, Greece and Italy – cited a need for EU-wide rules on labelling and tracking of food containing genetically modified ingredients, discussed below, before lifting it. The European Commission has criticized the ban increasingly loudly over the years, with health and agriculture commissioners calling on governments to 'show leadership' and allow new products to be approved (ENDS, 2001b). What the Commission has been most concerned about is a legal challenge to the ban in the WTO (ENDS, 2002b). These fears were confirmed in May 2003 when the US did file a formal challenge, discussed in the final section.

The approval of new EU rules on labelling and traceability, discussed below, was supposed to lead to the end of the moratorium and also to annul the US case in the WTO (FCN, 2004b). But agriculture ministers meeting at the end of April 2004 failed once again to muster the necessary votes for approval of the GM crop on their agenda. The only country to switch its vote from upholding the moratorium to supporting the approval of the GM crop was Italy; none of the remaining moratorium supporters changed their minds (FCN, 2004c). The European Commission, however, interpreted the rules of the Deliberate Release Directive as granting it discretion to intervene, and in May 2004 voted to approve the crop, a corn produced by Syngenta (ENDS, 2004). This ended the moratorium, but shortly after, member states were unable to agree on approving petitions for another GM corn and rapeseed, again leaving the decisions up to the Commission. In the face of this still-evolving EU position on GM crops, the US has maintained its opposition to the EU policies (FCN, 2004).

In the United States, USDA governs the commercial planting of modified crops and FDA regulates the marketing of food containing genetically modified organisms. Companies that have successfully completed field tests and otherwise demonstrated that a modified plant does not present a risk to the environment can petition the USDA to remove the plant from regulatory oversight. The USDA generally grants these petitions. Thus, once field tests have been conducted, modified crops are treated as identical to conventional crops in terms of safeguards for planting them.

Regulatory authority to market a food that contains genetically modified organisms falls under the jurisdiction of the FDA. The FDA is guided by its principle that 'The regulatory status of a food, *irrespective of the method by which it is developed*, is dependent upon objective characteristics of the food' (FDA, 1992; emphasis added). In other words, whether biotechnology is used in producing a food is not relevant to the FDA; rather, it is the characteristics of the end-product – the food – itself. Under the FDA's policy, foods produced through biotechnology are scrutinized under the same standard used to examine the safety of conventional foods. FDA's policy also provides for procedures for companies to voluntarily consult with and notify FDA before bringing foods to market, based on the recognition that the biotechnology companies wish for 'strong but appropriate oversight' (FDA, 1992: 22984). According to the FDA, the voluntary consultation process has been completed by all of the companies currently marketing food containing genetically engineered ingredients in the United States (Levitt, 2000). The FDA has proposed making these voluntary consultations mandatory (FDA, 2001a), but the issuance of final rules has been delayed for over three years while a new regulatory approach is considered (USDA 2004).

Labelling   Labelling of foods containing genetically engineered ingredients is mandatory in the European Union. Prior to 2004, several different regulations covered labelling, including the Novel Foods Regulation and separate regulations designed to provide for the labelling of the corn and soy varieties approved under the Deliberate Release Directive and for the labelling of additives or flavourings that contain genetically engineered ingredients (European Council, 1998a, 2000a, b). In 2004, the rules were significantly tightened when a comprehensive set of guidelines on labelling and traceability agreed upon in 2003 went into force (European Council, 2003a). For instance, all food, including vegetable oils made from GM crops such as soy, must now be labelled as containing genetically modified ingredients. Previously, the vegetable oils and other products that are derived from genetically engineered ingredients but contain no trace of those ingredients did not have to be labelled if they were 'substantially equivalent' to the conventional counterpart.

One of the biggest issues in developing the new EU guidelines was about thresholds: first, the threshold at which a food is considered to contain genetically engineered ingredients, and second, the threshold at which accidental contamination by non-approved genetically engineered varieties is allowed to occur. The first threshold acknowledges that conventional crops can, although unintended, become mixed with some genetically engineered crops during processing. The question then becomes at what point should a product derived from conventional ingredients be labelled as containing GMOs? The European Parliament and Council agreed on a threshold of 0.9 per cent, that is, 'the presence of GM material in conventional food does not have to be labelled if it is below 0.9 per cent and if it can be shown to be adventitious and technically unavoidable' (European Commission, 2004). The second threshold recognizes that some imported food products may contain trace amounts of genetically engineered ingredients approved in the exporting country but not yet approved in the European Union. The Council of Ministers battled with the European Parliament, which had proposed a zero-tolerance threshold, but ultimately they agreed that when products contain less than 0.5 per cent of unapproved GM material, they may still be sold on the EU market (FCN, 2003a).

The United States Food and Drug Administration also addresses food labelling, but in a very different manner. In its 1992 Statement of Policy, FDA calls for labelling only if food 'differs significantly from its conventional counterpart'. Hardly any food containing biotech ingredients has been labelled under this policy.[7] In 2001, the FDA proposed a new policy for voluntary labelling of food that is not genetically modified (Food and Drug Administration, 2001b). The FDA encourages statements that a product is not made using biotechnology, rather than statements that a product is free of genetically engineered food because, it maintains, the latter is virtually impossible to verify. Terms such as 'GM free' and 'modified' are not permitted in the draft guidelines; 'derived through biotechnology' and 'bioengineered' are acceptable. As with the proposal to make voluntary consultations mandatory, final confirmation of this proposal has been delayed for more than three years. The forthcoming regulatory changes being considered by USDA (2004) may well change this proposal for voluntary labelling.

Tracking   Tracking food throughout the production chain is essential to being able to label food as containing genetically engineered ingredients. Thus tracking and labelling are tightly linked. Traceability is the term used in the European Union to refer to a system or systems for tracking a genetically engineered product back through the production and distribution chains. In the United States, segregation and identity preservation refer to similar types of tracking system.

Along with its labelling guidelines, the EU adopted far-reaching, mandatory traceability regulations in 2003. The traceback system has three goals: to allow proper labelling to be verified; to monitor potential effects on the environment; and to be able to withdraw products that pose a threat to human health or the environment (European Commission, 2004). The guidelines require that information be collected at each stage of production and distribution on the particular type of genetically modified organism contained in the food, its characteristics, and where and from whom it was obtained. This includes a register of businesses that have bought genetically modified seed. These data should be stored for five years.

The United States in 2002 proposed developing an industry-funded, voluntary system to keep track of genetically engineered crops (US Department of Agriculture, 2002a). Currently, the vast majority of genetically modified crops grown in the United States are treated as being equivalent to conventional crops, and therefore they are generally not separated out from conventional crops. The stated rationale behind the proposed tracking system is to be able to differentiate 'value-enhanced' commodities – that is, next-generation biotechnology crops that may be nutritionally enhanced, lower in fat, and so on – from their conventional counterparts and from the non-genetically modified crops for the European and worldwide markets that demand them. This proposal is discussed in the final section of this chapter.

Seeds and feed

The EU has promulgated two separate initiatives to regulate genetically modified seeds and animal feed that contains genetically modified ingredients. Genetically engineered seeds must be approved under the Deliberate Release Directive like any other bioengineered product (European Council, 1998b), labelled, and comply with the traceback regulations. In addition, the European Commission plans to issue new rules for unintentional contamination of conventional seeds by bioengineered seeds in the near future (European Commission, 2004).

Under the EU regulations on animal feed, a genetically modified organism is either approved jointly for both food and feed or not approved at all. In other words, a food cannot be approved for use in animal feed without simultaneously being approved for use in human food. The approval is made for a period of ten years. Feed containing genetically modified ingredients is also subject to the traceability system (European Council, 2003b).

In the US, regulations governing animal feed changed after the *Starlink* corn controversy in 2000. *Starlink*, the brand name of a particular strain of Bt-producing corn, was approved by the EPA for use in animal feed only. EPA did not, however, permit *Starlink* in human food because of concerns about potential, although unlikely, allergic reactions. Nevertheless, in 2000, processed foods containing the *Starlink* variety showed up on supermarket shelves and in fast food eateries, although no adverse health effects were claimed or documented. As a result, EPA stopped issuing approvals for animal feed or industrial uses separately and now runs a joint-or-nothing approval system. In other words, current policies either approve genetically modified commodities jointly for human and animal consumption or do not approve them at all. There are no separate regulations governing seeds of genetically engineered crops.

Biotech foods on the trade agenda

The most visible effect of these differentiated regulatory policies has been the spread of biotech crops in the US, on the one hand, and their pariah status in the EU on the other. The EU has approved licences for sixteen genetically modified food crops, but no new GMOs have been approved since 1998 due to the moratorium. Twenty-four applications for GMOs, including nine for GM crops, are pending in the European Commission (European Commission, 2004). In the US, on the other hand, at least forty food crops containing genetic alterations have been approved for sale, from papayas to potatoes to squash (Biotechnology Industry Organization, 2003). The United States grows 68 per cent of the global total of genetically engineered crops, followed by Argentina, Canada and China, which together account for 99 per cent of all GM crops grown worldwide (ISAAA, 2002). In 2001, more than a quarter of all corn and more than two-thirds of all soy planted in the United States were of a genetically engineered variety. In 2002, those numbers increased by one-third and one-tenth, respectively (USDA National Agricultural Statistics Service, 2002).

Corn and soy are the two crops for which the trade implications of the vastly different regulatory approaches are most obvious, and on which this section focuses. They are two of the major food crops planted in the US and are used widely in all types of processed food as well as animal feed. Some varieties of GM corn and soy used in the US have been approved for use in the EU, but others have not.

While the drop in exports of corn has been precipitous, from $305 million in 1996 to $1 million in 1999 (McNeil, 2000), overall the EU represents a small fraction of the US export market for corn. A USDA Economic Research Service report issued in 2000 in fact pointed out that the pre-biotech value of trade in corn was simply not very high for the United States compared to that for other markets in East Asia (Ballenger et al., 2000). Moreover, most of the corn produced in the US is used domestically, at a rate of approximately 80 per cent in 1998/99. Prior to the biotechnology disputes, only about 4 per cent of the exported corn went to European Union countries. Once the moratorium took place, US exports of corn to the European Union fell to only 1 per cent of all corn exported from the US.

Soy presents a different case. According to the USDA's Economic Research Service, exports play a more important role in the market for soy than for corn (Ballenger et al., 2000). More than 40 per cent of US-produced soy is shipped abroad, and of this the European Union purchases about one-third.

Unlike corn, however, the biotech soybeans grown in the US as of 2000 were commercially approved in the EU. Although American soybean exports to the EU fell from $2.6 billion to $1 billion in 1999, this was due more to cheaper soy available from Brazil than to an opposition to GM soy. Indeed, in 2002, US soy exports reached record levels (US Department of Agriculture, 2002a), in part because of an increased demand abroad for soy in animal feed, which in turn stems from efforts in the wake of the BSE[8] crisis to remove meat and bone meal from animal feed (ENDS, 2001a).

In contrast to exporters of whole-grain corn and soybean, the trade implications for processed-food companies are less clear. Labelling rules in the EU have led some companies to drop biotech ingredients for fear that consumers will steer clear of items labelled as containing GMOs. In 2000, Gerber, Heinz, Bestfoods and Frito-Lay all announced that they would cease using biotech inputs in at least some of their products (Lin et al. 2000).

But more broadly speaking, the moratorium on approvals of GM crops has thus far not had a tremendous impact on either plantings or exports of US biotech crops. Moreover, European farmers are not benefiting from the reduction in US imports: the crops that the EU has ceased to import from the US are simply being replaced with non-GM imports from other countries. A protectionist motive, then, is not obvious. The row over genetically modified foods lacks the characteristics of many other trade disputes between the EU and the US. Why is it even on the agenda at all?

From the US perspective, biotech foods are on the trade agenda primarily due to concerns about the potential future impact of regulatory differences. First, the US is concerned about how European regulations could affect future generations of biotechnology crops. The Biotechnology Industry Organization, a trade association based in Washington, DC, touts consumer benefits ranging from non-allergenic peanuts to vitamin-A enhanced rice as up-and-coming possibilities for genetic engineering of food (Biotechnology Industry Organization, 2003). Proponents of biotechnology envision consumers clamouring for these next-generation benefits, but claim that the current European regulatory regime casts suspicion on them. Second, the various European proposals for very low tolerance levels of any genetically-modified ingredients in non-biotech imported food may be quite difficult to meet. Finally, not only the US but also biotechnology firms in the European Union are worried about the stringent regulations and the impact they will have on future development of the biotech industry in Europe.

The main reason that genetically modified foods are on the US–EU agenda, however, is the reaction of the public in various European countries to biotechnology in food. The visceral and strong reaction of the public in a number of European countries contrasted with that of the American public, which has remained relatively complacent about the existence of genetically modified food despite well-publicized events such as the *Starlink* corn episode. During the late 1990s, public outcry over the effects of genetically modified food spread across much of Europe. Officials in the UK established a cabinet-level committee to look into the effects of 'Frankenstein foods', as genetically modified organisms or GMOs are commonly referred to in the British press (Urry and Parker, 1998). Pictures of a 'Frankenstein potato' appeared on the pages of *The Economist* (*The Economist*, 1999a, b). In Germany, where over 80 per cent of the public expressed a negative opinion of GMOs (Jacob, 1998), the Social Democrats considered introducing a law to ban the use of genetically modified yeast in brewing beer (Atkins, 1998). Food writers also launched a campaign against GMOs, calling genetic engineering the equivalent of 'imposing a genetic experiment on the public, which could have unpredictable and irreversible adverse consequences' (Houlder, 1999).

Most officials who deal with biotechnology on both sides of the Atlantic believe that biotech foods are here to stay. As a result, when contemplating the future of agricultural biotechnology, they are very wary of public outcry. Again, this is quite a different situation from most other EU–US trade issues, which are less about public reactions and more about how businesses are affected.

Explaining regulatory differences

A number of authors have explored the reasons behind these regulatory differences in the EU and the US. Differences in culture and in the underlying, fundamental beliefs of policy-makers about the uses and potential concerns of biotech foods compared to traditional foods are one set of explanations offered (Echols, 2001; Pollack and Shaffer, 2001; Ramjoué, 2004). Vogel suggests that in fact we may be seeing the emergence of a new culture of risk regulation among European policy-makers. Other authors have pointed to how differences in both cultural norms and policy-making processes combine to produce different outcomes (McNichol and Bensedrine, 2003); to how coalitions are motivated by both public outrage and actors pursuing their own self-interest (Meins, 2000); and to how prior institutional choices constrained policy-makers on both sides of the Atlantic (Patterson and Josling, 2002).

On top of the factors listed above, it is also important to explore the European consumer reaction to the introduction of genetically modified foods, which as noted above is one of the driving forces that placed GM foods on the transatlantic trade agenda. The remainder of this section examines the myth that consumer reaction in the European Union is monolithically opposed to genetically engineered foods, and proposes two institutional explanations for the vehement public reaction in Europe.

Are European consumers completely opposed to genetically modified foods? Research conducted in a project on Public Perceptions in Agricultural Biotechnology (PABE) rejected the popular notion that European consumers are simply anti-biotech (Marris et al., 2001). One particular episode shows that the British public, at least, has been willing to buy a product containing genetically engineered ingredients. Zeneca, the British manufacturer of a tomato paste containing genetically engineered ingredients, spent an enormous amount of time communicating and preparing the public for the marketing of its product in British supermarkets in 1996. Zeneca labelled its paste as containing 'genetically altered tomatoes'. Two large UK supermarket chains touted the product as 'a world-first opportunity to taste the future' (cited in Charles, 2001: 168). The tomato paste cost less than the conventional brand, and proved to be very popular among the shoppers even though the product was labelled as containing GMOs. Thus consumers accepted a product labelled GMO prior to the outcry that characterized the late 1990s.

What, then, has led to the perceived anti-biotech reaction of European consumers? One explanation can be found in how genetically engineered foods were introduced onto the market in the mid-1990s. This has roots in both government regulation and private-sector behaviour. The PABE project found that consumers felt that they were not sufficiently informed about the foods or about how steps were taken to assess the risks. While the BSE crisis and timing played into the public's awareness of food-safety issues, the PABE report indicates that sources of mistrust lie much deeper in general misgivings about how experts and regulators balance public welfare against other competing concerns.

Moreover, consumers in Europe reacted strongly to what they perceived as an aggressive approach taken by Monsanto to marketing genetically engineered food in Europe. Monsanto is the US-based firm which is the major supplier of genetically modified seeds in the United States. Daniel Charles in *Lords of the Harvest* argues that Monsanto did not appreciate the differences in regulatory climate and attitude toward biotech food between the EU and the US (Charles, 2001: 100–1). Exports from the US arrived on markets with very little advance notice and no provisions in Europe for labelling it. The arrival of GM soy and corn from the United States at the end of 1996 and the beginning of 1997 attracted considerable media attention and significantly increased public awareness and concern throughout Europe, even in countries where the issues surrounding GM foods had previously attracted little public discussion, such as Spain and Italy. Zeneca tomato-paste sales suffered as a ban on GM foods was announced by numerous British supermarkets. The result of the US exports was a marked shift in views about risk assessment by regulatory authorities in a number of EU Member States. In response to public protests, both France and Britain began to include the effects of agricultural practices in their risk assessments. British newspapers called Monsanto the 'Frankenstein food giant' and the 'biotech bully boy'.

In addition to how biotech foods were introduced on the market, another explanation for anti-biotech sentiment among the European public is that openings in the political opportunity structure at the level of the European Union allowed NGOs to frame the issue of GMOs and encourage strong government action. Political opportunity structure refers to the political characteristics of the state which facilitate or deter the formation and main-tenance of social movements (McAdam et al., 1996). Changes in the rules of political institutions, at the national and supranational levels, can 'register, respond to and even shape the demands of social movements' (Kitschelt, 1986: 61–2).

In this case, structural changes at both the EU level and in some Member States facilitated opportunities for influence by European NGOs. First, the adoption of the Single European Act and the Maastricht Treaty on the Euro-pean Union strengthened the role and influence of the European Parliament, a body in which both Green Party members and European consumer and environmental organizations have been relatively influential (Bomberg, 1998: 40–2). The European Parliament represented an important source of pressure on both the European Council and the European Commission for more restrictive regulations on GM foods. Moreover in both Germany and Britain hearings were conducted on proposed legislation to regulate biotech-nology, which in turn provided an opportunity for both public participation and widespread media coverage (Levidow et al., 1999).

Second, the electoral strength of Europe's Green Parties also provided opportunities for NGOs. The German Green Party played a critical role in shaping German regulatory policies toward GMOs in the 1980s and by the late 1990s the Greens were represented in the governments of three Euro-pean countries, namely Germany, France and Belgium. They also enjoyed considerable representation and influence in the European Parliament. The efforts of European NGOs and the Green Party played a critical role both in raising public awareness of GMOs and in mobilizing political support for more restrictive regulatory policies in Europe.

European NGOs took full advantage of these openings in the political structure. In 1998, the European Bureau of Consumers' Unions, a Brussels-based federation of national consumer organizations from all the EU Mem-ber States, launched a major public campaign entitled 'Campaign for Consumer Choice'. It demanded strict labelling requirements that would enable consumers to choose whether or not to consume GM foods. (BEUC had earlier led a successful campaign to ban the use of growth hormones in beef.) Two other influential European NGOs, Friends of the Earth and Greenpeace, also waged highly visible public campaigns to pressure the EU to adopt stringent regulatory policies toward GMOs.

In the United States, conversely, political opportunities did not present themselves as easily, nor did NGOs jump into the debate over genetically modified food until much later than did their European counterparts. Dur-ing the 1980s when US regulatory policies were first being formulated, NGOs had other priorities, namely preventing the Reagan Administration from rolling back the enforcement of environmental laws. As a result, US reg-ulations toward GM foods and seed were adopted with virtually no public scrutiny: there were no Congressional debates or hearings, and there was not even a formal rule-making, just the issuance of the framework statement in 1986 by the White House. This helps account for the low level of public awareness of GM foods in the United States until the late 1990s.

Also, throughout much of the 1990s, American consumer and environmental groups were preoccupied with preventing the Republican-controlled Congress from repealing or weakening previously enacted environmental laws. They were hardly in a position to demand additional food-safety or environmental regulations, and even had they done so, they would have confronted a legislature controlled by a political party unsympathetic to their concerns. Numerous US NGOs, both large and small, have now made campaigning against genetically engineered foods a priority. But unlike in Europe, these efforts came relatively late: throughout the 1980s and the greater part of the 1990s, GMOs were simply not on the radar screen of American consumer and environmental organizations.

The differing emphases of NGOs on either side of the Atlantic is particularly striking in the face of past history of regulating public health risks. Research conducted on comparative regulation in the 1980s suggested that the United States was more likely to adopt stringent regulations than Great Britain or Germany, and this was due in part to more public access to information and decision-making procedures in the US (Brickman et al., 1985; Vogel, 1986). The opening of the political opportunity structure at the level of the European Union, coupled with a shift in focus of US NGOs, has contributed to the new 'European risk regime' (Vogel, 2004).

Unilateral and global paths toward resolution

The differences between attitudes in the EU and those in the US over genetic engineering, and particularly over genetic engineering of crops, have stimulated numerous efforts to reach agreement. Bilateral attempts at cooperation have included regulatory cooperation among agencies under the 1997 US–EU Mutual Recognition Agreement (see Steffenson, Chapter 8 in this volume), private- and public-sector transatlantic dialogues, and expert discussion through the EU–US Biotechnology Consultative Forum. None of these efforts has had a significant impact on resolving the regulatory tension (Patterson and Josling, 2002). The Organization for Economic Cooperation and Development has also served as a forum for discussion.

Current possibilities for resolution, however, have moved away from negotiations. In 2003, the US, joined by Canada and Argentina, initiated legal proceedings in the WTO against the EU, citing the European moratorium on approval of new GMOs as an illegal trade barrier. Hearings began in June 2004 and were not due to be completed until at least the end of the year. The US argues that 'the moratorium is inconsistent with the EC's obligations under the WTO Agreement' (US, 2004) and in particular violates the

WTO's Sanitary and Phytosanitary (SPS) Agreement because the approval procedures have led to an 'undue delay' in approving new GMOs. The US also contends that the EU moratorium is not based on a risk assessment, as is required under WTO rules (BRIDGES, 2004).

The US decision to take the case to the WTO was criticized on both sides of the Atlantic. The European Trade Commissioner denied the existence of a moratorium, and observers pointed to political pressure from Congress to explain why the White House decided to register its complaint to the WTO. Industry lobbyists also were not uniformly in favour of the case: the powerful Biotechnology Industry Organization in Washington expressed its preference for continuing to explore diplomacy options for resolving the tensions, rather than filing a WTO case (FCN, 2003b).

The outcome of the WTO proceedings could take several forms. On the one hand, the dispute resolution process may be rendered moot by the slow grinding of EU approvals for GM crops. The European Commission looked set to use its authority to override the deadlocked Council of Ministers on permitting GM crops. A steady flow of approvals would probably remove the rationale behind the US case. Yet this is not the only area where the US disagrees with EU policy, and in fact the US is already weighing whether to bring a separate WTO case against EU traceability and labelling rules (FCN, 2004d).

On the other hand, if the dispute resolution panel fulfills its task, and the US wins the case, the EU does not have to accept GM crops. First, if the EU loses, it may very well adopt the same remedy as it did in the WTO case over the use of growth hormones in beef: paying fines rather than changing its regulations (European Communities, 1999). Moreover, regardless of whether the US wins, threats and heavy-handed pressure from the US can only exacerbate the conditions that led to the situation in the first place: that members of the public across a range of EU Member States are suspicious of biotech foods, of the companies that bring them to market, and of the regulators that approve the process (Lofstedt, 2002). Attempting to resolve the differences through the WTO also fits into some European protests – such as the anti-McDonald's campaign in France – that lump US actions together with most negative aspects of globalization, including trade in genetically modified organisms.

The second path that may lead to at least an informal resolution of the trade tensions is the US government proposal to set up a voluntary system to track crops. At the urging of industry, the USDA offered a number of efforts to standardize the methods used to determine the presence of genetically modified crops in analyses of grains (USDA, 2002). It also proposed to set up voluntary systems of 'process verification' for seeds and bulk commodities that would track them throughout production and handling. The development of these systems is addressed primarily to processors seeking to separate out non-biotech crops for export (USDA, 2002a). Currently, the

US is considering a new round of biotech regulation (USDA, 2004), as dis-
cussed above. These new regulations hint that the regulatory agenda in the
US is, to some extent, being driven by concerns about the EU–US divergence
(Young, 2003).

Extensive technical and managerial changes will be needed to establish
such a system (Lin et al., 2000). Farmers must separate genetically engineered crops from conventional ones in crop plots at sufficient distances to
reduce pollen drift among the plants, and they must keep them separate at
harvest time and while storing and transporting them. Grain elevators will
likely need to make new investments, and their businesses are likely to see
slower turnover and reduced profits, at least initially, due to the difficulties
of keeping the crops segregated. Even if such a system is put in place, some
contamination will continue. Whether the low tolerance thresholds adopted
by the EU will pose a challenge to the separation remains to be seen. But if
such a system can be put into place and the tolerance threshold issue with the
European Union is resolved, this unilateral effort could go some way toward
reducing trade tensions between the EU and the US.

These unilateral and global paths toward resolution primarily address
the interests of the private sector in the US. US unilateral efforts to set up a
voluntary tracking system are motivated by industry desires to get their products to market in the EU, and will probably help resolve practical issues of
trade. But the tracking system does not address the continuing regulatory
divergence that is a source of tremendous concern for US officials. The WTO
dispute resolution is motivated by a desire to force the EU to lift its moratorium on GMOs, yet further outside imposition on the EU seems unlikely to
result in regulatory change. Neither pathway acknowledges the source of
public reaction to biotech foods – the widespread dissatisfaction with how
these foods have been introduced in Europe – nor do they recognize the
extent to which EU officials are tied by that public reaction (Levidow and
Marris, 2001).

The missing link in both of these potential resolutions is the concerns of
the European publics that have been so vocal about biotech foods. The
biotech food issue is different from other trade issues because of the participation of European publics. One potential solution that does address their
concerns is labelling. The downside to labelling, however, is substantial, for
two reasons. One, the costs to business of implementing the tracing system
that labelling would require would probably be quite high. Second, businesses are worried that any labelling of food as containing genetically modified ingredients will cause consumers to stay away from it. Nevertheless, any
valid arrangement for a long-term solution must recognize the concerns of
the European consumers.

Notes

1 This chapter draws on a conference paper co-authored with David Vogel. My grateful thanks to Michelle Egan, Javier Lezaun, Kate O'Neill and Gene Rochlin for helpful comments and insights.
2 Quoted in Urry (1997).
3 Quoted in Salman (1998).
4 This marker gene is often one that shields cells from being killed by an antibiotic or herbicide. The plant is then exposed to an antibiotic, and only cells with the inserted genes will survive the exposure. See Brown, 2001.
5 For in-depth discussion of the development of regulatory policies in the US and the EU, see Kraus, 1996 and Patterson, 1997.
6 These legislative acts are as follows: USDA regulates under the Federal Plant Pest Act, 7 USC 7B; EPA regulates under the Federal Insecticide, Fungicide, and Rodenticide Act, 7 USC 136, and the Federal Food, Drug, and Cosmetic Act, 21 USC 9; and the FDA regulates under the Federal Food, Drug and Cosmetic Act, 21 USC 9.
7 The only genetically engineered food to be labelled under this 1992 statement of policy was a canola (rapeseed) oil commercialised by Calgene containing lauric acid, which does not naturally occur in significant amounts in non-modified canola oil. Under FDA regulations, Calgene was required to label the product 'laurate canola oil'. Dr. Keith Redenbaugh, personal communication.
8 BSE stands for bovine spongiform encephalopathy. For a discussion of the case, see Jasanoff (1997).

References

Atkins, R. (1998), 'German Brewers in a Froth over Beer Purity', *Financial Times*, 3 June, 2.

Ballenger, N., M. Bohman and M. Gehlhar (2000), 'Biotechnology: Implications for US Corn and Soybean Trade', *Agricultural Outlook*, April, 24–8.

Becker, E. (2003), 'US Delays Suing Europe over Ban on Modified Food', *New York Times*, 5 February.

Biotechnology Industry Organization (2003), 'A World of Food and Agriculture: Biotechnology's Benefits', available at www.bio.org/foodag/brochure/cover.asp.

Bomberg, E. (1998), *Green Parties and Politics in the European Union*, London: Routledge.

Brickman, R., S. Jasanoff and T. Ilgen (1985), *Controlling Chemicals: The Politics of Regulation in Europe and the United States*, Ithaca, NY: Cornell University Press.

BRIDGES (2004), 'US Argues EC GMO Moratorium Hurts Developing Countries', *BRIDGES Weekly Trade News Digest*, 8:15, 28 April, available at www.ictsd.org [accessed 7 May 2004].

Brown, K. (2001), 'Seeds of Concern', *Scientific American*, April, 52–7.

Charles, D. (2001), *Lords of the Harvest: Biotech, Big Money, and the Future of Food*, Cambridge, MA: Perseus Publishing.

Echols, M. (2001), *Food Safety and the WTO: The Interplay of Culture, Science and Technology*, Boston: Kluwer Law International.

The Economist (1999a), 'Seeds of Discontent', 20 February, 75–7.

—— (1999b), 'Who's Afraid?' 19 June, 15–16.
ENDS Environment Daily (1999), 25 June.
—— (2001a), 30 January.
—— (2001b), 20 September.
—— (2002a), 3 July.
—— (2002b), 16 December.
—— (2002c), 19 December.
—— (2004), 19 May.
European Commission, DG XI/A/2 Biotechnology (no date), 'The European Community and the Contained Use of Genetically Modified Micro-organisms', Brussels.
—— (2002), 'Questions and Answers on the Regulation of GMOs in the EU', MEMO/02/160, 1 July, available at http://europea.eu.int/comm/press_room/index _en.htm.
European Commission (2004), 'Questions and Answers on the Regulation of GMOs in the EU'. MEMO/04/102, 30 April, available at http://europa.eu.int/comm/food /biotechnology/index_en.htm.
European Communities (1999), 'Measures Concerning Meat and Meat Products (Hormones)', Original Complaint by the United States, Recourse to Arbitrations by the European Communities under Articles 22.6 of the DSU, Decision by the Arbitrators, WT/DS26/ARB, Doc. No. 99–2855, 83–84 (12 July 1999), available at www.wto.org.
European Council (1990), Council Directive 90/220/EEC of 23 April 1990 on the deliberate release into the environment of genetically modified organisms.
—— (1997), Regulation (EC) 258/97 of the European Parliament and of the Council of 27 January 1997 concerning novel foods and novel food ingredients.
—— (1998a), Regulation (EC) 1139/98 of 26 May 1998 concerning the compulsory indication of the labelling of certain foodstuffs produced from genetically modi-fied organisms of particulars other than those provided for in Directive 79/112/ EEC.
—— (1998b), Council Directive 98/95/EC of 14 December 1998 amending, in respect of the consolidation of the internal market, genetically modified plant varieties and plant genetic resources, Directives 66/400/EEC, 66/401/EEC, 66/402/EEC, 66/403/EEC, 69/208/EEC, 70/457/EEC and 70/458/EEC on the marketing of beet seed, fodder plant seed, cereal seed, seed potatoes, seed of oil and fibre plants and vegetable seed and on the common catalogue of varieties of agricultural plant species.
—— (2000a), Regulation (EC) 49/2000 of 10 January 2000 concerning the compul-sory indication of the labelling of certain foodstuffs produced from genetically modified organisms of particulars other than those provided for in Directive 79/112/EEC.
—— (2000b), Regulation (EC) 50/2000 of 10 January 2000 on the labelling of food-stuffs and food ingredients containing additives and flavourings that have been genetically modified or produced from genetically modified organisms.
—— (2001a), Council Directive 2001/18/EC of 17 October 2002 on the deliberate release into the environment of genetically modified organisms.
—— (2001b), 'Proposal for a Regulation of the European Parliament and of the Council concerning traceability and labelling of genetically modified organisms

and traceability of food and feed products produced from genetically modified organisms and amending Directive 2001/18/EC', COM 2001–182 Final.

—— (2001c), 'Proposal for a Regulation of the European Parliament and of the Council on genetically modified food and feed', COM 2001–425 final.

—— (2003a), Regulation No. 1830/2003 of the European Parliament and of the Council of 22 September 2003 concerning the traceability and labelling of genetically modified organisms and the traceability of food and feed products produced from genetically modified organisms and amending Directive 2001/18/EC.

—— (2003b), Regulation (EC) 1829/2003 of the European Parliament and of the Council of 22 September 2003 on genetically modified food and feed.

FCN (2003a), 'European Parliament Accepts 0.9% Biotech Labeling Threshold', *Food Chemical News*, 7 July.

—— (2003b), 'EU Lashes out at U.S. Decision to File WTO Case against Biotech Moratorium', *Food Chemical News*. 19 May.

—— (2004a), 'USDA Seeks Comprehensive Overhaul of Biotech Regulations', *Food Chemical News*, 26 January.

—— (2004b), 'EU's Byrne Urges US to Allow Traceability Rules to Work', *Food Chemical News*, 29 March.

—— (2004c), 'EU Council of Ministers Fails to Approve Bt11 Corn Variety', *Food Chemical News*, 3 May.

—— (2004d), 'WTO Case against EU Labeling Regime Hangs Fire', *Food Chemical News*, 3 May.

—— (2004e), 'EU Lifts Moratorium but US Won't Drop WTO Case', *Food Chemical News*, 24 May.

FDA (1992), 'Statement of Policy: Foods Derived from New Plant Varieties', 57 FR 22984, 29 May.

—— (2001a), 'Premarket Notice concerning Bioengineered Foods', 66 FR 4706, 18 January.

—— (2001b), 'Voluntary Labelling Indicating Whether Foods Have or Have Not Been Developed Using Bioengineering', January 2001. Available at www.cfsan. fda.gov/~dms/biolabgu.html.

Houlder, V. (1999), 'Writers Sign up Against Modified Foods,' *Financial Times*, January 26, 7.

International Service for the Acquisition of Agri-biotech Applications (ISAAA) (2002), 'Global GM Crop Area Continues to Grow and Exceeds 50 Million Hectares for First Time in 2001', 10 January.

Jacob, R. (1998), 'Monsanto Research Finds Deep Hostility to GM Foods', *Financial Times*, 18 November, 10.

Jasanoff, S. (1997), 'Civilization and Madness: The Great BSE Scare of 1996', *Public Understanding of Science*, 6, 221–32.

Kitschelt, H. P. (1986), 'Political Opportunity Structures and Political Protest: Anti-Nuclear Movements in Four Democracies', *British Journal of Political Science*, 16, 57–85.

Kraus, M. (1996), 'Technology and Legal Systems: A Comparative Study of the Development and Regulation of Biotechnology in Germany and the United States', Department of Geography, UC-Berkeley, Berkeley, CA.

Levidow, L., S. Carr, and D. Wield (1999), 'Regulating Biotechnological Risk, Straining Britain's Consultative Style', *Journal of Risk Research*, 2: 3, 307–24.

—— and C. Marris (2001), 'Science and Governance in Europe: Lessons from the Case of Agricultural Biotechnology', *Science and Public Policy*, 28: 5, 345–60.

Levitt, J. (2000), Statement by Joseph A. Levitt, Director, Center for Food Safety and Applied Nutrition, Food and Drug Administration, Department of Health and Human Services, before the Health, Education, Labor and Pensions Committee, United States Senate, 26 September.

Lin, W., W. Chambers, and J. Harwood (2000), 'Biotechnology: US Grain Handlers Look Ahead', *Agricultural Outlook*, April, 29–34.

Lofstedt, R. (2002), 'Time to Sow Seeds of GM Harmony', *Independent*, 25 August, Business, 2.

Marris, C., B. Wynne, P. Simmons and S. Weldon (2001), 'Public Perceptions of Agricultural Biotechnologies in Europe', Final Report of the PABE Research Project funded by the Commission of European Communities, December 2001 [cited 11 June 2002]. Available at www.pabe.net.

McAdam, D., J. D. McCarthy, and M. Zald (1996), 'Introduction: Opportunities, Mobilizing Structures, and Framing Processes: Toward a Synthetic, Comparative Perspective on Social Movements', in D. McAdam, J. D. McCarthy and M. N. Zald (eds), *Comparative Perspectives on Social Movements: Political Opportunities, Mobilizing Structures, and Cultural Framings*, Cambridge: Cambridge University Press.

McNeil, D., Jr. (2000), 'Protest on New Genes and Seeds Grow More Passionate in Europe', *New York Times*, 14 March, A1.

McNichol, J. and Bensedrine J. (2003), 'Multilateral Rulemaking: Transatlantic Struggles Around Genetically Modified Food', in M. Djelic and S. Quack (eds), *Globalisation and Institutions: Re-Defining the Rules of the Economic Game*. Cheltenham: Edward Elgar (chapter 9).

Meins, E. (2000), 'Up or Down? Explaining the Stringency of Consumer Protection', *Swiss Political Science Review*, 6: 2, 94–9.

National Research Council (2000),*Genetically Modified Pest-Protected Plants: Science and Regulation*, Washington DC: National Academy Press.

Office of Science and Technology Policy (1986), 'Coordinated Framework for Regulation of Biotechnology', 51 FR 23302, 26 June.

—— (2002), 'Proposed Federal Actions To Update Field Test Requirements for Biotechnology Derived Plants and To Establish Early Food Safety Assessments for New Proteins Produced by Such Plants', 67 FR 50578, 2 August.

Patterson, L. A. (1997), 'Regulating Biotechnology in the European Union: Institutional Responses to Internal Conflict Within the Commission', Conference of the European Community Studies Association, Seattle, WA, 3–6 June.

—— and T. Josling (2002), *Regulating Biotechnology: Comparing EU and US Approaches*, Pittsburgh, PA: European Union Center, University of Pittsburgh.

Pollack, A. (2001), 'Gene Research Finds New Use in Agricultural Breeding', *New York Times*, 7 March.

Pollack, M. A. and G. Shaffer (2001), 'The Challenge of Reconciling Regulatory Differences: Food Safety and Genetically Modified Organisms in the Transatlantic Relationship', in M. A. Pollack and G. C. Shaffer (eds), *Transatlantic Governance in the Global Economy*, Lanham, MD: Rowman and Littlefield.

Ramjoué, C. (2002), 'Comparing Policy Paradigms: Genetically Modified Food Policy in the United States and the European Union', Conference of the European Association for the Study of Science and Technology, York, UK, 31 July–3 August.

Salman, S. (1998), 'Prince of Wales Speaks out on Genetic Foods', *London Times*, 8 June.

Urry, M. (1997), 'Genetic Products Row Worsens', *Financial Times*, 20 June, 4.

—— and G. Parker (1998), '"Enforcer" to Monitor GM Crops: Farming Cunningham Heads Committee to Monitor Tests on "Frankenstein Foods"', *Financial Times*, 22 October, 11.

US (2004), 'European Communities – Measures Affecting the Approval and Marketing of Biotech Products (WT/DS291, 292, and 293). Executive Summary of the First Submission by the United States', 30 April, available at www.insidetrade.com [accessed 7 May 2004].

USDA, Animal and Plant Health Inspection Service (1997), 'Genetically Engineered Organisms and Products: Simplification of Requirements and Procedures for Genetically Engineered Organisms', 62 FR 23945, 2 May.

——, Agricultural Marketing Service (2002a), 'Facilitating the Marketing of US Agricultural Products with New Testing and Process Verification Services', 67 FR 50853, 6 August.

—— (2002b) 'Outlook for US Agricultural Trade', AES-34, 31 May; and AES-36, 2 December. Available at http://usda.mannlib.cornell.edu/reports/erssor/trade/.

USDA National Agricultural Statistics Service (2002), Acreage, 28 June. Available at http://usda.mannlib.cornell.edu/reports/nassr/field/pcp-bba/.

—— Animal and Plant Health Inspection Service (2004), 'Environmental Impact Statement: Introduction of Genetically Engineered Organisms', 69 FR 3271, 23 January.

US EPA (2001a), 'Regulations under the Federal Insecticide, Fungicide, and Rodenticide Act for Plant-Incorporated Protectants (Formerly Plant-Pesticides)', 66 FR 37772, 19 July.

—— (2001b), 'Exemption from the Requirement of a Tolerance under the Federal Food, Drug, and Cosmetic Act for Residues of Nucleic Acids that are Part of Plant-Incorporated Protectants (Formerly Plant-Pesticides)', 66 FR 37817, 19 July.

—— (2001c), 'Exemption from the Requirement of a Tolerance under the Federal Food, Drug, and Cosmetic Act for Residues Derived Through Conventional Breeding from Sexually Compatible Plants of Plant-Incorporated Protectants (Formerly Plant-Pesticides)', 66 FR 37830, 19 July.

Vogel, D. (1986), *National Styles of Regulation: Environmental Policy in Great Britain and the United States*, Ithaca, NY: Cornell University Press.

—— (2004), 'The Politics of Risk Regulation in Europe and the United States', *The Yearbook of European Environmental Law*, 3 (January): 1–42.

Yoon, C. K. (2000), 'E.P.A. Announces New Rules on Genetically Altered Corn', *New York Times*, 17 January.

Young, A. R. (2003), 'Political Transfer and "Trading UP"? Transatlantic Trade in Genetically Modified Food and US Politics', *World Politics*, 55, July, 457–84.

8   *Rebecca Steffenson*[1]

Competing trade and regulatory strategies for the mutual recognition of conformity assessment in the transatlantic marketplace

Introduction

This chapter examines the EU–US Mutual Recognition Agreements (MRAs) as a key liberalization tool in the New Transatlantic Marketplace. The MRAs eliminate duplicate conformity-assessment procedures that require manufacturers to undergo multiple testing, inspection and certification of goods when they export products.[2] These duplicate control procedures, like diverging product requirements, form technical, non-tariff barriers to trade as they increase the costs faced by exporters, in terms both of time and resources, when selling their product in foreign markets. For example, a product with a twelve-month shelf life, such as a modem, loses one-twelfth of its expected revenue for every month it is held up by testing procedures (TIA, 2001).

The impact of different process requirements is most visible in the European Single Market where mutual recognition originally emerged as a strategy to facilitate the free movement of goods and services between the Member States in areas where harmonization had not occurred. The concept of mutual recognition was developed through the European Court of Justice's decision in the 'Cassis de Dijon' case, which overturned a German import ban on French liqueur. The ruling established that within reason producers and service providers who had complied with national requirements could sell their products or services in all of the other Member States. Mutual recognition became an important part of the EU–US strategy for regulatory cooperation in the 1990s under the New Transatlantic Agreement (NTA). EU–US relations in the 1990s contained a strong commitment to facilitating trade through the removal of non-tariff barriers to trade. Both the Commission and USTR consistently identify divergent conformity-assessment processes in their annual reports on barriers to trade. The Commission has complained about 'cumbersome' inspection and approval procedures used by US regulators, most notably the FDA in the case of pharmaceuticals and US Customs in the cases of food products. EU officials also argued against third-party certification, as opposed to manufacturers self-declaration of conformity-assessment in telecommunications and in electrical safety (European Commission, 2001).

USTR argued that the EU's sole acceptance of approval bodies located within the EU disadvantaged US companies. More specifically, it claimed that the EU policy of testing each batch of pharmaceuticals at the point of entry increased market costs, delaying market access for US manufacturers (USTR, 2002). In 1997, the EU and the US signed an overarching framework agreement with six sectoral annexes including telecommunications, medical devices, electromagnetic compatibility, electrical safety, recreational craft and pharmaceuticals (see Table 8.1).[3] Similar MRAs for professional-services sectors, including architecture, insurance and engineering, as well as new-goods sectors such as road safety, cosmetics and marine safety, were initiated with the Transatlantic Economic Partnership (TEP) in 1998. These agreements are of economic significance in the transatlantic relationship because they seek to eliminate redundant testing and certification costs affecting an estimated $180 billion of trade in goods and services.[4] In addition, they are arguably the most important deliverable produced by the NTA-TEP dialogue and a benchmark of EU–US regulatory cooperation. While the MRAs have introduced a degree of regulatory convergence into the transatlantic economic relationship, regulatory divergence is glaringly evident in a number of sectors, demonstrating the complexity of facilitating EU–US regulatory cooperation.

Table 8.1   The MRA annexes

MRA Umbrella Agreement (1997)	*New sectors (post-1998)*
Goods	*Goods*
Telecommunications	Road Safety
Medical devices	Cosmetics
Electromagnetic compatibility	Marine Safety (MRA +)
Electrical safety	*Services*
Recreational craft	Architecture
Pharmaceuticals	Engineering
	Insurance

The chief dilemma for policy-makers is how to facilitate trade at the transatlantic level when technical procedures for approving products are devised at the national and sometimes local level. This problem is most visible in the US where there are more than 2,700 state and municipal authorities that exercise regulatory authority. The Commission argues, for example, that different regulations produced by these authorities can account for as much as 15 per cent loss of sales for an individual company (European Commission, 2001). Furthermore, conformity-assessment procedures are shaped not only by market demands, which facilitate trade, but also by regulatory demands, which facilitate consumer health and safety in domestic constituencies. Given the competing interests of regulatory and trade mandates, convergence and divergence in the MRA negotiations is best understood through the roles played by different sets of actors – both private and public – at the domestic and international levels.

The chapter is organized with these different sets of actors in mind. The first section looks at the factors which explain regulatory convergence. It concentrates mainly on the role of trade officials in the EU and the US who facilitated the MRAs by negotiating the overarching framework agreement. Heavy emphasis is also placed on the role of the TABD, which closely followed the agreements, acting as a source of both technical support and political pressure. The following section turns to the factors that explain regulatory divergence. Here the impact of domestic regulatory agencies, consumer groups and national laboratories is discussed.

It is not just how these actors influenced the negotiations, but also the factors shaping their decisions that are relevant to the larger discussion on EU–US regulatory cooperation. The argument here is that a number of institutional and cultural similarities have allowed the EU and the US to pursue the MRAs. However, institutional differences have also acted as a source of regulatory divergence. In particular, the legal structure of the US regulatory system has precluded the possibility of MRAs in certain sectors. This system also empowers different regulatory agencies in the US, whose cultures of regulatory autonomy and regulatory superiority lead to the minimal application of mutual recognition in their respective sectors.

The MRAs as a force of regulatory convergence

The concept behind MRAs is summarized by the TABD's motto that products should be 'approved once, accepted anywhere in the transatlantic marketplace'.[5] However, the level of regulatory convergence to facilitate trade within MRAs is far less than in the case of other kinds of regulatory agreements. Unlike harmonization agreements, MRAs do not require regulators to alter and align domestic standards. Nor are the transatlantic agreements full-equivalency agreements, such as those found within the EU's single market, which allow regulators to approve products for export using the same standards applied in the domestic marketplace. Rather, the EU–US MRAs draw on mutual recognition only as a basic principle. What is mutually recognized is not foreign standards but the competency of foreign bodies to test and certify products. This means that firms still need to comply with two different sets of standards, but that the products do not need to be tested in two different markets and by two different sets of regulators. In short, the agreements impose a convergence of regulatory processes rather than regulatory standards. The MRAs constitute only limited transatlantic regulatory convergence. Nonetheless, the agreements represent a key trade strategy, advocated by both trade officials and business on both sides of the Atlantic, and they are an important step toward liberalizing the transatlantic marketplace.

This section concentrates on the factors that influenced policy-makers' decisions to pursue mutual recognition as a transatlantic regulatory strategy. As such, the emphasis is on those actors in the negotiation process with a demonstrated interest in facilitating trade. These include the Directorates General (DG) for Trade and Enterprise, who negotiated the overarching MRA framework for the European Commission, and the USTR and US Commerce Department who negotiated the agreement for the US. The influence of European and American firms, through the TABD, is also an important factor in MRA negotiations.

The EU's exportation of internal market opening strategies
The EU's interest in pursuing mutual recognition agreements with the US can only be understood in relation to developments within the single market. Though MRAs are embedded in international law in both the TBT Agreement and the GATS, the EU–US agreements are not the result of a WTO 'top down' strategy of liberalization. Rather, mutual recognition in the transatlantic marketplace is best explained as a 'spillover' from the European single market, where MRAs are most extensive and most developed (see also Nicolaïdis, 1997a and 1997b; Egan, 2001a and 2001b).[6]

More specifically, the transatlantic MRA agreements can be seen as an extension of the EU's new 'Global Approach' to the internal market (see also Egan, 2001a and 2001b). In 1990 the EU developed the CE mark, a product-certification stamp which assures acceptance of product assessment anywhere in the EU, with EU Member States retaining responsibility for monitoring testing-certification bodies. While mutual recognition within the EU ensures free movement of goods within the single market, it also alienates external trading partners because the CE mark requires conformity-assessment bodies to be located within the EU (Egan and Nicolaïdis, 2001: 464). However, the Global Approach gave the Commission negotiating authority from the Council to pursue external MRAs with the EU's trading partners.

The Commission's negotiating authority for external MRAs was based on the 'Model MRA' it presented to the Council (see also Steffenson, 2002). Its mandate limited the externalization of MRAs to trading partners with similar levels of regulatory competency and those sectors that were most likely to open markets and encourage deregulation. A number of agreements were initiated with the US, Canada, New Zealand, Australia and Japan, as these countries had the most compatible regulatory regimes and were likely to generate the most commercial interest. Since the US is the EU's largest trading partner, and transatlantic MRAs could save manufacturers an estimated 200 million euros a year, they were the most important MRAs for the Commission.[7]

The externalization of the EU's regulatory strategy can be viewed as both a normative and a strategic initiative (Nicolaïdis, 1997a, b). The EU is increasingly eager to export its internal policy models to external partners.

As a symbol of European integration, the externalization of mutual recognition fits into the broader European strategy of policy transfer (see also Steffenson, 2002). The Commission saw the external trade strategy as a way of using the EU's leverage to reduce technical barriers to trade in third-country markets (European Commission, 1996), and enjoyed a strong bargaining position in this area. It faced little opposition from the Member States in negotiating the agreements because mutual recognition had already been negotiated internally.[8]

The Commission was also able to shape the environment of the MRA negotiations by using 'first-mover advantage' (see Egan and Nicolaïdis, 2001). The model of the agreement and the MRA approval process is based on the Commission's internal MRA. The basic elements of the agreement including the 'umbrella' multi-sector agreement, the use of sector annexes, confidence-building periods and much of the language of the agreements is derived from the Model MRA.[9] In addition, the Commission also exported an institutional design for the agreements, establishing a process for the designation of procedures for mutual conformity assessment whereby European and American trade and regulatory actors were cooperated in Designating Authorities, Joint Committees and Joint Sectoral Committees (Table 8.2; see also Steffenson, forthcoming).

Table 8.2   The MRA institutions

Institution	Function
Designating Bodies	Monitor and Approve Private CABs
Joint Committee	Administrative and Dispute Resolution Forum
Joint Sectoral Committees	Technical Implementation

US interest in facilitating trade in the transatlantic marketplace

The Commission approached US regulatory agencies as early as 1992 to initiate the negotiation of MRAs, but faced strong opposition from some US domestic regulatory agencies. In particular the FDA argued from the start that the Commission's proposed strategy was inconsistent with its regulatory mandate. The negotiations remained deadlocked until the 'bottom-up' strategy – i.e., negotiations with individual regulatory agencies – was replaced with a new 'top-down' strategy. The 1995 New Transatlantic Agenda included a high-level commitment from EU and US chiefs of government to pursue regulatory cooperation broadly and identified the MRAs as a priority for liberalizing the new transatlantic marketplace. Their inclusion in the NTA brought the negotiations under an institutional framework whereby the task of facilitating mutual recognition was primarily delegated to US trade rather than regulatory agencies (Steffenson, forthcoming).

The Commission naturally found USTR more receptive to the MRAs than US regulatory agencies had initially been, because the first objective of the agreements is to facilitate trade. Implementation of the CE Mark also made mutual recognition with the EU an increasingly attractive policy option to trade officials both in USTR and the US Commerce Department, with US industry arguing that CE testing procedures acted as barriers to trade. Though the main motivation for negotiating the agreements was to open the European market to US manufactures, trade negotiators also argued that the MRAs could benefit domestic regulatory agencies. One USTR official argued that the pharmaceuticals MRA could save the FDA $1.5 million annually.[10]

The new institutional arrangements for negotiating the MRA led to increasingly intense discussions between US trade officials, who negotiated the overarching umbrella agreement, and US regulatory agencies, who negotiated the sectoral annexes. USTR's negotiating position toward the EU was constrained by the structure of the domestic legal system. Agency officials argued that they could not negotiate a full-equivalency MRA, because altering domestic regulatory mandates would require legal authority from the US Congress. A number of sectors suggested by the Commission were pushed off the negotiating table because they were not compatible with the US domestic legal system (see Ives, 1997: 28; Vogel, 1998). In particular, aviation, pressure valves, road-safety equipment, lawnmowers and personal protective equipment were problematic because the regulatory systems were not similar enough to negotiate or because they posed serious health and safety issues.

The different negotiating styles of the EU and the US were also reflected in the trade negotiations. The Commission sought a broader agreement with more sectors, arguing that a framework approach would encourage the spillover of mutual recognition to other sectors (Ives, 1997; Nicolaïdis 1997a, b). US negotiators were only willing to invest time and resources in negotiating sectors where they could realistically win over US regulators. They favoured sector-by-sector negotiations to limit the number of regulatory agencies involved and thus avoid an unreachable threshold for agreement (Egan 2001a and 2001b).

The sectors that were eventually included in the agreement reflected the bargaining power of both EU and US negotiators. As Horton (1998: 648) argues, 'the Commission would not agree to MRAs on telecommunications and recreational craft – viewed as advantageous to the United States – unless there also was MRA coverage of pharmaceuticals – viewed as advantageous to the EU'. Commission officials also argued that the MRAs for telecommunications and electromagnetic compatibility were useless without an agreement on electrical safety, because products such as PCs have to conform to multiple regulations.[11]

The TABD as a force of regulatory convergence
Business on both sides of the Atlantic took an active interest in the MRAs. Manufacturers noted that the duplicate testing of products by domestic and foreign regulators was slowing down the product-approval process, creating

extra costs for exporters and effectively creating a barrier to market access. Furthermore, reducing these exporting constraints benefited the exporters directly, with a TABD advisor arguing that a typical US manufacturer may spend $50,000–100,000 annually complying with foreign regulatory requirements (Stern, 1997).

The TABD became deeply embedded in the MRA decision-making process (Cowles, 2001; Steffenson, forthcoming). It offered technical support for the negotiation process and created the Transatlantic Advisory Committee on Standards (TACS), composed of industry experts from the TABD working group on regulatory cooperation to suggest measures reducing costs for exporters. Although the main focus of TACS is harmonization, the committee was able to provide EU and US officials with a clear outline of where EU and US industry felt MRAs would be most feasible and productive.[12]

Manufacturers involved in the TABD were also key to gaining US government support for the MRAs. In addition to devising policy options, the TABD became a powerful lobby, exerting constant pressure on both governments to negotiate and to implement the MRAs.[13] The TABD held frequent meetings with senior officials at the US Commerce Department and publicly criticized both sides for missing deadlines and failing to implement the agreements. In particular, the TABD Scorecard argued that the problems in both the medical-devices and electrical-safety annexes undermined the credibility of the entire process, because EU and US officials could not deliver the implementation of the MRAs once they were agreed (TABD, 1999 and 2000).[14]

Business strategies toward the MRAs were for the most part compatible with those of the European Commission, the USTR and the US Commerce Department. It is clear that TABD played a key role in obtaining support for the MRAs at the transatlantic level, where the overarching framework agreements were negotiated by trade officials.[15] European Commissioner for Trade Brittan noted 'the vital input of TABD' (1997). US Commerce Secretary Daley (1997) argued, 'TABD said it was important, we heard them and we acted.' President Clinton (1996) thanked the TABD, 'for their leadership in achieving these agreements' and USTR Barshefsky (1997) claimed, 'we could not have achieved this [MRA] package without the Transatlantic Business Dialogue'.[16] However, the capacity of the TABD to act as a force of regulatory convergence largely ended with trade agencies. It had far less influence with the domestic regulatory agencies which negotiated the sectoral annexes. FDA officials, for example, have downplayed the role of TABD in the negotiations, arguing that their interaction with the TABD resulted in little more than 'briefings'.[17]

The impact of institutions and culture on regulatory divergence

Major systemic and normative differences posed various obstacles to the annex negotiations, where domestic regulatory agencies exercised their negotiating authority. Trade officials faced heavy opposition from domestic regulators who were both strategically and normatively motivated. Distinct regulatory cultures and contrasting systems of regulatory accountability and regulatory autonomy surfaced in the negotiations, with many US NGOs and national laboratories supporting national regulators in their campaign to limit the application of mutual recognition at the transatlantic level (see also Egan, 2001; Nicolaïdis, 1997a; Shaffer, 2002: 7).

Incompatible conceptions of regulatory equivalency and accountability?
As applied in the transatlantic context, mutual recognition requires domestic regulators to accept the competency of their foreign counterparts to conduct product testing. However, regulators remain accountable to domestic legislators for product standards. Regulators on both sides of the Atlantic are thus generally reluctant to transfer authority to a foreign body, and the MRA negotiations demonstrated that some regulatory bodies are more reluctant than others. While European regulator agencies expressed general concerns about accountability in the US regulatory system, the main objectors to the process were the FDA, which negotiated the annex agreements for the medical-devices and pharmaceuticals sectors, and the Occupational Safety and Health Administration (OSHA), which negotiated the electromagnetic-compatibility MRA.

Problems arose initially from the use of private conformity-assessment bodies (CABs) in the EU. The FDA argued that it could not delegate authority to approve private third-party reports or manufacturing-facilities inspections (see also Ives, 1997: 30). This position changed only when the FDA underwent structural changes to its regulatory mandate via the FDA Modernization Act (1997), which altered the scope of FDA control and allowed delegation of authority to third-party assessment bodies (Egan, 2001b: 15).[18] In addition, Congress instructed the FDA, in consultation with the US Secretary of Commerce, to support USTR in reaching an agreement with the EU on all products under its jurisdiction where MRAs would not lead to a reduction in the quality of standards (Merrill, 1998: 742). Given this clause, the FDA stressed that the MRAs could not be considered a transfer of authority from the FDA to EU regulatory bodies but only as 'contracts of service' for foreign CABs. It maintained the authority to reject EU-approved CABs in both of the sectors it negotiated.

Further problems arose within the pharmaceuticals annex, which outlines 'Good Manufacturing Practices' (GMPs). The agreement requires regulatory authorities on one side of the Atlantic to rely on its counterparts to conduct on-site visits to manufacturing facilities. The Commission's interpretation of the agreement was that foreign regulators should then be able to expect a certification of the inspection reports regarding manufacturers' compliance. In contrast, the FDA argued that it could only certify GMPs after reviewing the full reports composed by national regulators. The FDA argued further

that all legislation, manuals, memoirs, administrative acts and reports must
be provided in English, but the Commission replied that it was simply too
costly to translate all of these documents.[19] The problem was defused when
the FDA accepted that it would 'normally' be able to accept certification. It
also agreed to work with European regulators to devise a common inspector-
report format.[20]

Because mutual recognition was already accepted within the EU, the MRAs
faced far less opposition from EU regulators, who argued that the
autonomous role of many US regulatory agencies blurred the lines of regulatory accountability in the US. They also expressed concern that regulatory
quality was undermined by the lack of standardized requirements (Nicolaïdis,
1997b; Egan, 2001b: 14).

From this perspective, US regulatory policy is both highly fragmented
(Egan, 2001b) and decentralized (Cowles, 1997). The FDA, the Federal
Communications Commission (FCC), the Federal Aviation Agency (FAA),
the Defense Department and the National Institute on Standards and Technology (NIST) all operate separately and are governed by individual statutes
from Congress. The US system relies heavily on voluntary conformity from
more than 400 federal and state trade and industry associations and scientific
and technical societies. The American National Standards Institute (ANSI)
does serve as an 'administrator' and 'coordinator' of the private-sector vol-
untary-standardization system. However ANSI does not set standards itself
and not all standards bodies are members (Egan, 2001b: 24).[21] The MRA
negotiations consequently prompted another structural change in the US. To
reassure European regulators, the National Institute on Standards – an agent
of the Commerce Department – created the National Voluntary Conformity
Assessment Program to accredit conformity assessment in the US.

Divergent regulatory cultures
The approach of US regulators to the MRAs also highlights larger cultural differences that challenge EU–US regulatory cooperation. The regulatory culture
within the EU internal market is considered 'trade-friendly', because EU and
national regulators operate with dual missions to promote free trade within
the internal market while ensuring public safety (Petriccione, 2001: 220;
Shaffer, 2002: 7). However, many US agencies have narrower mandates that
focus solely on public health and safety. In addition, both FDA and OSHA
have a developed culture of regulatory superiority vis-à-vis European regulatory agencies and regulatory autonomy vis-à-vis USTR (see also Nicolaïdis,
1997a), while US agencies that supported the agreements – such as the US
Coast Guard and the FCC – do not.

The culture of regulatory superiority emanates from idea that not only are
US standards and conformity-assessment processes superior, but no one outside the oversight of US regulatory agencies is qualified to implement these
standards. OSHA's culture of regulatory superiority is also evident in the

electrical-safety annex. It maintained not only that it had the right to refuse European certification of CABs, but that it alone holds the authority to approve these CABs. However, it has accepted only one CAB and rejected a number of other applications that were made in French and Spanish. One OSHA official argued, 'We're a domestic health and safety agency, we don't do translations' (Alden, 2001).

This culture of regulatory superiority is most evident in the case of the FDA, because the FDA considers its mark of quality to be the gold standard (Merrill, 1998; Horton, 1998). One FDA official confirmed that 'the FDA has a proud history. We felt no need to play in this – we are used to being authoritative.'[22] The FDA not only maintains that its standards as a whole are superior to European standards, it also refuses to accept that mutual recognition within the EU guarantees similar levels of regulatory protection across the Member States.[23] Rather, it insists on determining the equivalence for each Member State individually.

US regulatory agencies place an emphasis on defending national sovereignty because they benefit from a high degree of autonomy vis-à-vis trade agencies. Both FDA and OSHA argued that their sectors had been taken hostage in return for an agreement in the telecommunications sector. One FDA official argued that since it was a 'political decision to have internal MRAs, there was no option on the part of technical agencies'.[24]

Because regulatory agencies viewed the agreements as an imposition from trade authorities, they were adamant about maintaining clear lines of authority. One FDA official argued that the 'legal authority to regulate is placed with FDA, not Commerce, not USTR'.[25] In testimony before the House Committee on Commerce, Oversight and Investigations, FDA Deputy Commissioner for External Affairs Sharon Holston argued that: 'There were clearly times during the negotiations when DG-I (Trade) negotiators operated under the assumption that trade issues were paramount in the negotiations. It was made clear to them, however, that for legal and policy reasons health and safety issues would govern'.[26]

The FDA was opposed to setting up the Joint Committee to oversee conformity assessment because of the potential opportunity for trade agencies to dominate (see Ives, 1997). It requested a Memorandum of Understanding (MOU) with USTR to secure clear authority for the FDA in the sector annexes and reserved an 'observer' role for USTR in Joint Committee meetings where FDA annexes were discussed.[27]

Both the FDA and OSHA also questioned why regulatory agencies should bear the cost of negotiating and implementing a trade agreement, since the MRAs ultimately seek to reduce the cost of exporting to producers. While USTR argued that the cost of duplicate testing for domestic regulators should also be reduced, the FDA complained that the agency had spent 'significantly' in promoting MRAs out of 'nominal budgets'.[28] OSHA started charging a 'processing' fee for applications for conformity assessment to compensate for the costs of approving foreign CABs, whereby the Commission argued it had violated the agreement by creating a duplicating assessment fee.

Private-actor support for maintaining the status quo
A number of private actors supported the actions of US regulatory agencies to retain existing, separate conformity-assessment processes. NGOs, particularly in the US, shared fears about delegated governance, trade control over the regulatory process, and more specifically the TABD.[29] The groups protested that the MRAs transferred authority from domestically, politically accountable actors to the less transparent international level. They argued that this could instigate a downward spiral to the lowest common denominator of health, safety and environmental standards (de Brie, 1999).

These groups also opposed full equivalency agreements, the use of private conformity assessment bodies and the creation of overarching institutions such as the Joint Committee (see Steffenson, forthcoming). Both the Transatlantic Consumers Dialogue (TACD, 2000) and the Transatlantic Environmental Dialogue (TAED, 2000) argued that accepting foreign standards allowed for subjective comparison of what might be vastly different, democratically achieved regulatory standards. Consumer groups saw the use of private conformity-assessment bodies in the EU as a de facto privatization of government responsibilities (TACD, 2000). They argued, as the FDA had, that the Joint Committee gave trade negotiators control over regulatory policy.[30] These groups also questioned why regulatory agencies should bear the cost of negotiating an agreement that mainly benefited producers, and were particularly suspicious of the special relationship between the TABD and the Commerce Department in MRA negotiations. The high praise of the US Administration for TABD led one TACD member to argue, 'Our biggest fear is that the MRAs *are* TABD'.[31]

Not all groups that supported the US regulatory agencies on these issues were consumer or environmental. A number of laboratories were also happy to maintain the status quo. The American Council of Independent Laboratories (ACIL) expressed concern about the mutual recognition of CAB accreditation processes, sharing the FDA's view that American standards are higher than elsewhere. In response to claims that the US accreditation system is a barrier to trade, Joan Walsh Cassedy, the Executive Director of the ACIL argued that, 'the bottom line is public health and safety. And there the United States is undoubtedly a leader.'[32] Shaffer adds that many labs in the electrical-safety annex were unhappy with the MRA because they benefited from OSHA's approval system (2001: 19). Finally, many laboratories had already found the means to capitalize on the conformity-assessment process by providing quick product acceptance either through agreements with European laboratories or through European subsidiaries.[33]

The impact of different trade and regulatory strategies

Trade officials and US regulatory agencies with strong cultures of regulatory autonomy and regulatory superiority maintained distinct, often opposing strategies throughout the MRA negotiations. This section examines how these different strategies shaped the capacity of the EU and the US to cooperate in these sectors. In other words, what impact did these different actors have as forces of both regulatory convergence and divergence? The focus here is on implementation gaps in the MRA annexes, the extent to which the MRAs have opened the transatlantic market, and finally what the outcome of these negotiations means for future MRAs.

Patchy implementation of the MRA annexes
The strong bargaining position of US regulators driven by strategic and normative motivations to maintain control vis-à-vis other agencies and what they viewed as superior standards vis-à-vis foreign regulators is most clearly reflected in the patchy implementation of the negotiated sectors. Not surprisingly, the lowest application of mutual recognition has come in sectors where the FDA and OSHA objected to the agreements. Serious difficulties arose in implementing the MRAs for medical devices, the Good Manufacturing Practices of pharmaceuticals and electrical safety.

The FDA and OSHA have created serious obstacles to MRA implementation in their respective sectors through their tight control of CAB approval. As noted above, the FDA maintains the right to reject European CABs and OSHA maintains it has sole authority to approve European CABs. OSHA has yet to approve any CABs in the electrical-safety sectors; thus the agreement has essentially not been implemented. The lack of implementation in this sector has sparked heated debate between the US authorities and the Commission, which argues that the telecommunications and EMC annexes are essentially not functional without the electrical-safety annex. The medical-devices annex, which applies to a limited range of products, has faced similar deadlock. The three-year period for confidence building has expired without real progress, and again no European CABs have been approved. Thus, this annex is also not operational.

The Good Manufacturing Practices annex for pharmaceuticals applies mutual recognition only in its most minimal form. It requires the regulatory authorities on one side of the Atlantic to rely on the regulatory authorities on the other side to conduct on site visits to manufacturing facilities. Here the FDA's insistence on evaluating each Member State individually has delayed implementation, as inspecting manufacturing facilities in each of the Member States is costly and technically difficult to engineer. To date the FDA has conducted on-site visits only in the UK, a Member State it perceives to be the closest in terms of regulatory equivalence. See Table 8.3.

Table 8.3 Correlation between US regulatory positions and policy success

Annexes	US regulators	Position on MRAs	Policy success
Telecommunications Electromagnetic compatibility	FCC	Pro	Operational
Medical Devices Pharmaceuticals	FDA	Against	Not operational
Electrical Safety	OSHA	Against	Not operational
Recreational Craft	Coast Guard	Pro	Operational

The MRAs as a liberalization strategy

The most successful annexes are in sectors where US regulatory bodies supported the agreements and which were perceived as most advantageous to US companies. These include telecommunications equipment, electromagnetic compatibility and recreational craft. An agreement was reached in each of these sectors to recognize the testing and approval of products by foreign CABs and to use the joint institutions to determine the competency of CABs. The agreements were implemented after the allocated time for confidence building between EU and US regulators. For example, successful confidence building between the Coast Guard and its European counterparts led to new negotiations on a full equivalency agreement (the MRA +) in marine safety equipment. The MRA + is significant because it is the first EU–US agreement to allow products to be certified for foreign markets using domestic standards. The MRAs also prompted further deregulation in the telecommunications-equipment industry, and the FCC has used the experience it gained from the EU–US negotiations to commence similar negotiations with the Asia-Pacific Economic Cooperation forum (APEC) and the Inter-American Commission on Telecommunications (CITEL) (see Shaffer, 2002). The multilateral negotiation of MRAs in the telecommunications sector means that between the EU, the US, APEC, CITEL and the Asia-Pacific Telecommunity (APT), more than 90 countries are engaged in dialogue on how to apply mutual recognition.

The sectors that have been completed are considered most advantageous to the US, while the most glaring implementation gaps remain in the sectors pursued by the EU. Given this disparity, what did the Commission accomplish in initiating the MRAs? On the one hand it was able to draw important sectors into the MRA negotiations through the overarching framework agreement, and has used the relative success of the initial MRAs to initiate new MRAs for services.[34] On the other hand, the limited depth, scope and implementation of mutual recognition points to minimal strategic gains either in the bilateral negotiations or in multilateral fora.

It can be argued that the EU gained more normatively through, albeit restricted, policy transfer (Steffenson, 2002). The Commission was able to shape the negotiations by drawing on internal institutional design for the MRAs, for example by pushing to establish the Joint Committee as a decision-making and dispute-resolution structure. The Commission also benefited symbolically from the externalization of its internal market policy, as US rather than EU negotiators suffered from a capabilities gap.

Future strategies for mutual recognition in the NTM
Officials on both sides of the Atlantic have argued that the agreed MRAs are only the first step toward broader liberalization of trade through mutual recognition and that the agreements set the groundwork for future application of MRAs in new sectors. Transatlantic agreements on the mutual recognition of veterinary equivalence standards and national measurement standards have already been signed. The first full equivalency MRA in marine safety is well under way and new services agreements in architecture, insurance, and engineering have been initiated. However, movement in many of these sectors, particularly services, has been slow. The spread of mutual recognition in the transatlantic marketplace depends on a number of factors.

Many authors have argued that the transatlantic relationship lacks strong institutions with the depth to oversee and enforce the MRAs (see for example Egan and Nicolaïdis, 2001; Petriccione, 2001). Unlike the EU single market, there is no authoritative legal body – such as the ECJ – with the capacity to enforce mutual recognition. Although the Joint Committee is designed to act as a forum for dispute resolution, it has been unable to break the deadlock achieved by the FDA and OSHA in the implementation process. This underlines the need to strengthen the institutional foundations for transatlantic regulatory governance.

On the other hand, it is difficult to imagine, at least in the near future, a transatlantic institution with the authority to override domestic regulatory agents.[35] In the short term a stronger case can be made for focusing on institutionalizing contact between regulatory authorities. Increased dialogue between regulators is crucial because the agreements require not only the assessment of foreign standards, but also confidence in foreign regulators to apply those standards. Confidence building is key to both the deeper and wider application of mutual recognition in the transatlantic marketplace, even if it has not prompted regulatory convergence across the board.

Trade officials hope that confidence-building processes will lead to new MRAs as understanding is increased between regulators, particularly in new sectors where the regulatory culture is less autonomous. This confidence-building process is particularly important for the new MRAs on services, where EU regulators have to negotiate not with a single federal regulatory authority, but with numerous authorities at the state level. Confidence building in existing sectors also has the potential to spark further deregulation, once regulators gain trust for their counterparts, and some experts agree that harmonization is likely to be the direct result of MRAs, with the parties agreeing to standardize their compliance processes in order to save time and money.[36] According to Helen Delaney of Delaney Consulting:

> The greatest achievement by both governments, however hard won, may not have been the finalisation of a mutual recognition agreement, i.e., an agreement to preserve existing differences, but the first halting steps towards eliminating those differences, the international harmonisation of regulations and the use of international standards. What we certainly gained is an understanding of one another's processes that is deep enough to provide a foundation for achieving that end goal.[37]

Finally, continued business support for the agreements is key to the success of mutual recognition as a transatlantic regulatory strategy. TABD has played a critical role in the MRA negotiations, securing US support by lobbying USTR and the US Commerce Department. It offered technical support and exerted pressure on officials on both sides of the Atlantic to conclude the agreements. Furthermore, industry has the potential to increase the impact of mutual recognition as MRAs in existing sectors give firms leverage to demand agreements in others (see Shaffer, 2002).

Recent TABD reports, however, hint at lost momentum for the MRAs. Under the leadership of PriceWaterhouseCoopers and Electrolux (from 2001) the group's attention has turned to a number of new strategic issues including the growth of e-commerce, the WTO negotiations in Doha, dispute management, and mergers and acquisitions. The new services MRAs are not on the TABD's agenda. The implementation of the existing agreements remain key to maintaining industry support for the MRAs, as TABD members have continually complained about the problems in the electrical-safety and pharmaceuticals annexes. In addition, the group is seeking more government action on the harmonization of product standards or at least full equivalency of approval processes.[38] Without clear results in these sectors, there could be a shift away from MRAs in new sectors and in the overall EU–US regulatory strategy.

Conclusion

This chapter has examined different trade and regulatory strategies and their impact on the negotiation and implementation of transatlantic MRAs, with the aim of highlighting factors that explain regulatory convergence and divergence in the case of the EU–US MRAs.

Two coalitions have emerged during the MRA negotiations, divided not by the marketplace but rather by their respective mandates. To a large extent EU and US trade officials had a shared interest in pursuing the MRAs as a market-opening strategy. Convergence on this issue was secured because manufacturers on both sides of the Atlantic identified duplicate conformity-assessment testing procedures as barriers to trade, and because these groups were organized through the highly influential TABD. The second coalition consisted of domestic regulators, mainly the US FDA and OSHA, who argued that MRAs impinged on their domestic regulatory mandates.

The interplay between these actors points to both institutional and cultural differences as sources of divergence in the EU–US MRA negotiations. Institutional differences empowered US regulatory agencies, limited the negotiating authority of USTR and pre-empted cooperation in a number of areas. These institutional differences were heightened by cultures of regulatory autonomy and regulatory superiority in the US, which incited strong reactions from the FDA and OSHA. The impact of these different sets of actors is reflected in the outcome of the MRAs and their implementation. US regulatory agencies were drawn into the language, deadlines and institutions laid out in the overarching framework agreement. The FDA was forced by Congress to modernize, and thus accept the authority of EU private conformity-assessment bodies. On other hand, both the FDA and OSHA effectively delayed the implementation of the agreements in their respective sectors.

What does this case study tell us about the prospects for transatlantic regulatory cooperation more broadly? The MRAs demonstrate the complexity of negotiating regulatory agreements as a means of liberalizing trade. In this case interagency negotiations, particularly in the US, were as important as foreign-trade negotiators. The existence of separate and often competing trade and regulatory mandates highlights the need to build both regulatory confidence and stronger transatlantic institutions to facilitate regulatory cooperation.

Notes

1 The author would like to acknowledge Helen Wallace, the Robert Schuman Center and the European University Institute for the support she received as a BP Transatlantic Jean Monnet Fellow in 2001–2002. Gratitude is also due to John Peterson, Mark Pollack, Ricardo Gomez, Adrian Van den Hoven, Dave Allen, Michele Egan, Bill Burros and members of the European Forum (EUI) for their comments on earlier drafts of this chapter and related research.

2 Conformity-assessment procedures are used to assess that products comply with standards or regulations. These processes include sampling and testing; inspection; certification; management-system assessment and registration; accreditation of the competence of those activities and recognition of an accreditation programme's capability. (See the National Institute of Standards and Technology's website at http://ts.nist.gov/ts/htdocs/210/gsig/cainfo.htm.)

3 The framework agreement (a general mandate) introduced general language, timeframes and an institutional structure that applied to all of the individual annexes. The annexes were sector specific. They were negotiated by regulatory agencies and contained specific language for each policy sector.

4 The rough figures quoted from the US Mission and TABD are $50–60 billion in trade under the first framework agreement and $130 billion for a services framework agreement.

5 Nicolaïdis (1997a: 1) argues, '"The recognition" involved here is of the "equivalence", "compatibility" or at least "acceptability" of the counterpart's regulatory

system, the "mutual" part indicates that the reallocation of authority is reciprocal and simultaneous'.

6 Mutual recognition has existed in Europe from the 1950s, where the mutual recognition of professional services was outlined in the Treaty of Rome to facilitate the free movement of people. The ECJ *Cassis de Dijon* case gave legal credibility to the mutual recognition of goods, and mutual recognition underpins the Single Market today.

7 European Commission, 1996.

8 Interview, European Commission, September 1999.

9 Interview, European Commission, January 2002.

10 See Ives, 1997; White House, 1996.

11 Telephone Interview, European Commission, January 2002.

12 In May 1996 it released a progress report listing priority areas for regulatory cooperation. See www.tabd.gov.

13 Interview, USTR official, Washington DC, 2000; US Commerce official, Washington DC, October.

14 The TABD Scorecard is a report issued annually that marks government progress on its recommendations.

15 The *Financial Times* reported that 'The key to final approval of the MRA was the Transatlantic Business Dialogue', 19 June 1997.

16 All of these statements can be found under 'What They Said About the TABD', available at www.tabd.com.

17 Interviews, FDA, October 2000. See also Steffenson, 2005.

18 The FCC also modified its regulations in order to recognize private testing bodies (Shaffer, 2001: 15).

19 Interviews, FDA, October 2000; EU Commission delegation official, Washington DC, 2000.

20 Interviews, FDA, October 2000.

21 Including prominent organizations such as the American Society for Testing Material and the International Institute of Engineers (IIE) (Egan, 2001b).

22 Interview FDA, October 2000.

23 One official commented, 'FDA knew Europe was not "whole". Interview, FDA, October 2000.

24 Interview, FDA, October 2000.

25 Interview with FDA official, October 2000.

26 Statement by Sharon Smith Holston, Deputy Commissioner for External Affairs Food and Drug Administration Department of Health and Human Services, Before the Subcommittee on Oversight and Investigations Committee on Commerce, US House of Representatives, 2 October 1998.

27 Interview, FDA, October 2000.

28 Interview, FDA, October 2000.

29 Both the Transatlantic Consumer Dialogue and the Transatlantic Environmental Dialogue (TACD, 2000; TAED, 2000) issued statements on the MRAs. Public Citizen also reacted to the MRAs as part of its harmonization campaign. See www.citizen.org.trade/harmonization/MRA/.

30 Interview, US NGO, Washington DC, October 2000.

31 Interview, US NGO, Washington, October 2000.

32 Interview in *Standardisation News*, October 2000. See www.astm.org/SNEWS /OCTOBER2000/octinter.html.

33 For example, United Laboratories and DEMKO ran an advertising campaign urging companies not to wait for the MRA. See 'On the Mark, Don't Wait for the MRA', available at www.ul.com/about/otm/otmv3n3/mra.html.

34 In particular the Commission is pushing for an MRA in the insurance sector because EU companies argue that US federal and state regulation has blocked them out of the market. For example, in many states the insurance of large risks can only be placed with insurance companies established within that State. Interview, European Commission, March 2002.

35 The notion of a transatlantic treaty or a Transatlantic Free Trade Area (TAFTA), which would require ratification from the US Congress, has been continually rejected (see Steffenson, 2001).

36 Allen Bailey, Brand Consulting Group, Mutual Recognition Agreements, Globalisation of Product Standards and Compliance, see www.bcgiso.com/mra-article.html.

37 Impact of Conformity Assessment on Trade: American and European Perspectives, Speech made by Helen Delaney, Delaney Consulting, Inc., SES Annual Conference, 14 August.

38 Electrolux CEO Michael Treschow argued in a 2001 speech to the Swedish-American Chamber of Commerce that 'Governments have still not responded to the TABD request for a strategic commitment to the principle "approved once, accepted everywhere". This is a call for broad convergence of product requirements and approval procedures'.

References

Alden, E. (2001), 'Mismatch on Product Safety puts Accord on Danger List', *Financial Times*, 9 November.

de Brie, C. (1999), 'Watch Out for MAI Mark II', *Le Monde*, 21 May.

Cowles, M. G. (2001) 'Private Firms and US–EU Policymaking: The Transatlantic Business Dialogue', in E. Philippart and P. Winand (eds), *Ever Closer Partnership, Policy Making in US–EU Relations*, Brussels: Presses Interuniversitaires Européennes.

Daley, R. (1997), 'US and EU Reach Agreement on Mutual Recognition of Product Testing and Approval Requirements', US Department of Commerce Press Release, 13 June.

Egan, M. (2001a), 'Creating a Transatlantic Marketplace: Government and Business Strategies', Conference Report, The American Institute for Contemporary German Studies: Washington DC.

_____ (2001b), 'Mutual Recognition and Standard Setting: Public and Private Strategies for Governing Markets', in M. Pollack and G. Shaffer (eds), *The New Transatlantic Dialogue: Intergovernmental, Transgovernmental and Transnational Approaches*, Lanham MD: Rowman and Littlefield.

European Commission (1996), 'Mutual Recognition Agreements', Com (96) 564 Final.

_____ (2001), 'Report on US Barriers to Trade and Investment', available at http://europa.eu.int/comm/trade/pdf/usrbt2001.pdf.

Horton, L. (1998), 'Mutual Recognition Agreements and Harmonisation', *Seton Hall Law Review*, 29: 2, Seton Hall University.

Ives, R. (1997), 'The ABC's of MRAs', remarks at the conference on *Limits of Liberalization*, Washington DC, 16 January.

Majone, G. (2000), 'International Regulatory Co-operation: A Neo-Institutionalist Approach', in G. Bermann, M. Herdegen and P. Lindseth (eds), *Transatlantic Regulatory Co-operation: Legal Problems and Political Prospects*, Oxford: Oxford University Press.

Merrill, R. (1998), 'The Importance and Challenges of "Mutual Recognition"' *Seton Hall Law Review*, 29: 2.

Nicolaïdis, K. (1997a) 'Mutual Recognition of Regulatory Regimes: Some Lessons and Prospects', Jean Monnet Working Papers, Harvard University, available at www. Harvard.edu/programs/JeanMonnet/papers/97/97-07-1.htm.

_____ (1997b) 'Negotiating Mutual Recognition Agreements: A Comparative Analysis', paper presented at the 1997 Annual Meeting of the American Political Science Association, Washington DC, 28–31 August.

_____ (2001), 'Regulatory Co-operation and Manage Mutual Recognition: Elements of a Strategic Model', in G. Bermann, M. Herdegen and P. Lindseth (eds), *Transatlantic Regulatory Co-operation: Legal Problems and Political Prospects*, Oxford: Oxford University Press.

Petriccione, M. (2001), 'Reconciling Transatlantic Regulatory Imperatives with Bilateral Trade', in G. Bermann, M. Herdegen and P. Lindseth (eds), *Transatlantic Regulatory Co-operation: Legal Problems and Political Prospects*, Oxford: Oxford University Press.

Shaffer, G. (2002), 'Managing US–EU Trade Relations through Mutual Recognition and Safe Harbor Agreements: "New" and "Global" Approaches to Transatlantic Economic Governance?', European University Institute Working Papers, Robert Schuman Centre No. 2002/28.

Steffenson, R. (2002), 'The EU's Exportation of Mutual Recognition: A Case of Transatlantic Policy Transfer', European University Institute Working Paper, Transatlantic Series.

_____ (forthcoming), *The Institutionalisation of EU–US Relations: Decision Making, Institution Building and the New Transatlantic Agenda*, Manchester: Manchester University Press.

Stern, P. (1997), 'The Success of the MRAs', available from the Transatlantic Business Dialogue (TABD) at www.tabd.com/index1.html.

TIA (Telecommunications Industry Association) (2001), 'Guide to MRA Basics', available at www.tiaonline.org/policy/mras.cfm

TABD (1999), 'Mid-Annual Report', available at www.tabd.com

_____ (2000), 'Mid-Annual Report', available at www.tabd.com.

TACD (Transatlantic Consumers Dialogue) (2000), 'Principles of Harmonisation', TACD Trade Document, February. Available at www.tacd.org.

TAED (Transatlantic Environmental Dialogue) (2000), 'Mutual Recognition Agreements Draft Policy Statement of the Transatlantic Environmental Dialogue', presented at the Third Meeting of the TAED.

USTR (2002), 'National Trade Estimate Report on Foreign Trade Barriers', available at www.ustr.gov/reports/index.shtml.

Vogel, D. (1998), *Barriers or Benefits? Regulation in Transatlantic Trade*, London: Brookings.

White House (1996), 'Good Manufacturing Practices', Press Briefing, Washington DC, 16 December.

9 *Youri Devuyst*[1]

The EU–Canada dialogue: trend-setting for rule-based global governance

Introduction

In his classic *Discord and Collaboration*, Arnold Wolfers (1962: 73–4) draws a distinction between milieu goals and possession goals in foreign policy. While pursuing milieu goals, countries aim at shaping the international environment beyond their national borders. By strengthening the multilateral trading system and creating international security structures, for instance, governments try to establish a congenial external environment that will help them attain their long-term policy preferences. When pursuing possession goals, countries find themselves competing with others in a more short-term timeframe for a share of values of limited supply. Competition between countries for expanding export markets forms an example.

While countries are constantly pursuing both possession and milieu goals, the current dialogue between the EU and Canada can without hesitation be classified as one that puts milieu goals at the centre. During the Uruguay Round, EU and Canadian proposals were instrumental in creating the WTO as the new multilateral-trade policy structure. At the WTO's Seattle and Doha Ministerial Conferences, the EU and Canada again largely shared a preference for a comprehensive Round that would strengthen and expand the scope of the multilateral-trade regime. In the traditional foreign-policy field, the EU and Canada have actively joined forces in trying to create new international rules on such human-security dossiers as combating the spread of small arms and de-mining. Particular efforts were made by both parties to turn the entry into force of the International Criminal Court into a success. As such, the EU and Canada have been actively using their extensive bilateral dialogue to contribute to global governance.

Of course, the EU and Canada both continue to pursue specific possession goals, notably in their respective trade policies. Both defend their producers' interests when discussing such trade issues as agricultural subsidies or wine and spirits imports. But none of the recent trade irritants between the EU and Canada has escalated into trade wars fought out with unilateral economic sanctions and counter-measures. On the contrary, the EU and Canada have successfully managed their disputes in a rule-based manner in the framework of the WTO. Even the famous EU–Canada fisheries dispute – which in 1995 did literally lead to gun-boat diplomacy – was in the end resolved through a legal dialogue that contributed to the clarification of the international law of the sea regime.

By focusing on milieu goals, the EU–Canada dialogue can be seen as trend-setting for rule-based global governance. This forms an important reason to study it more in detail. In addition, both the quality and quantity of the EU–Canada dialogue is often underestimated in the current literature. Many books covering the so-called transatlantic relationship either completely overlook, or attach only minor importance to the Canadian dimension of the EU's relations with North America.[2]

The framework of the relationship

Soon after the entry into force of the European Economic Community (EEC) and the European Atomic Energy Community (Euratom) in 1958, Canada expressed an interest in establishing formal relations with the new legal entity. Already in 1959, Canada and Euratom concluded a Nuclear Cooperation Treaty. Also in 1959, Canada's Ambassador to Belgium was accredited to the Community as well. Canada's diplomatic representation in Brussels was upgraded in 1973 by the establishment of a separate Mission to the EC.

A major step toward the creation of the current framework linking the EU and Canada was taken in 1976 with the signing of the *Framework Agreement* for commercial and economic cooperation between the European Communities and Canada. It was the EC's first framework cooperation agreement with another industrialized country. The initiative for the Agreement had been taken by the Canada. When assuming office in 1968, Canadian Prime Minister Pierre Trudeau had immediately underlined that 'Canada should seek to strengthen its ties with the European nations.' Trudeau specifically proposed that Canada 'should seek to join with Europe in new forms of partnership and cooperation in order to strengthen international security, to promote economic stability on both sides of the Atlantic and . . . to balance our own relations in the Western Hemisphere' (cited in Mahant, 1981: 269). The underlying reason explaining Canada's desire for closer relations with the EC was the need to reduce its dependence on the United States. Canadian policy-makers had become particularly concerned about the growing dominance of US-based interests in the Canadian economy (Canadian Parliament, 1996: 68).

American ownership of Canadian industry had been growing and the US market represented over 70 per cent of Canada's international trade. President Richard Nixon's decision of 15 August, 1971 to end the Bretton Woods exchange rate system, accompanied by a 10 per cent US import surcharge, underlined Canada's vulnerability to changes in US policy and pushed the

Trudeau government into taking action. It came in the form of what Secretary of State for External Affairs Mitchell Sharp called the 'Third Option'.[3] Under that label, Canada adopted a long-term policy designed to strengthen the Canadian economy and reduce its vulnerability to the US through a diversification of Canadian foreign policy. In practice, however, the Third Option came to be associated solely with obtaining a treaty link with the EC (Mahant, 1981: 268–71). This argument has resurfaced on a regular basis. In June 2001, the Standing Committee on Foreign Affairs and International Trade of the Canadian Parliament expressed the view that, 'Canada has become quite dependent on its southern neighbour for its trade and investment, and the recent economic downturn in the US demonstrates that there is a danger in continuing to rely so heavily on one trading partner for our well-being . . . In this context, Europe could serve as a useful counterbalance to Canada's high degree of dependence on the United States' (2001: 13).

The Framework Agreement of 1976 did not create a preferential trade regime. In accordance with their normal GATT obligations, the parties undertook to accord each other Most-Favoured-Nation (MFN) treatment. In addition, the EC and Canada committed themselves to promote the development and diversification of their reciprocal commercial exchanges and to foster mutual economic cooperation in all fields. In institutional terms, the Framework Agreement created the Joint Cooperation Committee (JCC). The JCC – which is still meeting on an annual basis – was granted the task of promoting and keeping under review the activities under the Agreement. The conclusion of the Framework Agreement in 1976 coincided with the opening of the European Commission Delegation in Ottawa.[4]

The next important step in the framework for EU–Canada relations was the 1990 *Transatlantic Declaration* on EC–Canada Relations, issued in parallel with a similar Declaration on EC–US Relations. After the breakdown of the Iron Curtain in 1989, the political situation on the European continent was changing drastically. At the same time, European integration had regained momentum via the internal market initiative symbolized by its 'Europe 1992' slogan. In order to solidify the link between the US and the new Europe after the Cold War, and in light of the EC's '1992' dynamism, US President George Bush (1989) and his Secretary of State James Baker (1989) proposed the creation of 'a significantly strengthened set of institutional and consultative links . . . whether in treaty or some other form'. However, following US Secretary of Commerce Robert Mosbacher's (1990) request for 'a seat at the table' in the EC's internal-market deliberations, the Europeans proved most sceptical toward any US attempts at creating formal treaty ties. As an alternative, German Minister of Foreign Affairs Hans Dietrich Genscher proposed 'improving relations between the European Community and the two North American democracies . . . via a new declaration concerning the common challenges we face in the political, economic, technological, and ecological fields' (Potter, 1999: 82).[5] During the negotiation of the Declarations, Canadian officials insisted that the EC–US and the EC–Canada texts would be similar, both with regard to the principles of partnership and the institutional framework for consultation, 'so that Canada would not be viewed as a "second class" transatlantic citizen' (Potter, 1999: 102).

In the end, both Declarations underlined that the partners would consult each other on humanitarian, political and economic issues to ensure that their efforts would have maximum effect. They would also join their efforts in meeting such transnational challenges as terrorism, drugs trafficking, arms proliferation, environmental preservation and large-scale migration. Furthermore, both Declarations contained an important institutional part. The EC–Canada Declaration notably provided for regular meetings between the Canadian Prime Minister and the Presidents of the European Council and European Commission. These Summits have in practice taken place every six months. The Declaration also foresaw bi-annual Ministerial meetings between the Canadian Secretary of State for External Affairs and the Council Presidency and Commission.

The final component to the overall framework of EU–Canada relations was added in 1996 by the *Joint Political Declaration* and the *Joint Action Plan*. It was issued one year after a similar accord between the EU and the US on a New Transatlantic Agenda (NTA) and Joint Action Plan. Although the Canadian government had pressed for a trilateralization of the NTA negotiations, the parallelism in the development of the EU's relations with the two North American countries had been broken in March 1995. This was due to the political dispute over Canada's seizure of the Spanish fishing vessel *Estai* in international waters. While EU and Canada managed to avoid a further escalation of the conflict by reaching an agreement in April 1995 on fisheries enforcement and conservation, the issue continued to strain relations for some time. Already in October 1995, however, Canada and Germany – the EU Member State that had also been instrumental in the creation of the 1990 Transatlantc Declaration – formed a working group which helped to prepare the ground for the EU–Canada Action Plan.

Both the NTA with the US and the EU–Canada Action Plan were attempts to re-enforce transatlantic ties after an intense period of EU deepening and widening during the first half of the 1990s.[6] The ambitious Treaty of Maastricht on European Union, which entered into force in 1993, notably established the path to Economic and Monetary Union (EMU). Maastricht also gave a new momentum to the creation of a Common Foreign and Security Policy (CFSP) and to cooperation in the fields of Justice and Home Affairs (JHA). Furthermore, the EU's enlargement with Austria, Finland and Sweden in 1995 and the accession process with the countries of Central and Eastern Europe not only broadened the EU's market but also its geopolitical importance.

In a response to these developments, the EU–Canada Joint Action Plan of 1996 significantly expanded the scope and depth of the EU–Canada dialogue.[7] The Plan consists of four parts. The first part deals with economic and trade relations. Its purpose is to reinforce the multilateral trading system and the bilateral economic relationship. The second part concerns foreign policy and security issues. Its focus is on cooperation regarding Euro-Atlantic security issues and such global topics as disarmament, non-proliferation and human rights. Transnational issues are included in part three which aims at the preservation of the environment, Arctic cooperation, migration and asylum, and fight against terrorism. Finally, part four focuses on links in education, science and technology, business-to-business contacts and people-to people links.

During the EU–Canada Summit of 18 March 2004, a new Partnership Agenda was adopted. It was designed to further strengthen the ties between the EU and Canada. A key goal was to enhance cooperation in foreign and security policy, drawing on the shared commitment of both partners to effective multilateral institutions and effective global governance. To this end, the partners notably agreed to more systematic contacts between parliamentarians.

The institutional network

The bi-annual Summit and Ministerial meetings, as established by the Declaration on EC–Canada Relations of 1990, bring together decision-makers at the highest level and provide the necessary political impetus for the development of the EU–Canada dialogue. Summits and Ministerials also put EU–Canada relations high on the bureaucratic agenda in the preparatory and follow-up phases, thereby requiring constant formal and informal contacts both between EU and Canadian officials and between the European Commission and the EU's Member States.

In addition to the political dialogue at the level of Presidents, Prime Ministers, Ministers and Commissioners, European Parliament–Canada Interparliamentary Meetings have been taking place since 1974. In the European Parliament, the Delegation for Relations with Canada regularly reviews the EU–Canada dialogue. The Canada–Europe Parliamentary Association has a similar function on the Canadian side. Interparliamentary Meetings involve an intense exchange of information and viewpoints. The 24th European Parliament–Canada Interparliamentary Meeting in Brussels (19–25 March 2000), for instance, was preceded by seven meetings between the Canadian delegation and the chairpersons of the European Parliament's most important Committees. Moreover, the Canadian delegation attended two sessions of the European Parliament's Committee on Foreign Affairs, Human Rights, Common Security and Defence Policy during which they were seated 'on the floor' and participated in the debate. Furthermore, side-meeting were organized between the Canadian delegation and several European Commissioners.

At the level of officials, the EU–Canada dialogue centres around the annual meeting of the JCC which leads to a review of the entire relationship. In the margins of the JCC, the EU and Canada also hold consultations on foreign and security policy and on cooperation in justice and home affairs. In addition, a number of subcommittees have been constituted to assist the JCC in the performance of its tasks. The annual Trade and Investment Sub-committee (TISC) serves as the main forum for a discussion of outstanding bilateral trade issues and for an exchange of information on general trade-policy developments. While the JCC and the TISC are not problem-resolving institutions, they require senior officials in the EU and Canada to put EU–Canada relations on their agenda, to review the development of the relation-ship and to listen to each other's objectives. In addition to numerous indi-vidual visits and missions in both directions, the High Level Consultations on the Environment and on Fisheries provide a formalized context to raise specific questions in these two fields.

The foreign-policy dialogue between the EU and Canada is particularly well developed. No other third country, with the exception of the US, has such strong institutional foreign-policy links with the EU. In an average semester, the EU Troika will have at least ten formal meetings with Canadian diplomats to discuss issues of mutual interest. During a typical semester, meetings take place on such subjects as non-proliferation, small arms, human rights, the West-ern Balkans, Eastern Europe and Central Asia, the Middle East, Iraq, Africa, Asia and Oceania, and Latin America. These meetings allow for a coordination of positions on the most important topics in world politics. The human rights Troika with Canada, for instance, takes place a few weeks before the session of the United Nations Human Rights Commission, thus allowing the partners to systematically exchange views. In addition, in the field of justice and home affairs, Canada had meetings with the EU on crime, immigration information, and asylum information. Furthermore, during the first semester of 2000, Justice Canada seconded an official to the European Commission's new Direc-torate General for Justice and Home Affairs, underlining the importance attached by both parties to a productive dialogue in this area.

Within the EU, positions vis-à-vis Canada are prepared in the framework of the Council's Transatlantic Relations Working Group that reports to the Committee of Permanent Representatives. The Working Group consists of representatives from all Member States and the Commission. It meets approximately every two weeks in the Brussels Council building. The agenda of the Group always includes a Canada item as well as a US item. The inten-sity of the Group's activities increases dramatically when a Summit or Min-isterial meeting approaches. The Group allow the Commission and the Council Presidency to debrief the Member States on their contacts with Canadian officials in the run-up to the Summit or Ministerial. For each item on the agenda, the Commission and the Presidency present the Member States with an annotated agenda, including the proposed EU position for each item. The Member States also receive the draft joint declarations or draft agreements that will be signed or released at the end of the Summit or Ministerial. The Member States use the discussions on the annotated agenda, joint declarations and draft agreements to ensure that their points of view will actually be reflected. The annotated agenda, joint declarations and draft agreements always have to be discussed more than once before the Group can express its agreement on the EU position to be defended by the Commission and the Presidency. This agreement frequently arrives only a few days or hours before the Summit or Ministerial.

The economic dialogue: toward a new forward-looking trade and investment enhancement agreement?

Economic relations are by definition focusing on possession goals. Still, in their economic dialogue, the EU and Canada have paid special attention to the strengthening of structural links of both multilateral and bilateral nature.

On the multilateral stage, Canada and the EC have both been leading the way to the creation of the WTO during the Uruguay Round. In February 1990, the EC circulated a non-paper entitled *The Strengthening of the Institutional Basis of the GATT*, arguing that international trade deserved its own permanent institution alongside the International Monetary Fund and the World Bank (European Commission, 1990). The same theme was further developed in a Canadian proposal of April 1990 entitled *Strengthening the Open Multilateral Trading System* (Canadian Government, 1990). In this proposal, Canada for the first time explicitly came forward with the idea for the creation of a World Trade Organization as part of the Uruguay Round. While the EC gave strong support to the proposal, the Europeans preferred the name Multilateral Trade Organization (MTO). Throughout the negotiations the term MTO was used and seemed accepted. Only hours before the deadline of 15 December 1993 did a reluctant US delegation – which continued to fear Congressional criticism on the loss of sovereignty – make its acceptance of the new institutional framework conditional upon a last minute name change to WTO, thus returning to the title that had originally been proposed by the Canadian government in 1990.[8]

In preparation for the WTO's Seattle and Doha Ministerial meetings in 1999 and 2001, the EU and Canada again shared a significant number of preferences on some of the fundamental structural questions. They both made a public priority of better catering for the interests of the developing countries in the WTO system and argued for a comprehensive new Round that would extend the world-trade regime to such topics as competition policy and trade facilitation. In the field of services, the EU and Canada shared a particular sensitivity with regard to the right of each WTO member to promote 'cultural diversity'.[9] Agricultural subsidies, on the other hand, continued to divide the two partners. While rejecting the EU's export subsidies for agricultural products as a distortion of competition, Canadian Minister of International Trade Pierre Pettigrew warned in January 2003 that 'it is important for Europeans to know that there can be no real progress on Doha if there is no real and satisfactory progress in international negotiations over agriculture' (*Agence Europe*, 10 January 2003).

Bilaterally, economic relations between the EU and Canada are governed by the EU Canada Trade Initiative (ECTI) which was launched at the EU–Canada Ottawa Summit in December 1998 to further develop the trade chapter of the E –Canada Joint Action Plan of 1996. ECTI has proven to be an interesting framework for pragmatic step-by-step trade facilitation via cooperation mechanisms and mutual recognition among specialized regulatory and supervisory agencies. Under ECTI's umbrella, the parties have concluded four important agreements. The Customs Cooperation Agreement (1997) expands the exchange of information between Canadian and EU customs officials. The Veterinary Agreement (1998) provides for the mutual recognition of equivalent sanitary measures. It covers two-way trade in animals, animal products, fish and fish products. The Mutual Recognition Agreement (MRA, 1998) provides for the mutual acceptance of product approvals in the exporter's jurisdiction to the importing party's regulatory requirements by recognized Conformity Assessment Bodies. It covers telecommunications equipment and electromagnetic compatibility, recreational boats, medical devices and pharmaceutical good-manufacturing practices, and electrical safety. The MRA specifically aims at reducing regulatory burdens and transaction costs for firms operating on a transatlantic basis. The MRA's full implementation has been delayed by concrete technical obstacles. The ECTI progress report published on the occasion of the EU–Canada Summit in May 2002 mentioned that particular challenges were being encountered in the MRA's implementation as regards medical devices, electrical safety and pharmaceuticals.

The fourth agreement concluded under the ECTI umbrella is the EU–Canada Competition Agreement (1999) which establishes a cooperation system between the European Commission's Directorate General for Competition and the Canadian Competition Bureau. This is perhaps the most dynamic of the current agreements between the EU and Canada in the economic-policy sphere. The purpose is to increase the effectiveness of enforcement in transatlantic antitrust and merger cases, and to reduce the risk of reaching conflicting or incompatible decisions. The Agreement provides for the reciprocal notification of cases which may affect the other party. The EU and Canada may also request enforcement action by the other party against anti-competitive behaviour which is harming industry or consumers of the requesting party but which is initiated in the other's territory. The Agreement also foresees two formal bilateral meetings between the competition enforcers from both parties on an annual basis. In practice, a growing number of cases are being examined by the two competition authorities, resulting in increasing need for enhanced cooperation. Discussions have concerned both case-related issues, and more general policy issues.

In 2000 and 2001, a total of 17 formal notifications were made by the European Commission to the Canadian Competition Bureau. During the same period, the European Commission received 20 formal notifications from the Canadian Competition Bureau. Case-related contacts in cartel and merger cases have usually taken the form of telephone calls, e-mails, exchanges of documents, and other contacts between the case teams (European Commission, 2000 and 2001). In addition, the Canadian Competition Bureau and the European Commission have been crucial players in the creation of the International Competition Network (ICN). ICN was launched in October 2001 and is intended to provide antitrust agencies from developed and developing countries with a more focused network for addressing practical antitrust enforcement and policy issues of common concern. Its purpose is to facilitate procedural and substantive convergence in antitrust enforcement through a results-oriented agenda. The head of the Canadian Competition Bureau served as the first chair of ICN's Steering Group.[10]

To provide a further impetus to their economic relationship, the EU and Canada have actively pushed for the creation of business-to-business contacts, following the model of the Transatlantic Business Dialogue. This resulted in the creation by a number of large Canadian and European companies of the Canada Europe Round Table for Business (CERT). CERT was formally launched on 16 June 1999, in the margins of the EU–Canada Bonn Summit. CERT member companies conduct content work within a system of ad hoc working modules on specific markets such as biotechnology and food, or regulatory questions such as standards and mutual recognition. These working modules are round tables where recommendations are formulated in efforts to remove market-distorting inefficiencies in EU and Canadian trade and investment policies. These recommendations are consolidated into policy papers that are delivered to senior EU and Canadian political representatives on the occasion of the semi-annual EU–Canada Summits.[11] For policy-makers, CERT recommendations are an indication of the trade barriers that frustrate business people. While its recommendations are carefully considered, CERT has produced some ideas, but these ideas have, in practice, not resulted in much.

One of CERT's objectives is to achieve a free-trade agreement between the EU and Canada. Canada had pushed this goal on several occasions, long before CERT was created. In a September 1994 speech, then International Trade Minister Roy MacLaren asked why Ottawa would not initiate free-trade negotiations with its traditional trading partners in Europe after it had signalled a willingness to contemplate free trade with Latin America and with the Asia-Pacific region. Subsequently, Prime Minister Jean Chrétien, addressing the French Senate in December 1994, proposed the negotiation of a trade liberalization agreement between the NAFTA countries and the EU. Canadian Trade Minister Pettigrew returned to the question at the Ottawa Summit in December 1999; and at the Stockholm Summit of 21 June 2001,

Canada provided the EU with a study on the advantages of removing tariff barriers. Following their Toledo Summit of 8 May 2002, both parties announced that they were examining the question of non-tariff barriers.[12]

The EU remained skeptical, however, toward the creation of a traditional bilateral free-trade agreement with Canada. The EU argued that, after the multilateral developments in Seattle and Doha, starting traditional bilateral free-trade negotiations between industrialized countries to eliminate tariff barriers would send the wrong message to developing countries and to the world at large as regards the commitment of both EU and Canada to the multilateral process (Scoffield, 1999: B1–B6). Furthermore, the EU underlined that classical border measures such as tariffs and quotas are only minor barriers to EU–Canada trade. Trade Commissioner Pascal Lamy argued that a free-trade area would therefore be the wrong cure for existing problems. Instead of tackling tariffs, Lamy proposed to direct the attention to regulatory barriers such as the lack of transparency and divergence in technical and sanetary standards and the lack of recognition of professional qualifications. In Lamy's own words:

> I personally believe this kind of traditional free trade area of the 20th century, based on total market liberalisation, to be a formula that is today a little outdated despite its political symbolism. If we want the trade and investment relationship to reach its full potential, then we should tackle the regulatory obstacles and, for the time being, put our ambitions aside with regards to market access, leaving that to the multilateral arena where it belongs. Frankly speaking, the difficulty that Europe experiences with the idea of a free trade area is that it is not absolutely clear that this is what our trade relations need. (*Agence Europe*, 13 January 2003)

In this context, the EU–Canada Summit of December 2002 resulted in a joint statement in which the two sides committed to design a new forward-looking and wide-ranging bilateral trade and investment enhancement agreement covering inter alia the new generation of regulatory issues and outstanding non-tariff barriers.[13] Canadian Trade Minister Pettigrew placed the emphasis on the fact that such 'an original agreement of the 21st century' could serve as a model to the benefit of the international community (*Agence Europe*, 10 January 2003).

Contentious economic issues

Since ECTI was launched in December 1998, structural work on the various agreements has overshadowed the more conflictual aspects of the economic relationship. Still, economic 'possession' disputes have generally been managed in an orderly manner, in the framework of the WTO's dispute-settlement system and without upsetting the overall relationship.[14] One prominent case concerned the EU's ban on hormones in livestock farming. In 1996, following a similar complaint by the US, Canada requested consultations regarding the EU's ban on imports of meat and meat products from cattle treated with hormones. Both the Panel and the Appellate Body found that the EU's ban was inconsistent with WTO rules. In June 1999, Canada and the US requested authorization from the WTO's Dispute Settlement Body (DSB) for the suspension of concessions to the EU in the amount of Can$ 75 million (and US$ 202 million in the US case). Following an EU request for arbitration, the amounts were drastically reduced. The arbitrators determined the level of nullification suffered by Canada to be equal to Can$ 11.3 million (and to US$ 116.8 million in the US case). The DSB in July 1999 authorized the suspension of concessions in the respective amounts set by the arbitrators. Whereas the US case was constantly brought to the public's attention by threats from Washington for unilateral retaliation under Section 301 of the 1974 US Trade Act, the EU–Canada dispute ran its course through the WTO system, without threatening to disrupt the overall relationship.

While the EU lost the hormones dispute, it won in the Auto Pact case. The EU had lodged a complaint against the discriminatory aspects of Canada's legislation implementing the automotive-products agreement (Auto Pact) between Canada and the US. In February 2000, the Panel found in favour of the EU, and this was confirmed by the WTO's Appellate Body in May 2000. Other cases have also had mixed results.

In another Panel report of February 2000, regarding the case brought by the EU against Canada's alleged lack of protection of inventions in the area of pharmaceuticals, the Panel found partly in favour of the EU and partly in favour of Canada. In 2001, EU also won the so-called asbestos case. Canada had lodged a complaint against French measures prohibiting asbestos and products containing asbestos. Both the Panel report and the Appellate Body ruled in favour of the EU in finding that France did not violate WTO rules. At the moment this chapter was written, consultations were pending in the WTO in three other cases: Canada's complaint of 1998 against the EU's allegedly incorrect patent-protection scheme for pharmaceutical and agricultural products; Canada's complaint of 1998 against EU measures affecting the imports in the EU of wood from Canadian conifers; and an EU complaint of 1998 against Canada's measures affecting film-distribution services. The Canadian complaint of 1995 against the EU (French) trade description of scallops ('coquille Saint-Jacques') has been settled through a mutually agreed solution before the Panel circulated its report. The Panel established in 1995 at Canada's request regarding EU duties on wheat imports was allowed to remain inactive as the parties managed to negotiate reduced import duties for medium-grade durum.

The important trade and animal-welfare dispute on leg-hold traps was resolved outside the WTO framework. In 1991, the EC adopted a regulation which, starting in 1995, would have banned the use of jaw-type leg-hold traps in the Member States. The regulation also implied that imports of furs from third countries still using such traps would be banned. For Canada this was a difficult issue since the fur industry employs over 100,000 Canadians and many aboriginal communities rely heavily on the industry for their livelihood (Canadian Parliament, 1996: 29; Potter 1999, 242–3). Instead of entering in a tit-for-tat trade war that the implementation of the ban would probably have provoked, the European Commission instead chose to propose the negotiation of agreed standards for humane trapping. The EU–Canada Humane Trapping Agreement of 1997 establishes the basis by which standards will be applied to all trapping methods involving mechanical devices with respect to the capture of 19 species of wild mammals. These standards apply regardless of the reasons for capture, whether for pest control, conservation, fur or food (*General Report EU*, 1997: point 545). As such, the leg-hold trap question resulted in one of the first legally binding documents to specifically address international standards of animal welfare.

There has been one major exception to the EU–Canada practice of managing their 'possession' disputes in such a way that they do not upset the entire relationship: the fisheries dispute. On 9 March 1995, Canadian authorities – after having fired several warning shots – boarded and seized the Spanish trawler *Estai*, which was fishing in high seas outside Canada's 200-mile exclusive economic zone off the coast of Newfoundland. On 26 March 1995, the net warps of another Spanish fishing vessel, the *Pescamaro Uno*, were cut by the Canadian Coast Guard. These incidents touched off the worst dispute in the history of EU–Canada relations, with the Europeans accusing Canada of gunboat diplomacy. In fact, EU–Canada fishing relations had been deteriorating since the late 1980s. In 1988, as a measure to stop over-fishing in the NAFO (Northwest Atlantic Fisheries Organization) area, Canada had begun to prohibit EU fishing vessels from entering Canadian waters and ports. In 1992, a bilateral agreement had been negotiated that would have permitted EU fishing boats access to Canadian ports again. While the Europeans ratified the agreement, Canada did not and accused EU vessels of on-going violations of NAFO conservation measures. In 1994, the Canadian Parliament passed Bill C-29, amending the Coastal Fisheries Protection Act to provide the Canadian government with the 'legal authority to make regulations for the conservation on the high seas of straddling stocks that exist both within the Canadian 200-mile limit and in the adjacent high seas area beyond the 200-mile limit'.[15]

Most importantly, the legislation provided for the use of force, if necessary, to board, examine, inspect and arrest foreign vessels that were suspected of violating NAFO quotas either inside or outside the 200-mile zone. In March 1995, the Canadian government adopted implementing regulations expressly permitting use of force as regards Spanish and Portuguese ships on the high seas. Canada's action was the result of a dispute about the quantity of Greenland halibut, or turbot, being caught by European boats near Canadian waters. In February 1995, upon Canadian insistence, NAFO had allocated to the EU only 3,400 tonnes out of the 27,000 tonne total allowable catch of turbot. The EU's reaction had been to make use of the existing NAFO objection procedure and then to fix an autonomous quota of 18,630 tonnes. This proved unacceptable to Canada and resulting in unilateral enforcement measures against the *Estai* and the *Pescamaro Uno*. For Spain and the EU, however, Canada had violated the principles of international law which enshrine freedom of navigation and freedom of fishing on the high seas as well as the exclusive jurisdiction of the flag state over its ships on the high seas.

While Canada's coercive action created a very high level of political tension between Ottawa and the European capitals, the issue was resolved through a process of intense diplomatic and legal activity that, in the end, strengthened the fisheries regime of the North Atlantic.[16] The episode was resolved on 20 April 1995 when the EU and Canada signed an Agreed Minute on the conservation and management of fish stocks that straddle Canada's 200-mile limit (*International Legal Materials*, 1995: 1260). The parties agreed on conservation and enforcement measures to be jointly presented to the NAFO Fisheries Commission as well as on the total allowable catch for 1995 for Greenland halibut within the area concerned. As a result, Canada repealed the application of its enforcement regulations to Spanish and Portuguese vessels and discontinued proceedings against the *Estai*.[17] In September 1995, NAFO established turbot quotas in line with the agreement reached between Canada and the EU and also agreed to apply to all NAFO members new stringent control and enforcement measures inspired by the EU–Canada agreement. Furthermore, upon EU and Canadian insistence, discussions started with respect to effective dispute settlement within the NAFO regime.

The resolution of the EU–Canada dispute of 1995 was a crucial factor contributing to the successful conclusion of the negotiation of the UN Agreement relating to the Conservation and Management of Straddling Fish Stocks and Highly Migratory Fish Stocks of 4 August 1995 (*International Legal Materials*, 1995: 1542). In the framework of the implementation of this Agreement, however, fisheries questions resurfaced as a conflictual issue in EU–Canada relations. In view of the experience of 1995, the EU was most concerned by the extraterritorial aspects of the Canadian legislation (Bill C-27) that was adopted by the Canadian Parliament in 1999 implementing the UN Agreement. Spain in particular made it clear that the question needed to be resolved quickly. To underline its resolve, Madrid blocked the draft Joint Statement on Small Arms which should have been adopted at the Bonn EU–Canada Summit on June 1999.

Following a series of legal discussions and exchanges of notes verbales, Canada underlined, over the summer of 1999, that the terms used in Bill C-27 were fully consistent with those of the UN Agreement and would be applied accordingly. Canada's clarifications allowed Spain and Portugal to declare that their fundamental political concerns had been satisfactorily covered. This notably allowed for the adoption of the Joint Statement on Small Arms at the EU–Canada Helsinki Ministerial meeting of September 1999.

Some legal questions, on the relationship between NAFO rules and those of the UN Agreement, continued to be addressed in further contacts between the experts, bilaterally and in NAFO, with a view of clarifying the international fisheries regime. Both in 1995 and in 1999, the fisheries conflicts were managed by turning them into highly specialized discussions on international fisheries law, bilaterally and in NAFO, which in the end strengthened the international law of the sea regime.

The foreign policy dialogue

In the foreign policy field, the EU–Canada dialogue has focused on so-called human-security issues, a concept especially dear to the former Canadian Foreign Minister Lloyd Axworthy (1997; Canadian Government 1999c). Axworthy's starting point was that since the end of the Cold War, security for the majority of *states* had increased, while civil wars, large-scale atrocities and even genocide have shown that security for many of the world's *people* had actually declined (Canadian Government 1999c: 1–2). Preventive and remedial action to reduce vulnerability and minimize risks to human security must therefore take a central place in post-Cold War foreign policy. Canada's human-security agenda puts special emphasis on international regime-building. In Axworthy's words: 'Two fundamental strategies for enhancing human security are strengthening legal norms and building capacity to enforce them' (Canadian Government 1999c: 5). This implies the creation of new legal standards in combination with the improvement of the capacity of international organizations, in particular the United Nations.

While the EU's foreign policy has not been formulated in terms identical to Canada's human-security agenda, the priorities set out by Christopher Patten, the European Commissioner for External Relations, include many overlapping objectives. At the Helsinki European Council of December 1999, the heads of state and government have notably agreed to strengthen the EU's non-military crisis-response tools. The idea is to bring together and develop national and European capabilities, and to establish effective mechanisms for rapid coordination and deployment. Commissioner Patten (1999) has taken the lead in this coordination effort, focusing on such areas as humanitarian aid, election monitoring, police deployment and training, border controls, institution building, mine clearance, arms control and destruction, combating of illicit trafficking, embargo enforcement and counter-terrorism. The explicit purpose is to put conflict prevention and conflict management at the heart of the EU's foreign- and security-policy agenda. For Patten (2000: 2), 'with regard to every one of these . . . issues, it is difficult to think of a better partner than Canada to push the international agenda forward'.

Two initiatives in particular, the campaign to ban landmines and the effort to create an International Criminal Court, have demonstrated the potential of a successful Euro-Canadian collaboration in the strengthening of international regimes. With regard to landmines, the EU has for some time been the largest single contributor to the United Nations de-mining effort. In the period 1992–98, the EU committed over Euro 180 million to mine action world-wide. In addition, during the same period, EU Member States carried out bilateral actions on a similar scale. Furthermore, in November 1997, the EU committed itself to the goal of 'the total elimination of anti-personnel landmines world-wide' and its Member States have agreed a ban on the production and transfer of all anti-personnel landmines to all destinations.[18] Not surprisingly, the European countries proved Canada's most valuable ally during its attempt to gather the necessary support in favour of the Ottawa Convention on the Prohibition of the Use, Stockpiling, Production and Transfer of Anti-Personnel Mines and on their Destruction which was signed on 3 December 1997.[19] It was not a coincidence that Ottawa's commemorative ceremony in February 1999, marking the entry into force of the landmines Convention, took place on the occasion of the EU–Canada Ministerial meeting, in the presence of the EU Council President, German Vice-Chancellor and Foreign Minister Joschka Fischer, and Sir Leon Brittan, Vice-President of the European Commission.

Similarly, the negotiation of the Rome Statute establishing the International Criminal Court, adopted on 17 July 1998, depended in large measure on the persistence of Canada and the EU Member States.[20] While the Preparatory Committee meetings had been chaired by the Legal Adviser of the Dutch Ministry of Foreign Affairs, the Legal Adviser of the Canadian Department of Foreign Affairs chaired the Rome Conference itself. The US, which opposed the Statute, failed in its open attempt at persuading the United Kingdom and France – its fellow permanent members of the Security Council – to side against the Court too (Scheffer, 1999: 12–22). The United Kingdom and France both decided to support the Statute and the EU as a whole expressed 'its deep appreciation for the successful completion of the Rome Conference' and for the fact that all issues had been 'resolved in a satisfactory manner acceptable to all EU Member States' (*Bulletin EU* 7/8, 1998: point 1.4.22). Canada was the first country to introduce a comprehensive legislation implementing the Rome Statute in Canada (Canadian Government, 1999a). At the EU–Canada Toledo Summit of 8 May 2002, both parties declared that they welcomed the timely entry into force of the Rome Statute on 1 July 2002. They urged other countries to ratify or accede to the Statute in order to continue the process toward universal acceptance of the International Criminal Court.[21] In their attitude toward the Court, the EU and Canada thus defied the negative position of the US.

Another human-security area where the EU and Canada have been constructively cooperating is the combat against the spread of small arms. At the Helsinki EU–Canada Ministerial meeting in September 1999, a joint statement was adopted in which the parties agreed to consult closely during the preparatory process for the international conference on illicit trade in small arms and light weapons in all its aspects, convened by the United Nations General Assembly in 2001. In a new multilateral regime-building attempt, the two sides notably pledged to work toward the adoption of effective guidelines or legally binding instruments as well as a comprehensive international programme of action for the small-arms problem. At the same time, Canada declared that it shared the objectives of the EU Joint Action on small arms and of the EU Code of Conduct on Arms Exports. EU–Canada cooperation on small arms was taken a step further at the Ottawa Summit in December 1999 when both sides agreed in a new joint statement their intention to establish a joint working group to coordinate their approaches to the spread and destabilizing accumulation of small arms and light weapons. They also committed themselves to working together by supporting the implementation of initiatives and projects in the most affected areas of the world, with particular focus on Africa.[22]

During the Finnish Presidency of the EU in 1999, particular attention went to reinforcing EU–Canada cooperation on the so-called Northern dimension. This cooperation focuses on the Circumpolar and adjacent Northern regions with a view to promoting sustainable development as well as environmental and human security. In October 1999, Canada, the Finnish Presidency and the European Commission organized a joint seminar on Circumpolar Cooperation and the Northern Dimension in Ottawa. This gave the impetus for a joint statement on Northern cooperation that was adopted by the EU–Canada Ottawa Summit in December 1999. It underlined that the dialogue would be focused on cooperation that could engage other Northern countries such as the Russian Federation, acceding countries in the Baltic Sea Region as well as Norway and Iceland. Furthermore, rather than entering into competition with such fora as the Arctic Council, the Nordic Council, the Barents–Euro Arctic Council and the Council for Baltic Sea States, EU–Canada cooperation has tried to stimulate these existing multilateral and regional Northern organizations by drawing maximum benefit from their specific competences.[23]

Conclusion

This article has highlighted the productive and rather unknown EU–Canada dialogue that has been at the start of a several important regime-building efforts at multilateral level. The EU's own development has been a major factor determining the potential of joint EU–Canada initiatives at world level. In the trade field, the EU has long and effectively spoken through a single voice, bilaterally and in the WTO. But also in foreign- and security-policy matters, the EU is gradually showing that it can be an effective partner. The negotiations on the Ottawa Convention and the Rome Statute make this clear. Still, these negotiations also demonstrated the limits of the EU as a foreign-policy actor. During the discussions on the International Criminal Court, the sensitivities of the individual Member States continued to play an important role and it was only in the last phase of the negotiations that the United Kingdom and France decided to support the Statute. In the area of landmines, the EU had for years been the leading force behind their elimination, in particular in budgetary terms, and played a crucial role during the negotiations. Still, only 14 of the 15 Member States have signed the Ottawa Convention. To the degree the EU succeeds in strengthening its foreign and security policy, it is likely to become an even more effective partner.[24]

In their bilateral economic relationship, the EU and Canada have at the end of the twentieth century been focusing on pragmatic, step-by-step trade facilitation under the umbrella of ECTI. This has notably resulted in four important agreements dealing with non-tariff barriers and regulatory issues: the Customs Cooperation Agreement, the Veterinary Agreement, the Mutual Recognition Agreement and the Competition Policy Agreement. At the start of the twenty-first century, both parties agreed to work toward a new forward-looking trade and investment enhancement agreement covering in particular non-tariff and regulatory barriers. It is the intention of the EU and Canada to turn this new agreement into an alternative to a traditional free-trade agreement and to have it serve as a model for the world community. While pursuing their bilateral relations, the EU and Canada have also worked side-by-side in the multilateral arena, for instance during the creation of the World Trade Organization and the International Competition Network. Of course, the economic relationship has not been without conflicts. The fisheries dispute is the most prominent recent example. Still, even a conflict as tough as the fisheries question was managed in a direction intended to strengthen the international law-of-the-sea regime.

That the EU–Canada dialogue has been largely oriented toward milieu-goals, thus trying to improve the conditions for global governance, is not surprising. As open economies generating a major part of their GDP through international trade, the EU and Canada have a common interest in a predictable, rule-based world trading system. As largely civilian powers in world politics, their perspectives on security run parallel too, leading to joint initiatives that emphasize humanitarian goals. As respectively a federal state and an entity striving for an 'ever closer union', Canada and the EU also have the necessary internal experience with gradual community-building and compromise-formation that are essential to establishing international regimes and making them work.

Notes

1 The views expressed in this chapter are purely those of the author.
2 For excellent studies on transatlantic relations, see see Peterson and Pollack (2003); Philippart and Winand (2001); Pollack and Shaffer (2001). These books, however, do not go into the details of EU–Canada relations. A major exception, specifically devoted to Canada's perspective on the EU, is the excellent work by Potter (1999). See also Maclean (2001).

3 On the Third Option, see Pentland (1982); von Riekhoff (1978).
4 On the negotiation of the Framework Agreement, see Mahant (1976); Pentland (1977).
5 Potter, 1999, 82. For the negotiation of the Declaration with the United States, see Devuyst (1990); Krenzler and Kaiser (1991).
6 For the negotiation of the NTA, see Krenzler and Schomaker (1996).
7 For the negotiation of the Joint Action Plan, see Potter (1999, 213–18).
8 On the process of creating the WTO on the basis of Canadian and European proposals, see Croome (1999, 231–5); Jackson (1998, 14–19); Preeg (1995, 122–6).
9 See the Joint Statements on the WTO published after the EU–Canada Summits of Lisbon, 26 June 2000 and Stockholm, 21 June 2001.
10 See See www.internationalcompetitionframework.org.
11 For information on CERT, see its website at www.canada-europe.org.
12 EU–Canada Summit Statement, Toledo, 8 May 2002, para. 13.
13 EU–Canada Summit Joint Statement, Ottawa, 19 December 2002, 1–2.
14 For an excellent overview of the EU–Canada cases in the WTO dispute-settlement system, see WTO, 2002.
15 For a good summary of the main events, see International Court of Justice, 1998, para. 13–22; Barry (1998).
16 For the argument that the legalistic regime-building approach to the resolution of the EU–Canada turbot dispute was one of the key factors contributing to the successful conclusion of the UN Agreement, see Joyner and Alvares von Gustedt (1996).
17 On 28 March 1995, Spain had also instituted proceedings before the International Court of Justice contesting Canada's seizure of the *Estai*. On 4 December 1998, the Court declared that it had no jurisdiction to adjudicate upon the dispute. See International Court of Justice 1998. For an interesting comment, see Kwiatkowska (1999).
18 Joint Action 97/817/CFSP, OJ L 338, 9.12.1997. For a good overview of the EU's action against anti-personnel landmines, see European Commission, 2000.
19 For the interaction between the EU and Canada during the negotiation process of the Ottawa convention, see Axworthy and Taylor (1998); Thakur and Maley (1999).
20 For the interaction between the EU and Canada during the negotiation process of the Rome Statute establishing the International Criminal Court, see Benedetti and Washburn (1999); Kirsch and Holmes (1999). For Canada's approach towards the Court, see Axworthy (1998). For the EU's approach, see *Bulletin EU* 7/8-1998, point 1.4.22.
21 EU–Canada Summit Statement, Toledo, 8 May 2002, para. 10.
22 EU–Canada Joint Statement on Small Arms and Light Weapons adopted at the EU–Canada Summit, Ottawa, 16 December 1999.
23 EU–Canada Joint Statement on Northern Cooperation adopted at the EU–Canada Summit, Ottawa, 16 December 1999.
24 Ironically, at the same time, the development of a European defence and security policy has raised some questions in Ottawa on the evolution of the Atlantic link.

References

Axworthy L. (1997), 'Canada and Human Security: The Need for Leadership', *International Journal*, 52, 183–96.

_____ (1998), 'The New Diplomacy: The UN, the International Criminal Court and the Human Security Agenda', Address at the Kennedy School of Government, Harvard University, 25 April.

_____ and S. Taylor (1998), 'A Ban for All Seasons: The Landmines Convention and its Implications for Canadian Diplomacy', *International Journal*, 53, 189–203.

Baker, J. (1989), 'A New Europe, A New Atlanticism: Architecture for a New Era', Address to the Berlin Press Club, Berlin, 12 December.

Barry, D. (1998), 'The Canada–European Union Turbot War: Internal Politics and Transatlantic Bargaining', *International Journal*, 53, 253–84.

Benedetti, F. and J. L. Washburn (1999), 'Drafting the International Criminal Court Treaty: Two Years to Rome and an Afterword on the Rome Diplomatic Conference', *Global Governance*, 5, 1–37.

Bush, G. (1989), 'Boston University Commencement Address', Boston, 21 May.

Canadian Government (1990), *Crosbie Presents Detailed Proposal for Strengthening the GATT System*, Ottawa: Minister for International Trade News Release No. 82, 19 April.

_____ (1999a), *Canada Introduces New Act to Implement International Criminal Court*, Ottawa: Department of Foreign Affairs and International Trade, 10 December.

_____ (1999b), *Canada–EU Agreements*, Brussels: Mission to the European Union.

_____ (1999c), *Human Security: Safety for People in a Changing World*, Ottawa, Department of Foreign Affairs and International Trade, April.

Canadian Parliament (1996), *European Integration: the Implications for Canada*, Ottawa: Senate Standing Committee on Foreign Affairs, July.

_____ (2001), *Crossing the Atlantic: Expanding the Economic Relationship between Canada and Europe*, Ottawa: House of Commons Standing Committee on Foreign Affairs and International Trade, June.

Croome, J. (1999), *Reshaping the World Trading System: A History of the Uruguay Round*, The Hague, Kluwer Law International.

Devuyst, Y. (1990), 'European Community Integration and the United States: Toward a New Transatlantic Relationship?', *Journal of European Integration*, 14, 5–30.

European Commission (1990), *Non-paper – Strengthening the Institutional Basis of GATT*, Geneva, Delegation to the GATT, 6 February.

_____ (2000), *Action Against Anti-Personnel Landmines: Reinforcing the Contribution of the European Union. Proposal for a European Parliament and Council Regulation concerning Action Against Anti-Personnel Landmines*, Brussels, COM 111 final, 14 March.

_____ (2001), *XXXth Report on Competition Policy 2000*, Brussels.

_____ (2002), *XXXIst Report on Competition Policy 2001*, Brussels.

International Court of Justice (1998), *Fisheries Jurisdiction Case (Spain v. Canada). Jurisdiction of the Court*, 4 December.

Jackson, J. H. (1998), *The World Trade Organization: Constitution and Jurisprudence*, London: Chatham House Papers.

Joyner, C. and A. A. von Gustedt (1996), 'The Turbot War of 1995: Lessons for the Law of the Sea', *International Journal of Maritime and Coastal Law*, 11, 425–58.

Kirsch, P. and J. T. Holmes (1999), 'The Rome Conference on an International Criminal Court: The Negotiating Process', *American Journal of International Law*, 93, 2–12.

Krenzler, H. G. and W. Kaiser (1991), 'The Transatlantic Declaration: A New Basis for Relations between the EC and the US', *Aussenpolitik*, 42, 363–72.

Krenzler, H. G. and A. Schomaker (1996), 'A New Transatlantic Agenda', *European Foreign Affairs Review*, 1, 9–28.

Kwiatkowska, B. (1999), 'Fisheries Jurisdiction (Spain v. Canada)', *American Journal of International Law*, 93, 502–7.

Maclean, G. A. (ed.) (2001), *Between Actor and Presence: The European Union and the Future for the Transatlantic Relationship*, Ottawa: University of Ottawa Press.

Mahant, E. E. (1976), 'Canada and the European Community: The New Policy', *International Affairs* 52, 551–64.

—— (1981), 'Canada and the European Community: The First Twenty Years', *Journal of European Integration*, 4, 263–79.

Mosbacher, R. (1990), 'Address to the Columbia Institute Conference on the US Role in a United Europe', Washington DC, 24 February.

Patten, C. (1999), 'The Future of the European Security and Defence Policy (ESDP) and the Role of the European Commission', speech delivered at the Conference on the Development of a Common European Security and Defence Policy, Berlin, 16 December.

—— (2000), 'The EU's Evolving Foreign Policy Dimension', remarks delivered at the National Press Club, Ottawa, 7 February.

Pentland, C. (1977), 'Linkage Politics: Canada's Contract and the Development of the European Community's External Relations', *International Journal*, 32, 207–31.

—— (1982), 'Domestic and External Dimensions of Economic Policy: Canada's Third Option', in Wolfram F. Hanrieder (ed.), *Economic Issues and the Atlantic Community*, New York: Praeger.

Peterson, J. and M. A. Pollack (2003), *Europe, America, Bush: Transatlantic Relations in the Twenty-first Century*, London: Routledge.

Philippart, E. and P. Winand (eds) (2001), *Ever Closer Partnership: Policy-Making in US–EU Relations*, Brussels: PIE-Peter Lang.

Pollack, M. A. and G. C. Shaffer (eds) (2001), *Transatlantic Governance in the Global Economy*, Lanham MD: Rowman and Littlefield.

Potter, E. H. (1999), *Transatlantic Partners: Canadian Approaches to the European Union*, Montreal: McGill-Queen's University Press.

Preeg, E. H. (1995), *Traders in a Brave New World: The Uruguay Round and the Future of the International Trading System*, Chicago: University of Chicago Press.

Scheffer, D. J. (1999), 'The United States and the International Criminal Court', *American Journal of International Law*, 93, 12–22.

Scoffield, H. (1999), 'Europe Rejects Free-Trade Deal with Canada', *The Globe and Mail*, Toronto, 17 December.

Thakur, R. and W. Maley (1999), 'The Ottawa Convention on Landmines: A Landmark Humanitarian Treaty in Arms Control?', *Global Governance*, 5.

von Riekhoff, H. (1978), 'The Third Option and Canadian Foreign Policy', in B. Tomlin (ed.), *Canadian Foreign Policy: Analysis and Trends*, Toronto: Methuen.

Wolfers, A. (1962), *Discord and Collaboration: Essays on International Politics*, Baltimore: Johns Hopkins University Press.

WTO (2002), 'Update of WTO Dispute Settlement Cases', WT/DS/OV/7.

Conclusion

Trade negotiations, economic regulation and the transatlantic market

Recent tensions in the transatlantic relationship have received an unprecedented amount of commentary on both sides of the Atlantic. While developments in the security sector have highlighted disunity both across the Atlantic and within Europe itself, the economic sector has provided increasing cohesion and integration in both contexts.[1] The transatlantic economic relationship is a key anchor in the global economy, with a strong investment and trade basis moving towards toward a genuine transatlantic marketplace. This has been paralleled by the wide framework of consultations which the US and the EU have established over the past decade, demonstrating areas of political cooperation and policy cohesion, most notably in the trade sector.

Yet many differences persist between the US and the EU as economic actors, and these can obstruct or undermine further economic cooperation. Whether or not these principal trade partners can engage in collective decision-making to resolve their economic differences depends on a number of factors that influence the bargaining and negotiation process. A primary factor is the specific nature of the policy issue and its saliency on the political agenda. Conflicts over regulation are unlikely to emerge as long as regulation is viewed as largely technical and thus of low political salience. A second factor is the institutional network, both formal and informal, which serves to structure and channel dialogue among both government and non-governmental actors. A third factor is the calculation of interests that shape the nature and scope of any agreement (Wallace, 2000). The influence of proponents and opponents of regulation can vary significantly across issue areas. A fourth factor is the wider international context, which has played a critical role in shaping policy outcomes and responses. Both sides have made strategic use of other international institutions to enhance or impede international regulatory cooperation.

It is against this configuration of factors that we need to examine the development of policy cooperation between the US and the EU. The assessment of the chapters in this volume is that the broad section of policy sectors has generated not one, but several modes of policy-making based on specific constellations of interests, institutions and issues, which nonetheless have shared characteristics.

In particular, much of the driving forces of change has come from the international economy which has made it critical for firms to increase their competitiveness in both domestic and international markets. The impact of globalization has enhanced pressures for liberalization and market reform and led to some common trends. Both the US and the EU have implemented a variety of regulatory reforms as part of their effort to cope with and foster structural adjustment. They have adopted reforms to eliminate or simplify rules, increase the use of market incentives as alternatives to traditional regulation, and devolve regulatory authority to local administrations, courts, banks and regulatory agencies.

Paradoxically, both the United States and the European Union have also engaged in market intervention in terms of investment in infrastructure and human capital, subsidies and state aids. Public authorities on both sides continue to stimulate economic development. Since specific market interventions provide strategic advantages to their respective industries, there is increased attention to the impact of regulatory policy on both the international competitiveness of domestic firms and the effectiveness of such government controls over business. Because regulations rarely impact all firms or industries equally, transatlantic trade negotiations are subjecting a growing number of these policies to close scrutiny. Both the US and the EU have substituted new instruments of protection for traditional tariff or non-tariff barriers. Many of these highly protected activities are similar in both the US and the EU economies, suggesting that these sectors have been able to resist past trade liberalization (see Messerlin, 2001).

The challenge for the US and the EU is dealing with the competing dynamics generated by regulation of competition and regulation for competition. On the one hand, they must deal with the expansion of regulations and standards to protect public health and safety, improve environmental quality, safeguard financial and monetary markets, and reduce restrictive business practices. On the other hand, they must deal with the effects of regulated trade, which protects or subsidizes certain industries and sectors. Regardless of the actual motivations behind them, domestic regulatory policies are among the key domestic policy instruments that determine the openness of national markets to global competition. Though trade disputes and economic competition have been fundamental features of European–American relations for almost as long as there has been a European Community, the recent study, 'Partners in Prosperity: The Changing Geography of the Transatlantic Economy' suggests that trade negotiators have strong economic reasons to persevere in their efforts to improve market opportunities and reduce restrictive business practices.[2]

Different strategies for different sectors

Against this backdrop, many of the chapters in this volume provide analyses of the impact of regulatory policies in specific policy sectors. They have focused on the dynamics of competition and collaboration to illustrate they ways in which regulations constitute and define the market. In negotiating rules that will operate on a transatlantic basis, both sides are experiencing challenges to their external autonomy as the distinction between domestic and international governance is increasingly blurred. As significant areas of economic activity no longer coincide with national territorial boundaries, variations in the American and European regulatory models have generated competing pressures for regulatory alignment and regulatory competition.

The case studies can be classified according to their fit with the different types of regulation outlined in Chapter 1. In the case of airlines, European governments engaged in strategic regulation by protecting national firms from competition, and giving regulatory advantages to domestic industries rather than liberalizing and opening up markets. Competition is hampered by the existing international rules and regulations forcing American companies to respond through strategic bilateral agreements.

In the case of global satellites and wireless communications, efforts have been made to promote innovation and competitiveness through strategic regulation to leverage their dominant positions in high-tech markets. In the case of competition policy, regulations have been designed to improve the functioning of markets by avoiding duplication of competition rules. This has strengthened antitrust enforcement through increased coordination and codification of rules. For mutual recognition, pro-competitive regulations have been promoted to facilitate the effective operation of markets and remove restrictive non-tariff barriers through mutual acceptance of rules. In the case of data privacy, governments opted for self-regulation to respond with new political strategies that enables business to play a stronger role in monitoring regulatory compliance. In the case of biotechnology, Europe has extended regulations to new areas, and this differs from American efforts to use existing regulatory rules and procedures for ensuring compliance with current health and safety standards. What is clear in all of these cases is that risk and its management are increasingly critical in shaping the development and evolution of the regulatory process.

Many factors have contributed to the growing complexity of transatlantic economic governance. As the chapters demonstrate, the underlying causes of transatlantic disputes are varied. Some are more amenable to traditional processes of trade negotiation and dispute resolution than others. While the US and the EU have experienced trade tensions and disputes in the past, many bilateral disputes involve clashes in domestic values and priorities that emerge through differences in regulatory systems. Public concerns over new technologies and industries and different perceptions about government intervention and market conditions have repeatedly influenced policy debates.

As discussions take place simultaneously at different levels of government, the US and the EU must first coordinate their own positions to effectively promote their regulatory standards. This often requires a degree of policy coordination across different agencies as well as consultation with stakeholders, and this makes policy management an important factor in the resulting negotiations. Since the economic stakes are high, there is often regulatory competition (i.e. competition among rules) between the US and the EU in their efforts to gain strategic advantages for their firms in global markets. As the result, the transatlantic economy is the product of complex and sometimes contradictory pressures from government policies, competing corporate strategies and market dynamics, and prevailing societal and ideological preferences.

Future trends and prospects: managing the transatlantic market

Regulatory issues are increasingly at the heart of transatlantic trade relations. The chapters in this book give special attention to the search for institutional mechanisms to promote greater comity and cooperation in addressing potential regulatory conflicts. They emphasize the policy implications of the contemporary transatlantic relationship and the implications of economic coordination on their respective domestic polities. Underlying their assessments of specific cases and issues is the importance of managing transatlantic market challenges and creating new forms of transatlantic governance.

Many of the issues confronting the US and the EU are quite different from traditional tariffs and quotas – so-called at-the-border issues – since they concern deep-rooted domestic policies. Because these new dimensions of market access involve core issues of domestic governance, this has led to the search for new concepts and approaches to guide transatlantic liberalization efforts, often yielding joint or complementary approaches to regulating commerce through regular consultation and coordination. It has also revealed areas where political constraints are not amenable to resolution despite the existence of consultative mechanisms and procedures. Yet there are also some areas where improvement can be made or considered.

A great deal of the success in maintaining closer economic ties and resolving disputes is dependent on institutional capabilities and effective implementation. Yet this receives far less attention in studies of the transatlantic relationship, in part due to the absence of a legal foundation to promote compliance, than exists in other international arenas.

One important question which follows from this is whether the transatlantic relationship needs specific mechanisms that will promote compliance with negotiated agreements, or whether this is best left to existing multilateral institutions. The strong legal dimension in the European Union has played a key role in promoting market integration, providing a legal framework to tackle protectionist trade barriers. Although select mechanisms such as early warning systems and information exchanges have in some ways sought to address potential trade disputes in the transatlantic setting, they are limited to mitigating future trade conflicts and disputes. There is a lack of legal procedures to promote the resolution of existing regulatory differences in the bilateral context. While the multilateral framework is amenable to resolving traditional trade disputes such as tariffs and non-tariff barriers, there are concerns that this may detract from bilateral efforts to reach agreements. Though the US and the EU are increasingly managing their disagreements through the rule-based system of the WTO, there are concerns that the multilateral framework is far more problematic for settling regulatory conflict (Damro and Sbragia, 2003), and that litigation is not the best means to resolve transatlantic trade tensions. A record of well-managed dispute resolution and dispute prevention can perhaps enable the US and the EU to quiet some political tensions and better ensure that business and policy-makers remain engaged in promoting the political ambitions of a transatlantic marketplace.

A second issue that deserves further consideration is the changing way in which government is interacting with business and other civil society groups. The EU–US economic relationship has institutionalized new forms of consultation and dialogue with civil-society groups, redefining expectations for private-sector participation in trade negotiations. More significantly, this can have important effects on the nature of governance itself. Rather than viewing private sector involvement as undermining governmental capacities, we can see it as complementing government efforts to structure market outcomes to achieve both economic gains and specific political purposes. Challenges about the role of regulation in the economy have also generated new forms of consultation in the transatlantic relationship. The tremendous growth in economic ties has mobilized diverse interests demanding a policy response to the management of trade and regulatory conflict. Moreover, the demand for rules to govern commerce has given rise to a variety of sources of supply, and one of the most significant sources of market governance is the private sector itself. This does raise questions about how to combine a concern for accountability with a sensitivity to the full range of interests affected. Though there are grounds for believing that a number of processes in place will continue to foster a sustained dialogue, inevitably sharp differences will remain in the ability of different constituencies to influence negotiations. A model based on transparency throughout the regulatory process would encourage public and stakeholder deliberation.

A third issue to consider is the importance of implementation and evaluation. The proposing and making of regulations are often directed at issue management in formulating and agreeing new policies, but rarely address how those policies will be carried out (Löfstedt, 2004) Although bilateral official and private contacts have been crucial in enhancing regulatory cooperation, the regulators have not always been quick enough or able to respond effectively to problems encountered in implementation. Some problems have required continued deliberations and in some instances have generated discussions about a better regulatory framework. Many issues must still be analysed and resolved since they indicate a lack of mutual trust in their respective regulatory systems. Yet transatlantic efforts lack the legal strictures of domestic statutes and regulations coupled with the prospect of enforcement litigation. The role of various stakeholder groups – especially business – in seeking to push for the monitoring and enforcement of these agreements represents one potential avenue for sustained policy evaluation and implementation.

EU–US regulatory policies in global perspective

Government regulation now occupies an increasingly important place on the agenda of international relations (Vogel, 1997). This means that areas which were previously within the undisputed domain of national sovereignty are now subject to international scrutiny. As the process of global economic integration continues, not only have firms gained mobility across national borders, but governments are finding themselves losing regulatory control over corporate policies and practices. Long-standing national regulatory institutions and regimes are under increasing pressure to make sure existing regulations are not harmful impediments to an open competitive market economy, and the free flow of goods, service and technologies. As a consequence, governments are seeking new forms of international policy coordination, including the delegation of rule-making to non-governmental or self-regulatory bodies. Because divergent regulations can block competition and create trade friction, efforts are increasing to address differences in regulatory systems to improve trust and mutual confidence across borders, while still balancing market efficiencies with the goals of maintaining health and safety standards, protecting the environment, and upholding social values such as equity and responsibility to societal demands.

The United States and the European Union have been at the forefront of efforts to enhance regulatory cooperation and market access. In the case of the US–EU relationship, a broad range of institutional arrangements shape and influence economic behaviour, and allow us to evaluate the steps taken to coordinate their markets, integrate their economies and foster greater regulatory interdependence. As the chapters in this volume illustrate, no single approach can effectively address all of these challenges, given the difficulties of accommodating divergent legal and regulatory frameworks, as well as responding to different domestic interests. The transatlantic economy has been shaped by a mix of regulatory styles, instruments, and philosophies that reflect their respective policy styles and traditions. Yet their experience in coordinating markets can contribute to the development of deeper and more expansive liberalization of the multilateral trading regime and that of other regional economies.

Notes

1 Virulent ant-war sentiment did not discourage cross-border investment. Europeans invested $36.9 billion in FDI in 2003 in the US and in the same year Americans invested $87 billion in FDI in Europe – a jump of 30 per cent from the amount in 2002.

2 The report concludes that transatlantic economy generates roughly $2.5 trillion in total commercial sales per year and employs over 12 million workers on both sides of the Atlantic. Foreign affiliate sales, not trade are the backbone of the transatlantic economy. Roughly 60 per cent of American foreign assets are in Europe and 70 per cent of European foreign assets are in the United States in 2003.

References

Damro, C. and A. Sbragia (2003), 'The New Framework of Transatlantic Economic Governance: Strategic Trade Management and Regulatory Conflict in a Multilateral Global Economy', in M. Campanella (ed.), *EU Economic Governance and Globalization*, London: Edward Elgar.

Hamilton, D. and J. Quinlan (2004), *Partners in Prosperity: The Changing Geography of the Transatlantic Economy*, Washington DC: Center for Transatlantic Relations, Johns Hopkins SAIS.

Löfstedt, R. (2004), 'Risk Communication and Management in The 21st Century', Working Paper 04-10, Washington DC: AEI-Brookings Joint Center for Regulatory Studies.

Messerlin, P. (2001), *Measuring the Costs of Protection in Europe*, Washington DC: Institute for International Economics.

Vogel, D. (1997), Regulatory Cooperation Between the European Union and the United States, EUSA-AICGS Conference Washington DC.

Wallace, H. (2000), 'The Policy Process', in H. Wallace and W. Wallace, *Policy-Making in the European Union*, 4th edn, Oxford: Oxford University Press.

Index